I0332003

John Davis, William Westgarth

Tracks of McKinlay and Party Across Australia

John Davis, William Westgarth

Tracks of McKinlay and Party Across Australia

ISBN/EAN: 9783743319783

Manufactured in Europe, USA, Canada, Australia, Japa

Cover: Foto ©ninafisch / pixelio.de

Manufactured and distributed by brebook publishing software (www.brebook.com)

John Davis, William Westgarth

Tracks of McKinlay and Party Across Australia

TRACKS OF M^c^KINLAY

AND PARTY

ACROSS AUSTRALIA.

BY JOHN DAVIS,

ONE OF THE EXPEDITION.

EDITED FROM MR. DAVIS'S MANUSCRIPT JOURNAL; WITH AN INTRODUCTORY VIEW OF THE RECENT AUSTRALIAN EXPLORATIONS OF M^c^DOUALL STUART, BURKE AND WILLS, LANDSBOROUGH, ETC.,

BY

WILLIAM WESTGARTH,

AUTHOR OF "VICTORIA AND THE AUSTRALIAN GOLD MINES," ETC.

WITH MAP AND ILLUSTRATIONS.

LONDON:

SAMPSON LOW, SON, & CO., 47, LUDGATE HILL.

1863.

TO JOHN M^cKINLAY, ESQ.

MY DEAR MR. MCKINLAY,

To no one could I more appropriately dedicate this effort to portray the difficulties and hardships experienced during our trip across the Continent, than to you, our worthy Leader, who piloted us through the wilderness, and brought us again to the haunts of our fellow men, with such intrepidity and judgment.

Yours very truly,

JOHN DAVIS.

ADELAIDE, *February*, 1863.

PREFACE.

As we shall occupy the reader's attention at some length in the Introductory View, he may reasonably claim exemption from a long Preface. Our allusions here are confined to two subjects: our Chapters, and our Illustrations.

To have given three hundred successive pages of Journal without a break would have been tolerable to very few, and the less so from some degree of sameness that characterizes Australian scenery and incidents of travel. Mr. McKinlay, indeed, was fortunate in meeting with such weather as greatly dispelled this Australian sameness, and in many parts substituted for scrub, spinifex, and parched ground, the pleasant spectacle of lakes and running streams, waving grass and flowery meadows. Nevertheless, a subdivision of the Journal into Chapters will be found acceptable.

We have succeeded in finding demarcation lines for eleven Chapters, and at the beginning of each Chapter we have given a short *précis* of the subject. At the beginning of the last Chapter we give the very interesting account of an Englishman, James Morrill, who had lived seventeen years with the Aborigines of the lower Burdekin, and whose history lately reached us while occupied with this work.

With reference to the Illustrations, the Publishers are indebted to the courtesy of the Proprietors of the *Illustrated London News* for permission to make use of three of the Lake Views, and also of the Portraits of Burke and Wills, and J. McDouall Stuart. The latter is taken from a photograph by Mr. R. S. Stacey, North Adelaide, and is specially interesting from the fact that the background scene is a representation, sketched by Mr. Stuart himself, of the shores of the Indian Ocean, on the Northern coast of Australia. The other Lake Views are from sketches supplied by Mr. Davis; and the Portraits of McKinlay and party are from a photograph supplied by the same gentleman. As to the "little canvas camp flying in all directions," the Author, in his Journal, invokes "the spirit or the pencil of 'Crowquill,' or the *world-known George*, to scratch that ludicrous scene." It is hoped that our friend, Mr. C. H. Bennett, has not unworthily caught the spirit both of the scene and the invocation. The same gentleman has also, it is believed, adhered to nature and to truth in depicting the more serious scene of the alligators.

W. W.

LONDON, *June*, 1863.

CONTENTS.

Introductory View.

RECENT AUSTRALIAN EXPLORATORY EXPEDITIONS.

RESULTS OF RECENT EXPLORATION OF INTERIOR AUSTRALIA.

CHAPTER I.

CHAPTER II.

LIST OF ILLUSTRATIONS.

THE

LEADING EVENTS AND THEIR DATES

IN THE

DISCOVERY, EXPLORATION, AND SETTLEMENT OF AUSTRALIA.

THE reader may be interested in possessing for reference a concise view of the leading occurrences in the progress of the exploration of Australia, and the settlement of its colonies. There are now five of these colonies, which, in their order as to time of establishment, are as follows:—New South Wales, West Australia, South Australia, Victoria, and Queensland. We confine ourselves to a consideration of Australia, without alluding to Tasmania, New Zealand, and other adjacent islands that are comprised under the wider area of Australasia.

Year. DISCOVERY AND EXPLORATION.

1601.—Earliest authenticated discovery of Australia, by Manoel Godinho de Heredia, a Portuguese. This discovery was usually ascribed to the Dutch, in the year 1606, until Mr Major, two years ago (in 1861) had deduced the earlier date from a manuscript he found in the British Museum.

1770.—The Eastern coast made known by Cook, and called New South Wales.

1798.—Discovery by Bass that Van Diemen's Land is not a continuation of Australia, but is separated by a strait, which has since borne his name, Bass's Strait.

1802.—Completion of the coast outline by Flinders, by the discovery of Spencer Gulf, Port Phillip, and the intervening coast.

1828-31.—The Darling and the Murray, forming the largest river system of Australia, discovered by Sturt.

1840.—The Australian Alps, the highest mountain range of Australia, explored by Strzelecki.

1840.—Eyre's difficult and hazardous journey overland, from the colony of South Australia to that of West Australia.

1844-5.—Leichhardt's important journey overland from New South Wales to Port Essington in North Australia.

1845.—Sturt reaches from the colony of South Australia, the middle of Australia; dispels the notion of a great inland sea, till then prevalent, and substitutes that of a great interior desert. This unprecedently bold expedition, in connection with his previous explorations, have deservedly procured for him the distinctive title of the "Father of Australian discovery."

Year.

1860.—Stuart reaches from South Australia, the central point of Australia (Central Mount Stuart), and passes on almost to the opposite sea. He, in turn, dispels the notion of a great central desert.

1861.—Burke and Wills, from Victoria, reach the Gulf of Carpentaria, thus first crossing Australia from sea to sea.

1862.—Stuart, McKinlay, and Landsborough all accomplish this year the expedition across Australia from sea to sea.

SETTLEMENT.

1788.—Foundation of the colony of New South Wales, 26th January, when Sydney was founded.

1793.—Introduction of the fine-woolled Merino sheep by Mr. John M'Arthur, a step of unsurpassed importance to the whole of Australia.

1829.—Foundation of the colony of West Australia.

1835.—The Port Phillip District (afterwards the colony of Victoria) colonized from Tasmania; and the site of Melbourne, the capital, occupied.

1836.—Foundation of the colony of South Australia.

1840.—Cessation of transportation to New South Wales. (The colony had been founded in 1788 as a penal settlement to the mother country.)

1843.—Representative political institutions conferred upon the Australian colonies (an Assembly consisting of one third nominees of the Governor, who is always nominated by the Crown, and of two-thirds elected by the colonists.

1850.—West Australia made a penal settlement of the mother country.

1851.—Discovery of the Australian Gold Fields by Hargreaves, 12th February. Their existence was inferred, on scientific grounds, seven years previously by Sir R. I. Murchison.

1851.—The colony of Victoria established by separation of the district of Port Phillip from New South Wales, 1st July.

1851.—Ballarat, the earliest known of the great gold fields of Victoria, discovered in September.

1855.—Branch of the Royal Mint established at Sydney; came into operation on 13th May.

1855.—Responsible self-government conceded to the Australian colonies, West Australia excepted for the present. (Government by ministries with ministerial responsibility, as in the Home Government.)

1859.—The colony of Queensland established, by separation of the Moreton Bay District from New South Wales, December.

TRACKS OF M'KINLAY AND PARTY ACROSS AUSTRALIA.

INTRODUCTORY VIEW

OF THE

MORE RECENT AUSTRALIAN EXPLORATORY EXPEDITIONS AND THEIR RESULTS.

The present work records one of several successful expeditions that have lately resolved for us the long standing problem of Central Australia. "Who shall cross this great 'Terra Australis' from sea to sea?" was a question so long before our eyes, and so long unanswered, that we did not expect so overwhelming a response as the last three years have given. And yet, within that brief interval, this previously unattainable result has been accomplished no less than six times over, if we regard Stuart's first two journeys as a virtual crossing of the country; a distinction we can hardly withhold from them, although neither of them quite crosses Australia, as was the case with the third. So much for a bold pioneering, and the confidence that arises from some little experience of the way. So far these preliminaries may serve to show how imaginary are many difficulties, even those of a long standing, and how often the "will makes the way." Who, for instance, that read in times gone by of Commodore Anson's disastrous experience in rounding Cape Horn, would ever have anticipated a time like our own when "the Horn," with its awful region of eternal storm would be as familiar to every ordinary merchantman as the seas of Europe? And now it seems quite likely that in a few more years the once mysterious interior of Australia will be but a great public highway for the commerce and enterprise of the colonists.

We propose here to glance at the results of these later exploring expeditions. They throw much new light on the character of Inner Australia. Having, in this attempt, sketched out briefly the route and main incidents of each expedition across the country, we shall sum up the varied information given by the explorers, and thus endeavour to arrive at a conclusion as to what that vast interior, hitherto so little known, really consists of, and what to our practical colony-making people it is really worth. The question involves no less than a million of square miles of the earth's surface, and if we add to the account the northern coasts, which although not so unknown are also still uncolonized, we must increase this area by at least one-half as much more. The latter territory comprises the tropical region, which, with its comparative regularity of climate and generally better soil, is no doubt to prove much the most productive and valuable of the two. The other, with its more precarious features, is, however, on the whole more tolerable to the European constitution. Truly we have for our subject a magnificent domain, well worthy of many such exploratory efforts, and of all endeavours to ascertain with increasing accuracy what are its physical and climatic features, and to what varied purposes it may be applied!

The honour of being the first to accomplish the journey across Australia from sea to sea is due to Burke and Wills, the leaders of an expedition fitted out in the year 1860 by the colony of Victoria. The reading public have just been occupied with their sad fate. The most fortunate of explorers in accomplishing their object, they were surely the most unlucky of men in the way in which the personal fruits of their victory were snatched from them; for, by a series of *contre-temps*, grievous and almost incredible, they lay down to die of fatigue, exposure, and starvation, when they had well-nigh returned home, and were almost within hail of the friends and supplies that would have ensured safety.

This unfortunate issue however, was fruitful in results to the cause of Australian discovery. After an interval sufficiently long to arouse alarm as to the fate of the explorers, the Victoria Government despatched its armed steamer "Victoria" to the Head of the Carpentarian Gulf with suitable supplies, and organized two further expeditions, in the hope that Burke and Wills might be assisted, or at least that their fate might be ascertained. One of these parties, under Walker, proceeded from Rockhampton in Queensland to the Head of the Gulf of Carpentaria; the other, under Landsborough, landed in the Gulf itself, and beginning from the north, made a successful and very important journey southwards across Australia. The South Australian Government came also to the rescue, and equipped McKinlay and his party, whose journey across Australia northwards, equally successful and not less important, is the subject now before us. Indefatigable in his own exertions, and successful in the order and discipline of his party, Mr. McKinlay seems to have been eminently suitable for the mission entrusted to him.

STUART'S EXPEDITIONS, 1858—1862.

While McKinlay was proceeding north, in a direction suited to the special object of his expedition, the Government of South Australia had

[illegible]

[illegible] South Australian Government [illegible] rescue, and equipped McKinlay [illegible] whose journey across Australia [illegible] McKinlay [illegible]

[illegible]

While [illegible] direction [illegible] of his expe-dition, the [illegible] South Australia had

JOHN McDOUALL STUART.

also despatched another exploring party, which, in an independent track of their own, proceeded in parallel steps somewhat to the west of McKinlay. This was the expedition under Stuart, and the third which that veteran explorer had led across Australia. Stuart took the path that he himself had discovered, and that, after so many crossings and recrossings, he may be said to have already beaten to his own use.

Stuart's expeditions mark an era in Australian discovery. All that activity of the last two or three years to which we have alluded, and which has made us now almost as familiar with central as with sea-coast Australia, is really due to him and to the success and importance of his earlier journeys. Commencing in the year 1858 by making a comparatively short expedition to the north-west of the colony, he made known, for the first time, that a very extensive country suitable for colonization existed in that direction, diversified with numerous lakes and running creeks, and comprising millions of acres of land available and ready for pastoral occupation. These unexpected results supplied a timely counterbalance to accounts of a very different tendency received from Gregory, who, in the very same year, had descended upon the colony from its opposite or north-east corner, in following the course of the Victoria or Barcoo into the Cooper. This considerable length of river system, whose head waters—discovered and traced by Mitchell twelve years before far into the northern interior—were sanguinely conjectured to be the Victoria of North-west Australia, were now traced southwards, emerging through Strzelecki Creek and Lake Torrens into the sea at Spencer Gulf. Here was a pretentious river system truly, if estimated by the length of its course, and the capacity and depth of its rocky and rugged bed. But, like the mineral that had all the characters of coal excepting combustibility, the Barcoo wanted the one element of water, and the traveller experienced difficulty at times in finding in its spacious channel enough to sustain his party in existence.

Stuart's first success emboldened him to deeds of higher daring. In the year 1860, assisted mainly by private friends, he set forth to make the traverse of Australia. This was an exploit requiring at that time rare nerve and courage. Fifteen years had elapsed since Sturt, the experienced and indefatigable Australian traveller, had been baffled in the same attempt, Stuart himself having been one of his party. The sterile desert which Sturt then described as hopelessly interrupting his progress—an arid, burning, lifeless waste, from which he with difficulty extricated himself, and which has since borne his name—had given a very problematical aspect to the great Australian journey. Then, again, Gregory's expedition, in the year 1856, to explore the river Victoria of North Australia, had been brought to an end by apparently another portion of the same desert, equally dried up, and equally destitute of life. The fate of the gallant Leichhardt, too, some years before Gregory, seemed a climax of discouragement to Stuart's project. After his successful and highly important journey, in 1844-5, through the north-eastern districts of Australia to Port Essington, Leichhardt entered upon the bold project of an expedition across Australia, east and west, from the present colony of Queensland to that of West Australia. With characteristic ardour and resolution, he plunged with his party into the trackless bush, but he never emerged from its then unexplored and unknown expanse.

Stuart, then, in the year 1860, resumed this forlorn hope. He passed the centre in a line about five degrees to the westward of Sturt. He encountered no great desert, but on the contrary much good country, watered by many springs, ponds, and running streams. Well grassed plains and forest lands were intermingled with tracts of poor and sterile soil. On the whole, his entire route presented a fair average of the Australian soil as already known in the settled parts and their explored vicinities. Stuart had made for the dynamic centre, if we may so speak, of Australia, and he had the good fortune both to step through the mystical region and to find in its immediate vicinity a hill of destinctive appearance, to bear the name of Central Mount Stuart. This was in south latitude about 22°. Proceeding successfully northwards, he made latitude 18° 40′, when his further progress was stopped by the numbers and threatening aspect of the aboriginal natives, with whom his very small party, consisting only of two persons besides himself, was quite inadequate to cope. His position was provokingly tantalizing. He had made a point about equidistant between that which Gregory had reached southwards from the Victoria River on his left, and the head of the Gulf of Carpentaria on his right. In point of latitude he had surpassed Gregory's position above a hundred miles, and was short of the Gulf by about seventy, while he was about two hundred and fifty miles from the nearest part of its shores. There was now no resource but that of returning by the way he had come, that he might the sooner organize a more suitable force for another expedition.

The second expedition was undertaken in the following year, and after reaching successfully the position of the previous journey, and about one hundred miles in advance, Stuart was once more foiled. This time it was an impenetrable scrub and forest that barred his way. Failing supplies of food compelled his return a second time, but, nothing daunted, the year 1862 sees him for the third time traversing what had become to him a familiar road. The impenetrable scrub once more opposes. It is tried here and tried there, and long in vain for a practicable passage. This search embraces a detour of sixty miles to the westward in hopes of a more open country in that direction, by which he might accomplish one great object of his journeys, namely, a practicable passage from South Australia to the river Victoria, of the north-west. In this particular object he was defeated, but he did at length find a passage northwards through the forest barrier, and continued his march in that direction. He had in this last stage entered upon the finest and most interesting country of the journey. Amidst plains covered with luxuriant grass, which sometimes rose above the heads of the party, amidst picturesque diversities of hill and dale, woodland and river scene, where a profuse tropical vegetation showed generally the rich character of the soil, Stuart pursued his way until he emerged upon the Indian Sea.

He did actually emerge upon the northern ocean, and in having thus seen its waters and trodden its shore, he was more fortunate than his competitors. They had only witnessed its tides near the mouth of one of the northern rivers, and tasted its salt waters. The low, swampy surface at the head of the Carpentarian Gulf had, unfortunately, denied the longed-for and final triumph to the other weary travellers from the south. Landsborough, by taking his start from Carpentaria itself, had certainly defeated this difficulty, but the parties both of Burke and McKinlay were unable to advance further than within some four or five miles of the coast. Their further course was arrested by boggy ground and deep mangrove creeks, impassable to the travellers, with the few means at their command. The sea was not visible when they were compelled to turn from it, but its near vicinity was amply indicated by the tidal rush of sea-water, and by a rise and fall of from ten to eleven feet.

Indeed, to say the truth, neither this muddy shore nor yet that of the Van Diemen's Gulf trodden by Stuart, at all satisfy the demands of poetry or imagination, when these fanciful impersonations will roam over the sparkling waters and pebbly beaches of an Indian clime, or through far-off scenes which arouse hope and expectation in proportion to the difficulty of reaching them. Stuart seems to have paced along a very ordinary sea-beach. Swamp and bog combined their obstacles to arrest him also, and decided him not to waste the remaining strength of his party in an effort to proceed coastwise westerly to the mouth of the important river Adelaide, although distant only about fifty miles beyond his furthest seacoast progress.

Here he halted, reared the flag of his country, and drank to the health of his sovereign. And yet, even minus the poetry, we must envy Stuart the luxury of his rare triumph.

Let us recall his account of the day on which the party reached the sea. Preserving his reckoning, Stuart was aware that the coast must at last be close at hand, but with the view of giving his party a pleasant surprise, he had withheld the information from nearly all. Already his attentive ears had detected the low boom of the still ocean in front. But the sounds are lost upon his unwitting comrades, and little do they anticipate what is to greet their eyes when they have stepped through that coast fringe of scrub that now confronts them. The narrow belt is soon passed, and to their surprise and delight, the great Indian Ocean, the object of their constant thought for months previous, is expanded before them ! *

* On the interesting question of actually reaching and beholding the opposite sea, we deem it worth while to cull the following extracts bearing on the point from the journals of the expeditions of Burke and Wills, McKinlay, and Stuart. The subject is matter of history. Stuart's achievement is not merely his having stood upon the northern beach, viewing the sea at his feet, but his having reached the veritable outer ocean, while his competitors made for the head of the great inlet of Carpentaria.

BURKE AND WILLS NEAR THE MOUTH OF THE FLINDERS.

"At the conclusion of report, it would be well to say that

Stuart's third expedition acquires additional importance, from his having been accompanied by a naturalist, Mr. Waterhouse, whose observations upon the various regions passed through give us a very clear idea of Australia along its central line. Unfortunately the expedition was disappointed of its thermometers, so that we have no thermometric data of the peculiar and precarious

we reached the sea, but we could not obtain a view of the open ocean, although we made every endeavour to do so."—*Expedition by Jackson*, p. 223—Burkes' notes.

"Proceeding on our course across the marsh, we came to a channel through which the sea-water enters. . . . We moved slowly down about three miles, and then camped for the night. . . . Next morning we started at daybreak."—*Ibid*, p. 91—Wills' Diary. The Diary has no further allusion to the sea.

MCKINLAY NEAR THE MOUTH OF THE LEICHHARDT.

"*Sunday, May* 18*th*. (Camp lix.) Crossed, the sea running in through mangrove creeks into the flats like a sluice. . . . We are now perfectly surrounded by salt water, the river on one side and the mangrove creeks and salt flats on the other. I question much whether we shall be able to get to the beach with the horses. . . .

"19*th*. Started out this morning, with the intention of going to the beach . . . but was quite unsuccessful, being hindered by deep and broad mangrove creeks and boggy flats, over which our horses could not travel. I consider we are now about four or five miles from the coast; there is a rise here in the river of ten and two-thirds feet to-day, but yesterday it was a foot higher."—*Official Report*, p. 40.

"19*th*. Mr. McKinlay, Middleton, Poole, Wylde, and Kirby, started very early to get to the sea-shore, but found it climate. Probably so delicate an instrument could not have long survived the rough horseback travelling, the expedition having had no vehicles. From this cause a number of the collected specimens—shells and novel small fish—could not be preserved. Mr. Waterhouse divides the country passed through into three great regions, which differ in soil and other features as well as in latitude and

quite impossible. . . . The horses got up to their bellies in the swamp.

"*20th.* Mr. McKinlay said that any of us who liked to try on foot to get to the sea could do so, but none of us did, as we all thought if it had been practicable, that he would have done it himself."—*Davis's Journal.*

STUART AT VAN DIEMEN'S GULF.

"*July 24th.* At eight and a half miles came up in a broad valley of black alluvial soil covered with long grass; from this I can hear the wash of the sea. On the other side of the valley, which is rather more than a quarter of a mile wide, is growing a line of thick heavy bushes, very dense, showing that to be the boundary of the beach. Crossed the valley, and entered the scrub, which was a complete net-work of vines. Stopped the horses to clear a way, whilst I advanced a few yards on to the beach, and was gratified and delighted to behold the water of the Indian Ocean in Van Diemen's Gulf, before the party with the horses knew anything of its proximity. Thring, who rode in advance of me, called out, 'The Sea!' which so took them all by surprise, and were so astonished that he had to repeat the call before they fully understood what was meant, hearing which, they immediately gave three long and hearty cheers."—*Official Report*, p. 24.

climate. The first extends from the outside settlements of the north-west to between 27° and 28° of south latitude, and is a country watered by springs and available for pastoral use, although subject to great heat and drought in summer, and in many parts sandy and with but little vegetation. The second division comprises Central Australia, extending for 700 miles to the southern part of Newcastle Water. The soil here changes, generally, for the worse; it is "somewhat sandy, and occasionally sandy and loamy," and the water supply seems more precarious. The third division extends from Newcastle Water to the sea at Van Diemen's Gulf, and is of a most superior character. It is generally well watered and grassed, having valleys of rich black alluvial soil, and a beautiful and luxuriant vegetation on the banks of the rivers.

The first region extends from Gooloo Springs to about 27° 18′ of latitude, and may be distinguished as the country of springs and "salt-bush." As cattle can live upon the salt-bush, this country is thus suitable for pastoral pursuits, and is being occupied by squatters. The springs by which it is characterized are very remarkable features, as they are found issuing forth from the surface of plains, or from the very top of little conical hills, which are evidently volcanic, and through which the water seems to find its way upwards by the direction once taken by the lava.* These waters, however, are mostly impregnated with certain gases which give them an unpleasant flavour, usually that of a hard-boiled stale egg, but by pouring the water several times from one vessel to another the gases pass off, and the water is improved. The settlers have opened some of these springs, and on one occasion they dug up some huge fossil bones of an animal, which proved, by reference to Professor Owen, to be the *Diprotodon Australis*, an extinct quadruped of the huge pachydermatous order, but also of marsupial character, whose remains had already been found in New South Wales. In many places of this country even salt-bush is so scanty that the plains can maintain but few live stock, and the heat in summer on these plains is so intense, and the air so arid, that thirst is almost insatiable. Such areas, Mr. Waterhouse says, may well be regarded as the source of the well-known hot winds.

The second region extends from lat. 27° 18′, a little north of Hanson's Gap, to Newcastle Water, in latitude 17° 30′. The vegetation that charac-

* These are Mr. Waterhouse's remarks. Sir R. G. MacDonnell, the late governor of South Australia, who has also personally examined these curious cones, gives another view of their origin. He regards them as the successive deposit of the waters of the springs rising from the plains, and charged with soda and lime. Their size is from that of a beehive to that of a large hill.

terizes this vast area is chiefly a coarse grass of a pungent flavour, having very sharp prickly-pointed leaves, and therefore called by the settlers the porcupine grass. There are several species of this grass. It is the spinifex of Stuart's journal, the *Triodia pungens* of Gregory. The cattle will eat its tall thin seed stalks. It grows usually in the scrubs, and is always the indicator of a poor soil. Good grass is to be found only in the hollows of creeks, and rarely beyond these limited spaces do we find the few gum trees of this country. These trees, reared in precarious climes, are seldom large, or straight or well grown in the stem. The country is characterized by some hill ranges, the chief of which, however, are not more than from 1,500 to 2,000 feet above the plains. The culminating height is Mount Hay, in south latitude 24°, but the country had the appearance of gradually rising towards this point for several hundred miles southwards. Chambers' Pillar, in this part of the country, is a remarkable natural object, resembling a monument, with perpendicular sides, 105 feet in height, and surmounting a small hill, the whole elevation being about 250 feet. There were others near it similar but of less striking appearance, and on examination they proved to be eminences composed of soft argillaceous rock, capped by a thin silicious stratum. The sides were shelving away causing the flinty top gradually to break off, and thus to cover the surface of the country around with small flint stones.

The supply of water seemed to be precarious in both of these regions, but especially in the second. The season of 1861-2, that in which the expedition started, had evidently enjoyed a better rain fall than the following season, when the party returned. All along the route, as far into the tropics as even Newcastle Water, the ponds, creeks, and rivers were found greatly reduced in their contents on the party's return, as compared with the supply they presented on the outward journey, and this, too, notwithstanding that the summer was less advanced when the expedition re-passed homewards. Even the Bonney, in latitude 20° 24', a fine running river as seen in March, was by September following dried up into a few long shallow water holes. The Hamilton, with its long deep ponds, was all but dried up on the return, with many dead fish floating on the diminished surface, while the water of the Lindsay stood six feet lower in level. There was no water in the bed of the Upper Neales, and as the tracks of the previous year's expedition were still visible, there would seem to have been no rain in that part since that expedition passed. Most of the water courses, in fact, had the appearance of not having had water in them for many years. All these indications tend to show that there are no general rains or settled rainy season, and the great defect of these vast areas of the interior seems to be that the evaporative power is greater than the supply of moisture.

The third region extends from the north end of Newcastle Water, in latitude 17° 16′, to the sea at Van Diemen's Gulf, in latitude 12° 12′. "This country," says Waterhouse, "comprises (1) an extensive portion of Stuart Plains, the soil of which is of a fine lacustrine deposit, and is well grassed (the timber on these plains is generally of a very stunted species of swamp gum); (2) the Roper River and some of its tributaries—the valleys of which are of a fine rich black alluvial soil, well timbered and grassed, and with a tropical flora growing on the banks of the river of a most beautiful appearance and luxuriant growth; (3) from thence to the Adelaide River and the sea coast, comprising a considerable extent of well wooded and watered country, with a very varied vegetation."

Stuart states that in this fine country fires were very frequent around the party; the long, close, dry grass burning with great fury. The natives must be numerous in this country, judging from the frequent smoke of their fires, although few of them presented themselves to view. The constant firing of the grass by these natives, a custom also observed by McKinlay, in Northern Australia, seems to have had, for one object at least, to frighten and repel the white intruders from the country. Many of the beds of the creeks were dry, and there was a continuous absence of rain, indicating in a country still so full of vegetation, that the time of the party's visit, June to August, was the dry season of the tropical climate. The weather was exceedingly hot in the day time, as much so as if in the middle of summer, but the nights were cool. On 25th June the party came upon the Roper, a copious and beautiful river, and so deep as to cause much trouble and delay in finding a crossing place. On 10th July they struck the Adelaide, after enjoying, from a rocky and precipitous platform, a magnificent prospect of the luxuriantly wooded and grassed vale through which it flows. But these pleasures of the day were marred by the torment of mosquitoes at night. On the 24th July they reached the sea, as has been already related.

These exploits of Stuart exceed, alike for their extent of travel and adventure as for the importance of their results, those of all preceding Australian explorers. Of the very considerable legion that now claims to have aided the cause of Australian discovery, Stuart is indisputably the prominent figure. He has disencumbered the vast interior of Australia of its repelling awe and mystery; and he has shown that it is not only readily accessible to the colonists, but to a large extent available for immediate colonization. And towards facilitating this colonization, he has shown how little of all those costly paraphernalia of vehicles, baggage, and retinue that were deemed unavoidable for previous government expeditions, is really necessary to a good Australian bushman. If the "through route" of central Australia is some day to be Bradshawed after its own fashion, and to be accounted as the easily accomplished business or pastime of a well-mounted party of hardy colonists; we must never forget how difficult, nay, even impossible, the feat was long held to be, until Stuart's pioneering journeys practically demonstrated its facilities.

BURKE AND WILLS, 1860-61.

Stuart had aroused a general attention towards Australian discovery. While upon his first great expedition in 1860, a movement was made in the adjacent colony of Victoria with the view of fitting out another with the same object as that of Stuart. A private colonist, who concealed his name for some time, but who proved to be Mr. Ambrose Kite, of Melbourne, offered £1000 towards this object. Others of the public, and subsequently the Government, assisted, and a large and well-provided expedition was the result. Amongst other adjuncts of the party were a number of camels, which the Victoria Government had shortly before

R. O'HARA BURKE.

imported from India, and which were thus promptly to be put upon trial as to their merits for Australian purposes. They have well stood this trial, both in this expedition and in the subsequent journey of McKinlay, in which they also formed a part of the stock. They are therefore already a feature associated with Australian travel. They are, at all events, indelibly so associated in the minds of the aboriginal natives, who everywhere beheld them with alarm and astonishment in their unexpected irruption into the solitudes of the interior.

The command of the expedition was given to Burke. It had swelled out into large dimensions, and formed quite a public spectacle as its numerous and varied components poured forth from Melbourne upon the long journey. But delays had occurred, and the season was advanced beyond the most favourable time for action. Leaving Melbourne on the 20th August, 1860, it was the middle of December, that is to say, almost the middle of summer, ere Burke found himself on the foreground at Cooper's Creek ready to start for Carpentaria. Difficulties had already arisen; the company was too large and too much encumbered. Burke had early pushed on with a section of it, leaving the remainder to follow. At Cooper's Creek he still further reduced this party, taking only Wills, his second in command, and two others with him, and leaving the rest to await his return from the north. Taking with them six camels, one horse, and twelve weeks' provisions, the little party sallied forth on the 16th December. They took a direction mainly north, and nearly on the 140th degree of east longitude, arriving at the mouth of the Flinders River on 11th February, 1861, without, however, being able to get a glimpse of the sea.

After a wearisome march, in the later stages of which one of the party sank through fatigue and want of sustenance, they made the Cooper's Creek depôt again on the evening of the 21st April, in the joyful anticipation of finding at last all their troubles at an end. The camp, however, was deserted, and although they looked yet again for some indications that the absence must surely be but temporary, they looked in vain for any such symptom. An adjacent tree was marked "Dig," and on digging at the foot they found a small supply of provisions, and with them a note to the effect that the party in waiting had left for the River Darling, homewards. The note was dated the 21st April, at noon; the same day on which it was read by Burke, and only seven hours previously!

What was to be done? Attempt in their worn-out state to follow this fresh party for 400 miles to the Darling! There was a difference of opinion on this point, but Burke's view was that they should make for the nearest pastoral station of South Australia, which he had understood was at Mount Hopeless, about 150 miles to the southward, and accordingly they started in this direction the next day. Mindful of exploratory discipline, they place a note in the *cache* at the foot of the tree, stating their arrival, and their proposed route, and their inability, in their exhausted state, to make more than four or five miles a day. They also take the provisions left for them, but they do not deem it necessary to leave any external indications of their visit. Slowly they toil along in the new direction. Two of the six camels had survived hitherto, but they also sink early in these renewed labours. Their flesh is carefully preserved as a last addition to the scanty stock, but no water can be met with on the new route after they have turned off southward from the main bed of the Cooper. They struggled forward in vain hope, but were at last compelled to return. They believed they had made only about forty-five miles, but they were in reality much further on. "They decided to return at a point where, though they knew it not, scarce fifty miles remained to be accomplished, and just as Mount Hopeless would have appeared above the horizon, had they continued their route for even another day."*

* Governor Barkly to Duke of Newcastle, 20th Nov., 1861.

There is yet the climax of mishap. Brahe and the Cooper's Creek party, after eight days' march, met Wright with the rest of the expedition, coming on at last from the Darling. The two leaders agree to return to Cooper's Creek, as a last chance for the missing travellers, and they arrive there on the 8th May, but, unable to detect any change in appearances at the depôt, after remaining a few minutes, they return to Melbourne.

With still a very small remnant of provisions, including a little dried camel's flesh, Burke and his party had yet a faint hope of saving themselves, and they even contemplated a second attempt towards Mount Hopeless. They eked out their stores of food by a seed called "nardoo," which, following the natives' example, they ground with a stone and baked. But even this operation required more strength than they had left, and the only resource appeared to be to find a camp of natives, who are in considerable numbers on the Cooper, and to trust to their precarious hospitalities until assistance might arrive from the colony.

Getting feebler and feebler in this final march, Wills first lies down to die, requesting the others to go on. This was on the 28th June. Burke was similarly exhausted the second day after, and died the following morning. Four days after leaving Wills, King, now the sole survivor, returned to ascertain his fate. He had been left in a native "gunyah," with a small supply of nardoo, but poor Wills, too, had expired.

King succeeded in reaching the natives, by whom he was kindly received and cared for during two months and a half, until rescued on the 15th September, by the party under Mr. Alfred Howitt, despatched in search of the missing expedition by the Victoria government. King's narrative is favourable to the natives, who gave him regularly food and shelter, and even showed him acts of kindness. At first, indeed, they seemed to get soon tired of him, and made signs for him to be off. But King was not disposed to take these hints, and when they themselves decamped, with the view of being rid of him, he followed them.

At last they looked on him as one of themselves, sharing with him their fish and nardoo, while he on his part would amuse and gratify them by shooting crows occasionally, cooking the birds, and sharing the repast. Their kindly disposition was shown when King having, at their request, conducted them to the spot where Burke's body lay, they all shed tears, and covered the body over with bushes. He made them understand that the white people would come for him shortly, and would give them tomahawks and other good things. They were impatient for these promised presents, and when Howitt and his party approached they informed King, and went themselves readily to meet the party.

The records of this important journey are scanty and imperfect, but sufficient to guide us as to the character of central Australia, in the particular direction that was taken. Burke passed through some good and grassy country north of the Cooper, and before entering "the Desert." From the Desert to the tropic was generally stony and poor, but from the tropic to the Gulf there was a large proportion of richly grassed and well watered land, interspersed with hill ranges. In the dry central region, the party noticed in repeated instances that there were marks of flooding along the banks of creeks, and over parts of the country they passed through, although at the time of their visit everything was burnt up. Their experiences of the Desert were of a less inhospitable kind than those of Sturt. A week after leaving the Cooper they are within its limits, and they thus describe it:—

"*Sunday, Dec. 23rd.*—At 5 A.M. we struck out across the Desert in a west-north-west direction. . . We found the ground not nearly so bad for travelling on as that between Balloo and Cooper's Creek; in fact I do not know whether it arose from our exaggerated anticipation of horrors or not, but we thought it far from bad travelling ground, and as to

WILLIAM JOHN WILLS.

pasture, it is only the actual stony ground that is bare, and many a sheep run is in fact worse grazing than that."*

This view agrees with that of Howitt, who went into the "Stony Desert" from Cooper's Creek, in July, 1862. He describes the sand and stones as diversified with remains of grass, and with many pools of rain water. He says that on the whole, "the celebrated Desert" is very little different from large tracts in the colony of South Australia known as the "Far North," and "North West."

LANDSBOROUGH, 1861-2.

Landsborough's expedition was despatched in the year 1861, by the Government of Victoria, with the view of affording aid to the missing party of Burke and Wills. He was to proceed from the Gulf of Carpentaria southwards, while another expedition under Walker, was appointed to go overland from Rockhampton in Queensland, to the Gulf. A small brig of 200 tons, the "Firefly," was sent round from Melbourne to Queensland with supplies for the two expeditions of Landsborough and Walker, and after embarking a number of horses at Brisbane, sailed with Landsborough and his party for the Gulf. At Hardy's Islands the little brig was driven upon the rocks, adding one to the many previous casualties of the

* Expedition by Jackson, Diary of Wills, pp. 72, 73.

ill-reputed Torres Straits. The timely arrival of the "Victoria," however, enabled the "Firefly" to get afloat again, and she was taken round to the Albert. Ascending that river twenty miles to a convenient landing-place, a depôt was formed, and the horses, by this time reduced to twenty-five by the loss of some of their number in the late mishap, were safely unshipped, and the expedition was begun on the 17th October.

Landsborough's instructions had been that he should proceed in a south-westerly direction towards Stuart's Central Mount, and accordingly he makes a start upon that course, following up the Albert to its head. Thence diverging a little more to the westward, passing through a very dry country, and over a number of creeks, most of them waterless, as it was far on in the dry season, he is at last arrested by a total failure of water. Leaving this country, which he named Barkly's Tableland, and turning more towards the south along the river named the Herbert, he is compelled by the threatening indications of the natives, to return with his small party to the depôt. His company consisted but of two colonists besides himself and two aborigines. He had succeeded in attaining to about 210 miles from the coast, and had passed through what was, on the whole, a most promising country, well deserving the name of one of its districts, the "Plains of Promise." "The character of the country is," he says, "plains, with the best grasses on them." At Barkly's Tableland he seemed to have come upon the upper waters of a considerable river, or rather what would have been a river at the opposite season of the year, for at this time it was merely a chain of ponds. The ponds were full of fish. The channel took a south-westerly course. The Albert proved to be a fine running stream for 100 miles up to its source, where it gushed forth in a copious spring. About eighty miles from the sea a branch went off from the Albert to join the Nicholson. During the passage up and down the Albert, from October to January, or during the first half of summer, the temperature varied between 74° and 94°, and was usually about 80° in the daytime. The nights were agreeable, more especially as the travellers were not troubled by either mosquitoes or sandflies.

Commencing his return march on the 30th of December, Landsborough made the depôt on the 19th of January. Here he found that Walker had safely arrived from the east coast during his absence. He had made the depôt on the 7th of December, bringing the interesting intelligence that he had come upon the tracks of Burke's party at the River Flinders. This information induced Landsborough to alter the course originally laid out for him, and on the 10th of February,

1862, he started on a course across Australia by way of the Flinders.

Reaching the Flinders on the 19th of February, he was disappointed in finding all tracks obliterated by the rains that had fallen since Walker's visit. This fine river, which was struck at about 100 miles from the sea, he followed further upwards in a south-easterly direction for 280 miles, where it still presented a bed 120 yards wide, with a shallow stream flowing over it. He estimated the Flinders to be 500 miles long, which makes it probably the most considerable of the rivers of Northern Australia. From this fine stream a short journey of twenty miles across a low dividing range, brought the party to the head waters of the Thompson, where they found that some colonists from the Queensland settlements had preceded them, in search of suitable pastoral stations. Following this river for the greater part of its course, they crossed from it eastwards to the upper part of the Cooper or Barcoo, and thence to the Warrego. Here a change in the features of the country takes place. While the north, under the influence of genial rains, has been covered with verdure, this more southerly district has been suffering from a rather long continued drought, and all the fine grass has disappeared. An effort is made to maintain a southerly course to Cooper's Creek, in order to reach the depôt established there by Burke; but this endeavour is unsuccessful, owing to the want of water, and in the vain attempt the horses undergo the severe ordeal of being seventy-two hours without drinking. Landsborough therefore makes for the settlements on the Darling, and on the 1st of June arrives at the station of the Messrs. Williams on that river, where he learns for the first time of the sad fate of the expedition under Burke. His own expedition is finished by his arrival in Melbourne in August following.

Landsborough's description of the country between the gulf and the Thomson presents to us a new world. This extensive area he describes as magnificent, consisting of basaltic plains of good soil, very thickly grassed. There is no mention of any alloy of desert so common further south and west, so that we infer that this fine country prevails over the large area between 20° and 25° of latitude. A practical confirmation of its qualities appears in the fact that a foal which had been born at the Flinders, had followed its mother with the expedition to the station on the Darling. One of the most conspicuous of the grasses had a resemblance to sorghum, and the horses fed upon it with great avidity. With rare exceptions water was always abundant, and the climate was healthy as far as the brief experience of the travellers could decide. The whole country, however, was exceedingly flat—the highest land along the Flinders being not more than from 1000 to 1500 feet in elevation, while the dividing range itself was not of greater height.

The rainy season of this promising country was found to begin in January, and end in April or the beginning of May; and as there had been considerable rainfall prior to the expedition's visit, everything looked to great, and, perhaps, more than usual, advantage. Leichhardt, who about seventeen years before, traversed all the country bordering on the Gulf of Carpentaria, gave a less favourable account, as he saw it during the dry season. He alludes to the creeks as being salt, and to the vast plains as imperfectly supplied with fresh water; remarking, however, at the same time, that the indications of a numerous aboriginal population would augur better for the country's qualities. The drought which Landsborough found prevailing at the Warrego and Darling rivers had extended eastwards into those parts of the settled territory of Queensland and New South Wales that were situated in the same latitudes.

Landsborough speaks rather more disparagingly than his fellow-travellers of the aborigines, regarding them as alike insatiably greedy and incurably treacherous. While the expedition was at the Herbert, about a hundred of them came swarming around the camp, all fully armed after their own style, and all apparently so bent on mischief that the leader deemed it imprudent, with his very small party, to persist in going further. Fortunately there was a great awe inspired by the horses. Again, at the Barcoo, he was compelled to use fire-arms to repel the furtive attacks of the natives; and it would appear that about this place they had tried similarly to surprise Gregory several years before. Landsborough found that the best plan was to give them nothing, in which case they seldom troubled him with their presence. When presents were given them, the more they got the more they wanted. They did not seem to be numerous in the districts passed through.

The kangaroo were seen to be numerous near Carpentaria, and emus were chased on the banks of the Flinders, one of their number having been caught and dressed as food. As McKinlay's party observed a Platypus (*Ornithorhyncus paradoxus*) in the water of the Upper Burdekin, we have thus the remarkable fact that the three distinguishing types of Australian fauna range through the widely-separated latitudes of the country, from Carpentaria and its vicinity far into the tropics in the north, to the southern extreme of the colony of Victoria, extending to south latitude 39°. The typical vegetation, too, seems equally pervasive. Dr. F. Mueller of Melbourne, in giving, by way of appendix to

Landsborough's account of his expedition, a list of the plants known to exist at the Gulf of Carpentaria, remarks upon the general similarity of these intra-tropical productions to those of the extra-tropical part of Australia. He says, "that a vast predominance of phyllodinous acaciæ, and especially of *eucalypti* (gum-trees) impress on the vegetation a character by no means dissimilar to that of the extra-tropical tracts of Australia; that plants indicating a high mountainous character of the country are absent; and that amongst grasses and other herbaceous plants, very many occur of nutritious property, and of perennial growth, readily renewed by judicious farming, when, after the rains of the summer months, a fresh pastoral green will be desired for the future herds and flocks of the gulf country during the cool and drier season of the year."

Mr. Landsborough's successful journey, more, perhaps, than that of any other before him, will stimulate pastoral colonization, already advancing with a wonderful progress from the southern settlements towards the north and west, into that vast and vacant expanse of a pastoral empire through which the explorer passed. The herbage and the climate are found suited to the sheep even in these low latitudes; nor is the Australian squatter much disturbed by the assertions of scientific theory that the close fine warm fleece cannot continue upon the sheep under a tropical sun. The Australian colonists have had many years' experience of wool-growing in latitudes close to the tropics; and latterly they have passed with their fine-woolled sheep several hundred miles within the tropical boundary. And yet they shear annually a fleece of the finest quality from the still healthy and thriving sheep.

Mr. Landsborough is not less impressed than his fellow-colonists that the pastoral empire of the future is to be projected yet much further into tropical Australia. Science, sitting at home, speaks in one way on this subject; experience, working upon the actual scene, speaks in another. The following passage-of-arms between these two opponents occurs at a meeting of the Royal Geographical Society, held in London on the 11th May last (1863), at which Mr. Landsborough was present, and it is quite a refreshing variety to the monotonous dignity of more ordinary procedure:—

"Mr. Landsborough stated that, from his experience of sheep-rearing, Queensland was eminently adapted for the growth of wool, and the climate suitable for European constitutions; the Plains of Promise (part of the fine country above spoken of) were as fine a pastoral country as he had seen.

"Mr. Crawfurd was of opinion that wool could not be grown in the tropics; sheep were intended for a temperate climate, and the fleece was given to protect them from the cold. In the tropics the fleece was not required.

"Mr. Landsborough.—'You are theorizing. Who, of all

the human race, have the most wool on their heads—is it not the inhabitants of the tropics?' (Roars of laughter.)"

As to this difference of opinion, Australian experience has amply shown what can be done for a sheep and its fleece, within or without the tropics, by strict attention to breeding, regular shearing of the fleece, and careful shepherding. How a flock would fare in tropical Australia, if left for some time to its own shepherding, and if its breeding incidents were consigned to Mr. Darwin's general provision of "natural selection," is a question we have no data to answer. But in truth our data on Mr. Crawfurd's question are still less complete, for the region of Australia in which we have as yet experimented upon these pastoral problems is really not a tropical country in the climatic sense of the words. Far within the tropical boundary the country still retains the peculiarities of its extra-tropical features. Waterhouse, as we have seen, pushes the line of central non-tropical Australia northwards as far as 17° of latitude—that is, six and a half degrees within the tropical limit. Although in the parts of this immediate region near the sea, there seems a somewhat regular rainy season, as Gregory inferred at the River Victoria (North-west Australia), and as Landsborough observed towards the Gulf of Carpentaria, yet, on the whole, there is a general resemblance throughout in climate and physical features to the more southerly districts, a resemblance extending even to the irregular and rather scanty rain-fall. There is the dry atmosphere that results from this imperfect rain supply. There are heavy dews, with chill and even frosty nights. McKinlay, for instance, in descending the Burdekin, found ice on three different mornings, while the other nights or mornings were also mostly very cold. This was in July, mid-winter, no doubt, but in a latitude between 19° and 20°. Arnhem's Land, forming the west shore of the Carpentaria Gulf, and the Cape York peninsula, forming the opposite shore, have alone decidedly tropical features; and even in these comparatively restricted areas, it is not improbable that we may discern something of the "Australian feature" still imparting its peculiar expression to the tropical countenance.

McKINLAY—1861-2.

McKinlay left Adelaide on the 16th August, 1861. Proceeding in a direction due north, it was not until the 24th September that he had passed the furthest settlements of the colony, then extending in that direction to upwards of 400 miles from Adelaide. Some interest attaches to these remoter parts of the colony, as exhibiting extremes of flood and arid sterility. Twenty years before, Eyre had seen and described a kind of inland sea, shallow apparently, but of vast expanse, being twenty miles wide, and extending, in a horse-shoe or serpentine form, 400 miles into the interior. He named this watery expanse Lake Torrens, and Lake Torrens has ever since figured upon our maps with a vague and mysterious outline that has been gradually softening into those uncertain marks that may represent the traditionary and mythic. The sea in question was the sudden effect of heavy rains, such in fact as McKinlay's party encountered further on in the journey, and disappearing perhaps as suddenly as it came. On the present occasion there was nothing but a dry desert. "Got all safe across the Lake Torrens," says the explorer on 27th September, "no water being at our crossing nor in view." Indeed, the next fifty miles was the most veritable desert that was experienced on the journey.

Lake Hope succeeded, and the expedition entered a country remarkable for many such sheets of water, and for a soil clothed with luxuriant grass whenever the supplies of rain gave support to vegetable life, but at other times parched and waste with the excessive heat of summer. Here, at Lake Buchanan, the expedition halted for some time, until its leader had explored this lake district, and in particular had followed up the traces afforded to him by the reports of natives of the missing party under Burke. In the midst of his researches, he received intelligence that the fate of the party had been ascertained. He resolved, however, still to pursue the journey across Australia, a contingency for which the expedition had been fully fitted out.

Amongst the lakes and creeks of this country, the natives were found to be, comparatively speaking, exceedingly numerous; as many as from 200 to 300 would be found around some one of the lakes, and from 400 to 500 upon a creek, all being in good physical condition, and apparently amply supplied with food, chiefly the fish of these waters. There seemed to be large numbers to the eastward, upon the Cooper and in its neighbourhood, some of whom on one occasion, during McKinlay's search at Lake Massacre, were disposed to be hostile. In estimating numbers some allowance must be made for the fact that these natives were not stationary at the places where they were respectively seen. They doubtless wandered freely about over a certain range of country occupied by tribes mutually friendly, or connected with each other; so that bodies of natives successively met with may have consisted to some extent of those who had been previously seen. Thus at Lake Jeannie many "old friends" came about, whose acquaintance had been made at Lake Buchanan, fifty miles away. We must also bear in mind that Stuart in his preceding expedition in these latitudes could see no aborigines, a circumstance alluded to by Mr. McKinlay as most unaccountable. On the whole, however, these later Australian expeditions warn us that we must extend somewhat our estimates, vague as they previously were, of the Australian aboriginal population, and no longer imagine that an area equal to two-thirds of that of Europe, had contained, before the inroad of our colonization, no more than about 200,000 human beings.

Quitting the lake region, the party had to pass through Sturt's Desert, lying north and west of their position. Explorers since Sturt have successively contracted the dimensions, and mitigated the bad repute of this region. While Eyre, in 1841, witnessed the effects of deluge, Sturt, four years afterwards, encountered the opposite extreme of drought; and again, in a region where the latter had nearly perished with thirst, McKinlay and his expedition were all but swept away by a flood. Had these, in their turn of incident, been floated safely down for 300 or 400 miles, they might have witnessed Lake Torrens once more, assuming its *impromptu* existence; only, however, to suffer an equally rapid disappearance under that extraordinary evaporative power of the Australian atmosphere alluded to by both Waterhouse and McKinlay. The flooded state of the country on the left compelled the party to make a considerable detour to the eastward or right of the intended direction, which they had afterwards to rectify as they proceeded northwards.

Emerging from this region of inundation in about 25° south latitude, an extensive country of high promise was passed through, consisting in a great degree of grassy plains, intersected by rivers, and bounded by hilly ranges. The abundance of water, indeed, suggests that this particular season may have been one of unusual moisture. The travellers were impeded by swamps, and while in the daytime the air was perfumed by the odour of innumerable flowers, in the night it was infested by still more numerous mosquitoes. Patches of scrub, too, were not unfrequent, and the ever-recurring spinifex grass indicated its accompanying poor soil. What appeared to be the dividing range of the country was passed about latitude 22°, a little further north than Stuart found it in his line of march, seven or eight degrees to the westward.

After passing the tropical line, and entering what is geographically tropical Australia, the aspect of the country does not greatly vary until quite near to the gulf. No country perhaps retains its similarity of feature throughout so great an area, and through so many degrees of latitude, as Australia. A change of country begins where the regular rains of a tropical season call forth a profuse vegetation, and create a more uniformly good soil than is found under the precarious climatic conditions of the rest of Australia. The River Leichhardt was struck on the 6th of May, in about 19° south latitude, and at a distance of a hundred miles from its mouth. The stream was at this point only from twenty to thirty yards wide, but about thirty miles from the gulf the bed was from 500 to 600 yards wide, and about half of this space was filled by the water. There was a large sand-spit at this place, a feature that indicated the tidal influence, and a tidal rise of four feet was observed. McKinlay proceeded northwards as far as the state of the country would allow, but was at length arrested by interposing deep and broad mangrove creeks, and boggy flats. At this point he judged the sea to be still from four to five miles distant, and observed a tidal rise and fall of from ten to eleven feet. This was on the 19th of May, and on the 21st the party commenced the return homeward, which the leader had already decided should be by way of Port Denison and the eastern colonies.

For nearly 150 miles eastwards the country preserves the general Australian character. Beyond that distance and nearly to the sea-coast it presents almost a continuous succession of hill ranges, forming a country most difficult for locomotion, and where the remaining bullocks, horses, and camels of the expedition rapidly sank under their increased toils. The fine River

Burdekin was made on 5th July in about 19° south latitude and 145° east longitude; at which point it presented a fast running stream twenty yards wide, and knee-deep of water. Following its course, a party of natives are disturbed in the act of cooking food, which consisted of roasted roots and a kind of fruit. The deserted board was promptly cleared by our travellers, who, by this time reduced to horse and camel, found the native larder fully as attractive as their own.

The marks of dray-wheels and bullocks' feet—those sure indications of pastoral settlement, were repeatedly passed as the travellers descended the Burdekin; but, although cheered by the knowledge that they were once more amongst the habitations of their countrymen, they were never fortunate in coming upon any station, and they were unwilling to deviate from the direct course for any special search. It was only after leaving the river at the point where it makes its great sweep from a south-east to a north-east direction, that in their course for Port Denison they at length descried one of the pastoral homesteads. This station was about seventy miles from the port, and belonged to Messrs. Harvey and Somers, who received the party with the full measure of squatting hospitalities. The new seaport settlement of Bowen, upon Port Denison, is for the present the frontier township upon the advancing wave of colonization northwards. From this remote outport McKinlay and his party gradually made their way southwards through the three intervening colonies of Queensland, New South Wales, and Victoria, with little other impediment than the repeated gratulations and fêtes awarded them by the colonists.

RESULTS OF RECENT EXPLORATION OF INTERIOR AUSTRALIA.

PHYSICAL FEATURES AND CLIMATE.

We have now some reliable knowledge of the character of the interior of Australia. The features of the vast expanse seem latterly to have improved upon every successive acquaintance we have been enabled to make with them. We may at length conclude, in a gathering up of all our data, that the Empire possesses in Australia a very much larger territory available for the use of its people than was supposed to be the case several years ago. Then where is and what is the great Desert—that arid waste supposed to comprise the greater part of this interior space? Is it a phantom that has at length been dispelled? and were all the toils and sufferings of Sturt a mere imagination? By no means; for the "hot wind" that is still, with more or less of fiery breath, wafted down every summer to the south and south-eastern coasts proclaims that the arid region still exists, and still can make its existence known at many hundreds of miles distance.

The Desert is there still, but we have now gained a somewhat different view of its character. Lying to the south of the latitude of the centre is a wide sub-tropical region, comprising that part of the Australian continent which presents in the widest range of its extremes the irregularities of the country's very peculiar climate. Remote alike on one side from the moderating tropical rains, on the other from the equalizing influences of the sea, destitute of high mountain chains and extensive forests to draw down and retain moisture, the whole expanse is virtually a naked plain, basking under a semi-tropical sun. The rain supply is in the main inadequate for so warm and exposed a country; besides that it is of capricious occurrence; the evaporative force, therefore, is mostly in the ascendant, and the high winds that often scour the vast and open expanse acquire their dry and hot character as they pass over the dessicated country. Meteorological conditions cause these hot winds to blow towards the southern seas, where they are at length arrested, changed in their character, or destroyed by the supply of moisture they take up. The colonies to the south and south-east, namely, South Australia, Victoria, and New South Wales are thus in the direct route of these winds, and exposed to their full force. To these colonies they come usually as the climax to some days or weeks of preceding hot and dry weather, and they are as usually the precursors of a change of this weather—of cool southerly winds and rain.

These dry hot winds are due, then, to a region which is in general deficient in moisture and water surface, and which, at the same time, lies under a powerful sun. This usual condition is subject to occasional aggravation from unusual drought; occasionally, too, on the other hand, from an unusual rainfall this arid condition of the country is entirely, although but temporarily reversed. The result in this latter case is a rapid and wonderful change, alike in the country's aspect and in the character of its climate. Wherever there is a soil, the moist ground, fostered by the warm and now genial air, is promptly covered with vegetation; even the slopes of the sand hills sprout out with flowers; life teems forth in air, earth, and water. The hot winds are sensibly modified, and, if the rainfall is general, they are even entirely suspended. The colonies adjacent experience promptly the effect of these extremes of change that take place in the large and problematical area behind them, whose condition is at all times so important to their respective climates. Thus they occasionally enjoy an unusually cool season, as they occasionally also at other times suffer one that is unusually hot.

It does so happen that our accounts of the Australian interior as received from its various explorers are chequered by these very extremes. Several of the principal expeditions happened to have been undertaken in seasons presenting one or other of these extremes. The summer of 1844-5, during which Sturt was repulsed from the Desert, was one of great and unusual drought, as we ourselves well recollect with reference to the colony of Victoria, where scarcely a drop of rain fell during the four months from December to April. On the other hand, the season of 1861-2 was unusually moist and cool. In Victoria this season was considered to be the wettest the colonists had experienced in the country. This was the season in which Landsborough careered through the interior—that dry and thirsty land of Gregory and Sturt—almost as though it had been one universal grass park; and in which McKinlay found his difficulties to arise, not, as with Sturt and Gregory, from drought and arid waste, but from water.

The water supply is, indeed, the key to the whole question. This sub-tropical area, with all its precarious climate, is yet not to be accounted the mere desert that Sturt has impressed upon our minds; but neither is it to be depended on as the blooming, well-watered surface of later explorers. It may be urged, indeed, to its disadvantage that, as the country is liable to such extremes of condition, the bloom of one favourable season will hardly compensate to life and property for the uninhabitable waste that may be caused by its unfavourable successor. We are reminded of the saying that the strength of a whole cable is just that of its weakest link; and so a practical Australian squatter who ventures himself and his live stock into the far interior, may prudently interpret the country by its worst seasons. Mitchell in the year 1846 describes the district of the Upper Barcoo, or Victoria, as a grassy scene, similar to that which had captivated Landsborough in his course somewhat further westward and northward; but Kennedy in the very next year, as well as Gregory in 1858, found these verdant lawns of the Victoria only a dessicated waste; and now again in 1862 we learn that the country thereabouts is once more luxuriantly clothed, and beautiful as the "plains of promise." From this chequered scene, however, we can turn with re-assurance to the results of Stuart's expeditions. Having accomplished three successful journeys across Australia during three successive years, we have some guarantee as to the permanent features around at least one great dividing line of the interior country.

We are warranted in concluding that this vast interior Australia is habitable and available enough in its ordinary, or average seasons. The question remains with the occasional seasons of extreme drought. One such occurred, as we have seen, in 1844-5; another, six years later, the Victoria colonists can well remember, at least in its culminating effect on "Black Thursday," the 6th of February, 1851, when many parts of the arid country almost simultaneously took fire. Experience, however, seems to establish the fact that when this changeable interior is visited by such climatic extremes, the entire area is not simultaneously affected. This is a very important consideration for the expanding colonies of the south and east, whose increasing population and property are either clustered close around the precarious area in question, or are placed by successive steps of colonization further and further within its boundaries. The case practically amounts to this: that when one or two of the colonies suffer, and are, consequently, short in their harvest, the others have escaped, and can make up the deficiency; and, when one section of the pastoral interior may be scorched and destitute of pasturage, the live stock may all still be preserved by a temporary transference to another. A rather severe drought affected New South Wales and the southern parts of Queensland in the season of 1861-2—the very season that proved so moist further to the south and west, and that covered Victoria with universal verdure. Again, the three years' drought of 1837-39—of terrible memory in New South Wales—did not extend into Victoria. What is still more encouraging, this intolerable scourge, whose effect now upon the extended and multiplied interests of the colony would be tenfold more destructive than before, has not since re-appeared.

The most sterile portions of this precarious interior region are not those which are far removed from the settled country, although this has been the common notion. The country that originates the hot wind really extends much nearer to the settlements than the colonists had supposed; they have, in fact, already, by means of their squatting outposts, penetrated in some directions far into its depths, and they are occupying and making available to their purposes even the least favourable parts of its ill-reputed area. Such is the hot, dry, salt-bush country to the northward of Adelaide described by Waterhouse, who accompanied Stuart, and such is the kind of country McKinlay passed through, 400 miles north of the same capital, and already occupied by squatting stations. At Blanchewater, the furthest, for the time being, of these settlements, the party had to prepare to encounter in their northerly march fifty miles of the worst desert that was met with during the entire journey.

The interior of Australia, therefore, is a country we can make use of, and there is every reason to believe that the greater part of it will soon and with marvellous rapidity be overspread by pastoral settlements. There is sufficient rainfall and vegetable growth to cover by far the greater part of its wide surface with some kind of soil. Where the quartz, sandstone, and granite come to the surface, there is a poor account of results. These spaces are the scrub and spinifex country, so often recurring upon the explorers' maps, or they are the patches of mere sand and stones, which also often occur, and which in one particular region, where they are the prominent feature of a considerable area, have established a distinction as the "Stony Desert." On the other hand, the basaltic outcrop of rocks and the clay surfaces are the better class of soils. These are ever ready to spring into verdure. They await the providence of the clouds, and are never slow to respond whenever opportunities are showered upon them.

It is not improbable that the country may be found better and less subject to extreme changes further to the westward than McKinlay's or even Stuart's line of march. In that direction lies nearly one-half of the Australian interior still uninvaded. But this conjecture as to its qualities has to encounter that arid desert that arrested Gregory beyond the sources of the Victoria of the North-west, and that looks down ominously over this unexplored expanse from its northern margin. The conjecture, nevertheless, is based upon an opinion, somewhat general, that an inlet or strait of the sea has covered, recently perhaps, the flat or hollow country between Spencer Gulf and Carpentaria. The low sandy region that continues northwards from the head of Spencer Gulf may have been at no remote time (geologically speaking) the shallow channel of a sea dividing Australia into two great islands. This recently raised and sterile sea-bed is still marked out by the line of the fitful Lake Torrens and the lower course of the Cooper. Towards the Gulf of Carpentaria there is still the low flat country, but the rains and vegetation of a more regular and tropical climate have covered the surface with a better soil.

THE ABORIGINAL NATIVES.

We quit the subject of soil and climate for that of the living occupants who are in the midst of both, to enjoy or endure the ordeal of their extremes. Our information regarding the aboriginal race, derived from the recent expeditions, tends, as already stated, to enlarge our previous estimates as to their numbers. Few still, however, are these numbers, even if we double the former reckoning, and sprinkle some four hundred thousand individuals over the great "Terra Australis." And this small number is still diminished each year with each advancing step of the colonist into the aboriginal homes. The natives generally cannot retreat before the colonial invasion, because their exclusive tribal system surrounds each separate native community with aliens or enemies of its own race; each tribe ever watchful of its own territorial boundaries, each often at variance with its neighbours, and many of the tribes, in consequence of these alienating circumstances, speaking a dialect mutually unintelligible. They remain in the colonized districts, and gradually die off. Many tribes have thus nearly or entirely disappeared within the present colonies.

They are decidedly low in the scale of human attainments. A controversy occurred lately as to whether the true Australian invented and used the canoe.* He emerges from the degradation

* See the "Athenæum" of March 1st, 8th, 15th, 22nd, and 29th, 1862, where Mr. Crawfurd and Capt. Jukes contend for the negative, and Mr. Brierly, and Sir D. Cooper for the affirmative, which is the true version. Twenty years ago, the writer, in confirmation of both the latter authorities, saw the natives of Twofold Bay, at the south-eastern extremity of Australia, sporting in their little canoes, which were neatly made of stout thick bark, and managed with some dexterity.

implied by this question with a ray of triumph. He does make use of a canoe, tiny as its structure is, and one of the spoils collected by Stuart was a small native canoe model. The Australian can probably claim to have fashioned and navigated a canoe of his own, independently of the example of the superior vessels that are constructed by the more intelligent races adjoining the northern coasts. Some of his customs are curious. How came he to practise the rite of circumcision? Our travellers allude to this rite as observed in the South, but not in the North. Leichhardt, however, expressly states that it was practised by all the tribes he met with in the year 1845, around the Gulf of Carpentaria. The knocking out of two or four of the upper front teeth as a sign of adult manhood is very general, although not universal.

The accounts given us of the natives, their friendly, mischievous, or hostile purposes, are somewhat various and contradictory. They have evidently the Japanese quality of a dislike to be intruded upon by outside and unknown barbarians, with their sickly unnatural skins, and their uncouth, anomalous, unkangaroo-looking attendant quadrupeds. Our travellers and their temporary camps, it is evident, were repeatedly in the way of the natives, disturbing their fishing and their other arrangements. To conduct amicable intercourse with these sons of nature, much depends upon tact and firmness, and even more upon a thorough mutual understanding of aims and objects. The desire to appropriate is as inveterate in the black as, according to our police, it is in the white, and this impulse is perhaps the most fertile of all occasions of differences. A large property, of a nature kindred to blankets and tomahawks, fishhooks and bead necklaces, and a small party to defend it, forms a sad stumbling-block in the way of aboriginal virtues. The kindness shown by the Cooper's Creek natives to King, the survivor of Burke's party, as well as their sympathizing lament over the body of Burke, are pleasing and encouraging traits. A persistently hostile character like that of Keri Keri, encountered at Lake Massacre, a kind of Australian Hannibal, as he seemed, in his mortal antipathy to those intruding Romans, the colonists, seems the exception to the general rule.

Cannibalism is now but a too well ascertained custom of these Aborigines. New Zealand and Fiji afford analogous and perfectly authenticated confirmation of such customs, as well as New Caledonia. The report or rather confession of the Lake Massacre natives that they had dug up and eaten the body of Gray, another of Burke's party, who had died of fatigue on the return route, is not at all unlikely to be true. Nor is it necessarily a hostile indication on the native's part. Morrill, an English seaman, who had been wrecked seventeen years ago (in 1846), on the North-eastern coast, about Cape Upstart, and had lived with the natives thereabouts during all that time, brings us the latest accounts of this and other of their customs. He re-appeared amongst his countrymen at the northern out-stations at Queensland in February last (1863). The natives had treated him kindly after their own rough fashion. But he is clear on the subject of their cannibalism. He says: "My experience with the blacks proves that they are cannibals; parents eat their own children, and usually they eat the bodies of those killed in fight, and I would not trust them generally."* All these Aborigines seem to have a great difficulty in procuring any other food than fish, and the scanty edibles of the natural vegetation. This circumstance, together with the keen appetite given by the Australian air, to which our travellers repeatedly testify, may supply the original motives to cannibalism, according to the conjectures of some writers. The pursuit of a foe has the double stimulus of a feast and a revenge. "O for the kidney-fat of an enemy!" is the motto of aboriginal knight-errantry. But romance is sadly exploded in the fact that friend

* A further account of Morrill, derived from his own narrative, is given in Chapter XI.

and foe seem indistinguishably appreciated, and are sent with equal zest to a common bourne.

THE OTHER NOTABILIA OF THE WAY.

Comparatively few of the larger birds or animals were met with in these interior journeys. Australia is not, as a whole, densely filled with these objects any more than with man. The shy kangaroo keeps well within woods and hill ranges, where, however, with its somewhat gregarious habits, it is often in large numbers. The wild Australian dog spreads over the plains, but is venturesome only at night, when he frequently prowled about the camps of the travellers, being occasionally found dead in the morning, poisoned by the strychnine baits used for the purpose. He vies in ferocity with his congener, the wolf, for although partial to a sheep, he will as readily turn upon a wounded brother as upon any other attainable prey. This animal is remarkable as the only non-marsupial quadruped of noticeable dimensions in a world of kangaroo, and the question has long been debated as to his indigenous origin, so to speak, or the apparently more probable solution of a late introduction into the country by man's agency. There comes just recently from Australia a new light on the question, in the fact that amongst remains of the animals, extinct and non-extinct, of the Australian drifts, those of the dingo or native dog have been at length detected. This discovery might be supposed to have settled the question of man's intervention, were it not that a like antiquity to that just indicated for the dog, claimed now so generally for man himself, may afford grounds for regarding the interesting problem as still unsolved.*

Australia having broken through her exclusive kangarooism in the instance of the dog in the south and the central region, is again cosmopolitan in the north with the alligator; the *ornithorhyncus paradoxus* is in the north also, as well as in the south. The emu appears at intervals throughout. Tough, rank, and oily in his flesh, he is not a coveted morsel by way of variety to the fare of the explorers, although most of them have, on occasions, been glad to eke out their scanty supplies with an emu supper. A bird, distinguished as Sturt's pigeon, appears to have been most abundant. There were great numbers of cockatoos, including the black macaw, and many pelicans where there was water. But on the whole, in a thoroughly practical view of the country's fauna, the opportunities of subsisting by the products of the way were by no means frequent to the travellers, and the main reliance was ever upon the supplies taken with them, and in the

* For this geological information as to the dingo, I have to thank Dr. Falconer.

last resource upon the animals that carried the general outfit.

THE OUTFIT OF AN AUSTRALIAN EXPLORATORY PARTY.

What is the most suitable outfit for an Australian exploratory expedition? is a question that is now likely to be of some interest, if such expeditions are to go on at the rate of the last three years; and that they will be kept up is not at all improbable. An emulative spirit has been aroused on the subject in the colonies. These later expeditions have shown an unexpected facility in accomplishing such great journeys, and nearly the western half of the island-continent remains unknown. There is still enough left of the "*Terra Australis Incognita*"—to use the old words of a century past—to supply stimulative occasion for at least two great expeditions; one to proceed from the head of the Great Australian Bight, in a direction a little west of north, to the point reached by Gregory from the opposite direction in 1856; the other from a point several degrees westward of the Bight in a northwest course towards Nickol Bay, whose rather promising vicinities were explored by Mr. F. T. Gregory two years ago (1861). As Victoria is possessed of an armed steamer, happily not in request for any purposes of war, and therefore available for other and happier uses, that colony can hardly do better, towards assuming the duties of the metropolitan position to which its people aspire, than to organize these expeditions. Stuart and his compeers have satisfactorily proved that such expeditions need not be very costly undertakings, and that, with such men as McKinlay and himself, they are not likely to fail of success.

Stuart's first expedition comprised a party of but three persons, including himself, with thirteen horses for the carriage of stores and baggage. This force was too feeble to encounter safely any considerable body of hostile Aborigines, as the result showed. Landsborough, also, with the same force, the two Aborigines he had in addition not probably counting for much, was under the same necessity at the River Herbert, above the Albert. But again he was successful with a like force subsequently in crossing Australia. Burke and Wills ventured across the country, also successfully, with a total of only four persons. Security, however, cannot be assured with such small forces. On the second occasion Stuart made up his party to twelve, and on the third to ten; that of McKinlay was nearly as strong; such a force seems quite adequate to all the contingencies of the way.

In regard to supplies, Stuart, who preferred a troop of horses as his only carriers, limited himself to what could be conveyed by this means.

McKinlay, on the other hand, took with him sheep and bullocks as well as horses, together with the variety of four camels; the bullocks were designed for carriage as well as food. Our traveller specially recommends the sheep, which he thinks no expedition should be without. The little creatures were easily managed, and they bravely held their way, keeping abreast of the party even on the longest marches. Next to this supply of animal food, the great staple is flour. With this the Australian traveller turns out his simply baked "damper" from the hot ashes; and hardly less important than the damper is the unfailing accompaniment of tea and sugar; some bacon, some rice, some *et-ceteras* follow, including of course, tobacco; with medicines (charitably including the rum in this particular division), lucifers, signal rockets, ammunition, rifles, and other defensive arms. These, with the canvas, the poles, the cords, and the fastening pins of the indispensable tents, a supply of blankets, and a very limited assortment of personal attire, comprise the main stay of the outfit.

The use of a cart or dray on these expeditions is a convenience hardly to be resisted. It was an indispensable component of the old official expeditions of any importance into the interior. The convenience of the cart, however, is sadly chequered by the delays and difficulties it brings to the expedition. Stuart would have none of it. McKinlay took it in hand, at first with horses, afterwards with a team of bullocks. Nothing equals the slow steady pull of the bullock for mastering the thick and thin, the log, stump, and stone of nature's road in Australia. With the skilful bullock-driving of Ned Palmer, a marvellously long step of the rugged journey was accomplished; but although the cart did wonders, it must needs be given up. It was slow as the tortoise, but rarely as sure. All Ned's skill could not pilot "the wheels" against the laws of gravitation. Yesterday they were over their axles in Jones's swamp, and to-day they disappeared like a shot over the perpendicular ledge of Smith's Creek. To recover from disasters, indeed, is as much the *forte* of a true bullock-driver as to avoid them. The dray ever emerges triumphant from everything. Ned, like a geologist, only requires time; but time, in a flying march across Australia, is a costly requirement. The cart has been daily weighed in a balance of accumulating deficiences, till at length the climax of its fate comes with the heavy rains encountered in the desert country. Conveyed to the top of a sand hill, it is buried along with such of the outfit it had carried as cannot be otherwise provided for. So the cart is abandoned, and poor Ned, freed from his ever-troublesome charge, is left, who knows? with the mixed emotions of the fond mother mourning for her rickety offspring, the object of all her past toils, anxieties, and affections.

Both Burke and Wills, and McKinlay, had the novel addition of a troop of camels to the live stock of their respective expeditions. The Victoria Government, shortly before the departure of the former, had imported a number of camels from India, and their merits were thus promptly put on trial by the opportunity of the Victoria expedition. Of these, Burke selected six with which to push on from Cooper's Creek, leaving the others, together with the bulk of the expedition, behind on the way. These camels in fact, and but a single horse, were the sole attendants of his small party. McKinlay took four camels, in company of a goodly quadrupedal assemblage, consisting besides of twenty-four horses, twelve bullocks, and a hundred sheep. The camel disputes with the horse the palm of usefulness in the Australian expeditions. In powers of endurance the camel seemed quite the equal of his rival, but he was more unruly and troublesome, and very uncompanionable with the other animals, his fellow travellers. McKinlay found a decided convenience in the height of his back, as compared with that of the horse, in keeping the supplies of the party out of the water on the occasion of traversing the flooded parts of the march.

But both horse and camel alike proved useful in other ways less premeditated. Necessity cures many prejudices, and hunger is a sauce to reconcile us to a very miscellaneous diet. As tho stock diminished, and as the appetite increased, even horse-flesh proved no unsavoury morsel, lean, tough, and jaded as it too often was. Horse after horse fell under the "jerking" process, consisting of cutting the flesh into long strips, to be dried in the sun. The camel, too, took his turn under the knife, and our travellers were ever far more anxious to secure an adequate quantity than to differ about the quality of their fare. Only once was the case otherwise, when one of the camels, "old and worn out, with sores all over him," was doomed to the knife and the jerking. Refractory even in the pot, the tough liver and kidneys defy the teeth of the hungry travellers, and the cook is enabled to boast for once on the journey that there was superfluity on the board.

TRIBUTES TO THE EXPLORERS.

The Australian colonies may well be congratulated not only upon their taking upon themselves the entire cost and management of the exploration of this part of the empire, but upon the vigour with which they are prosecuting their exploratory duties—a vigour that promises ere long to make the whole of Australia about as familiar to us as the other parts of the colonial empire. Meanwhile, well-merited honour has been done to the distinguished explorers we have been speaking of. Their services have been acknowledged and rewarded by their respective governments, while they themselves have been fêted by the colonists. Stuart, returning to Adelaide from his third expedition, greatly impaired in his health, was received with a welcome calculated at all events to renovate his spirits, for he was met by nearly 20,000 colonists, headed by the colonial governor. An interesting episode occurs with McKinlay. A public dinner is to be given him in Adelaide, and on the same day, it is said at the very hour fixed for the entertainment, the arrival of Howitt is announced in the city, on his return from his special expedition to Cooper's Creek for the purpose of bringing down to Melbourne the remains of Burke and Wills. This unexpected but timely visitor is of course a welcome and conspicuous guest on the occasion.

The South Australian Legislature, in the year 1859, agreed to bestow a public reward of £2,000 upon the colonist who should first traverse Australia from sea to sea. Stuart has received and well earned this reward. The area of his colony is traversed by the central line, north and south of Australia, and we have seen that the colony has been laudably and specially alive to its duties in the long pending solution of the Australian problem. A sum of £1000 has also been awarded to McKinlay. As it is pleasant to narrate the liberalities of Governments, we go on to say that the relatives of Burke and Wills, as well as King, the survivor of the party, have received very considerable gratuities and pensions from the Government of Victoria. The relics of the heroes themselves, recovered as we have said by a special mission to the interior, were committed to the grave with the honours of a state funeral; while a grant of £4,000 has been made from the public revenue for the construction of a suitable memorial of their achievements and misfortunes.

WHAT IS IN THE FUTURE?

With pleasure we also observe, from a recent intimation of the Secretary for the Colonies, that the part of these Northern Australian regions continuous in a northerly direction with the colony of South Australia—the part, in fact, traversed and explored by Stuart—is to be annexed to that colony. The large remainder of North Australia, to the eastward, falls in the meantime naturally into Queensland, whose colonists, after the galloping fashion of pastoral settlement in Australia, have already advanced their squatting outposts beyond Port Denison, in latitude 20°, and the mouth of the Burdekin in latitude 19°—places unknown to the world within the last three years. We augur well of this Imperial arrangement, not merely because it forms a fitting acknowledgment of colonial enterprise, but because we may venture to see in it the beginning of a new policy, by which the Home Government frees itself, once for all, from the imaginary, or, at any rate, to it, the needless costs and difficulties of founding new colonies. Colonies already established and prosperous may be left to perform this duty, and they may be so left all the more readily when, as in this case, they are prompt to take the duty in hand, with all its outlay and trouble.

We may surely hope that the Imperial Government will not find itself necessitated to repress or prevent the extension of the Colonial Empire. And yet this has been the course for some time past, otherwise Northern Australia would already have been colonized. The contemplated arrangement we have just alluded to respecting that vast but waste colonial domain, will, we trust, for the future, have the effect of putting an end to this repressive system. Difficulties there may be as to new colonies, their land regulations, and the question of their preliminary expenses, but they are real difficulties only to the inexperience and remote position of the Imperial Government. South Australia and Queensland will deal with their respective portions of tropical Australia. In founding new settlements so remote from head-quarters, these colonies must foresee the time when these, their far-off daughters, will demand separate establishments of their own. The Imperial mother may virtually go to sleep, until aroused at this stage of her children's and her grandchildren's growth by a call to adjudicate, as the supreme parent, upon the impending and, perhaps, contentious question of separation, while she finds at the same moment that a forty-fifth or a fiftieth member is about to be added to the world-wide colonial family.

Let us here advert to what may prove a very important contingency of the future, namely, the question of the particular form of government for these tropical regions. At the proper time this should form a special subject of Imperial consideration. The European may no doubt undertake various kinds of labour in these latitudes, but he is probably unsuited to field labour. The labouring hands of the dark races will be eagerly invited by the colonists, and, perhaps, the response on the part of the former will be as ready as the invitation. The superior race will then be exposed to the temptation of legislating for its own interests at the expense of the inferior. The temptation will ever lean in the direction of a coercive power in the hands of employers, and towards constituting a slave instead of a servant. The prevention of this possible evil will be much easier than its cure, and the prevention lies in withholding from tropical Australia that complete self-government that now distinguishes the energetic colonies of the temperate latitudes. The Imperial Government thus retains an effective control over all the colonial legislation—a control it has virtually parted with in the self-governed colonies. Having once, by these free institutions, transferred the reins to the vigorous colonial grasp, we fear that the mere abstract Imperial supremacy, which, with all its strength of legal theory, still unites the Empire under one Government, would prove of small avail in regulating an exciting domestic question of colonial legislation. In the North Australia of the future no question, probably, will be more exciting than that of the regulations of the labour supply. Imperial views in such a question would take an equitable and humane direction for the necessary protection of the labourer; but we may rest assured from much previous experience that the views of a tropical Australian constituency and their legislators, all exclusively of the white and employing race, with their own direct interests and convenience involved, would take a direction quite different.

Already are associations projected in Victoria and South Australia for the colonization of the northern shores, and even a complete political constitution is amongst the items and attractions of the business prospectus. Melbourne is the Australian head-quarters of capital and enterprise, and will now, probably, with its large population of colonial youth, be fertile in genial adventure of this kind. For years past such associations have been kept in abeyance by the indifference or opposition of the Home Government. Melbourne enterprise will now enjoy a better chance, having an authority to deal with at Adelaide instead of Downing Street. We recommend the two sisters to a reciprocity of good offices and to mutual usefulness. Only let us no longer neglect that magnificent domain which has now been familiarized to us, and at the cost of so much effort and suffering, by Burke and Wills, Stuart, Landsborough, and McKinlay; no longer leave its bright streams to sparkle in a waste of sunshine, or its luxuriant grass to be annually burnt by the Aborigines, in the wanton riot of superabundance.

CHAPTER I.

ADELAIDE TO BLANCHEWATER.

Occasion of the Burke Relief Expedition—Start from Adelaide—Incidents and Accidents by the Way—Refractory Camels—Daily Troubles with the Cart—Pastoral Stations and Hospitalities — Buchanan's, James', Marchant's, Jacob's, and Chambers'—Arrival at Blanchewater.

THE reader has learned from our Introduction the lamentable mischance that left Burke and his party to perish at Cooper's Creek. The intelligence received in the colonies that Brahe and Wright had left the depôt at the Cooper without learning anything of the missing party, excited general concern. The Victoria Government took prompt measures to prosecute a further search; and in order to make this search as complete as possible, expeditions were organized to proceed by both the north and the south. Mr. Alfred Howitt, an experienced Australian explorer, was ordered off at once to Cooper's Creek, while further expeditions were being prepared for a march to commence from the Gulf of Carpentaria. Mr. Walker was fitted out for a journey from Rockhampton, on the eastern coast of

Queensland, to the River Albert, at the head of the Gulf, and Mr. Landsborough was despatched from Brisbane in a small brig, the "Firefly," also to the same part of the gulf, where he was to begin a journey towards the south. The government armed steamer, "Victoria," was also sent to hover about the same rendezvous with suitable supplies for rendering assistance to the cause generally.

Howitt, as we have seen, accomplished the object of all this enterprise by finding the unfortunate party in the person of its sole survivor, King, who for between two and three months since the death of his leaders, had been living with the Aborigines of the Cooper, kindly enough cared for, indeed, by the natives, after their rude fashion, but so haggard and emaciated as to be hardly recognizable as a human being. This intelligence arrived too late to prevent the other expeditions, a circumstance the less to be regretted when we consider the important results they accomplished. Walker executed his mission successfully, reaching, on the 7th December, 1861, a depôt formed on the Albert by Landsborough, after detecting the traces of Burke's party at the Flinders, on his way. Landsborough set out from this depôt in October, and after proceeding 210 miles in a southerly direction towards the Central Mount Stuart, returned to the depôt, apprehending danger to his small party from the Aborigines, and also finding a scarcity of water, as the time (December) was towards the end of the dry season. The country otherwise, however, was of the most promising description. He reached the depôt on the 19th January, 1862, and on the 10th February took his course across Australia by way of the Flinders, guided to this course by the information given by Walker. It was only on reaching the settlements of the Darling, four months afterwards, that he learned the fate of Burke's party.

The Queensland Government co-operated with that of Victoria in forwarding the northern expedition. That of South Australia organized a special "Burke Relief Expedition" of its own. The parliament of the colony promptly voted the necessary funds, and the charge of the party was offered to Mr. John McKinlay. That gentleman being at the time in Melbourne, the offer was made to him through the electric telegraph. It was accepted as quickly as made, and within three weeks, as Mr. Davis tells us, of the parliamentary vote, Mr. McKinlay and his party were already at Kapunda, fifty miles beyond Adelaide, all prepared for the great journey before them. It was not indeed contemplated at starting that they would have to cross the entire of Australia, but they were equipped for that contingency, and their leader having decided further on to accomplish that object, they did accomplish it most creditably, and have proved, continues Davis, that the unsettled parts of the interior, between Blanchewater and Carpentaria consist of something else than a howling desert.

"Started from Adelaide with the camels, etc., on 16th August, 1860," says Mr. McKinlay, in his official journal, "and overtook the remnant of the party, horses, cart, etc., nothing of any particular note occurring on the journey to Blanchewater (Mr. Baker's station) more than ordinary on such journeys." This is all very well in an official document. Not so, however, with Mr. Davis, who finds a world of pleasant incident in the region of the settlements, and a great deal more of hospitality than in the unexplored world beyond. Here are the occurrences *en route* to Blanchewater, the outside settlement for the time being in the colony's progress, Mr. Davis being narrator.

On the 14th August, 1861, the horses, carts, and six of the "Burke Relief Party," under the command of Mr. John McKinlay, started overland for Gawler, a town some twenty-five miles distant from Adelaide, where they were hospitably received by Mr. R. T. Poole, of the Willaston Hotel, and whose son, Mr. R. Poole, better known as "Bobby," formed one of the party. Nothing could exceed the kindness shown to Mr. McKinlay and his six companions by Mr. and Mrs. Poole, who did everything that could conduce to their comfort and enjoyment—pigeon match in the morning, champagne lunch after, and other little pleasantnesses for the jolly fellows who were there.

16*th*.—On the 16th Mr. McKinlay and two others of his party started by train with four camels to Kapunda, some twenty-five miles further, where the horses, with the detachment, would be ready to receive him, having preceded him the day before. On arrival at Kapunda, a little incident occurred to one of the crew—a young lady stepped out of the train, who proved to be the idol of his affections. Poor fellow! his look of agony! little did he think he should have to say again the word farewell. But the lady was not to be deprived of her "last fond look," and she pressed to the front at the start in the morning, seeing us all off, and one of us more particularly, with a reciprocal good-bye, and a vigorous agitation of kerchiefs.

An accident happened just now, the cart, after having been packed as full as possible, was found, on its arrival at the "Sir John Franklin Hotel" from the railway terminus, to have its axle bent to that extent that it would not be safe to proceed; so that Mr. McKinlay, with the driver, was obliged to remain to get new axles, wheels, etc., whilst the camels and horses proceeded on to a sheep station some nine miles up country named Anlaby, where the greatest kindness was shown to all by Mr. Buchanan, a fine specimen of the Australian sheep farmers, and a friend of Mr. McKinlay's. Let us here pay a passing mark of respect to him and his excellent wife, and thank them for the hospitality they lavished on us. The worthy host brought forth the "stirrup cup," and long will his fine, open, manly face be remembered by all, as he drank "God speed." May his shadow never be less, and may prosperity ever attend him and his!

At Kapunda we were met by a member of the clerical profession, a wandering preacher, a most curious specimen of the order; his stories were all harmless, only a bore, though he doubtless meant well. He subsequently joined the party at Buchanan's, and then ensued the most charming religious controversy, with one of our party, ever heard — the parson in downright earnest, and his opponent, I must say, very much the reverse. It served to pass away the evening; but as most of those arguments generally end, so this did also, both were, at the close, exactly of the same opinion as they were at the beginning. This parson was somewhat of an oddity.

17*th and* 18*th*.—On Sunday afternoon, after

we had had a sermon from his reverence, Mr. McKinlay arrived with the cart.

19th.—Monday; started for Tottle Creek; roads very bad indeed, and the cart got bogged up to the axle, causing much delay; and during the detention the camels thought they would have a little fun on their own account, and so they did, for they commenced fighting like fury, till they were separated and tied up. Soon, however, the order was given to start with them and horses, and not wait for tho carts; so off they went, got to Tottle Creek, put up at a roadside public house, where bottled porter was the order of the evening, and very acceptable it was.

Here very nearly occurred a sad accident, and had it not been for Mr. McKinlay, who fortunately happened to be standing close by, Mr. Hodgkinson would have been trampled to death by one of the camels, a very spiteful one; he (Mr. Hodgkinson) was hobbling him, when he struck him with his foot with such force as to knock all the wind out of him, and would have proceeded to trample on him had not Mr. McKinlay caught hold of our comrade and pulled him from under the feet of the infuriated beast, tho man who had hold of the brute's nose-string pulling the camel round the other way; thus he was saved and soon recovered, and then put on the hobbles in spite of him. This camel was very unruly for a long time, the man in charge of him did not like fondling him as was done with all the others.

20th.—Cart came in about 11 P.M. Up and stirring early, and after packing the animals started for "Gum Creek," one of Mr. Levi's stations, under the management of Mr. Love, a very jolly, good fellow, who tried to make everybody as comfortable as possible, and he succeeded. This was a long stage of twenty miles, and here again the cart got into a mess, and bullocks were obliged to be sent to drag it out of the bog.

21st. Started for Booberowie, a station of Dr. Brown's, where the party had to sleep in the kitchen; this would probably not have happened had the Doctor been at home, but unfortunately he was absent from the station, and the nice little beds they saw through the windows, in which they hoped to have rested their weary limbs, remained untenanted, kitchen table and floor being used instead.

McKinlay went, it was omitted to be mentioned, to the Burra, a small town some few miles to the east of this track, for some odds and ends that had been forgotten; here he joined again, and here the pastor took his final leave of us for the Burra. He is a natural wonder.

22nd. We left this station. A few blessings, not loud but deep, were devoted, to the hospitable or *kitchentable* beds, to say nothing of the hard floor, and everybody as fatigued in the morning as when he turned in the night before. The cart, *of course*, soon got bogged, and caused a delay on a plain for several hours; the sun very hot. Here they were overtaken by a good Samaritan, who shared his fine damper, mutton, and tea with them. He instituted quite a pic-nic alongside his cart. Men remained, with the horses and the camels lying down, all jolly and happy.

On the move again as soon as the cart came up, and camped on Mr. James' Run, Kanowie. Did not go up to the house, but for the first time erected tents in a paddock, and all turned in after a good supper. But, alas! man proposes, and God disposes; for all had to turn out almost as soon as they had got between the blankets, to go off after the horses and camels, as there was the greatest row with them possible, as the camels had got amongst the horses and started them off at score. The night too was rather dark, and, dear reader, you may imagine it was no sinecure to go after them, tumbling down holes and over stones, logs, etc. However, after a long hunt, found and brought them all back but one, which we supposed had been beaten by the savage fellows, and thinking discretion the better part of valour, had bolted. Brought back the tidings to McKinlay, who said it could not be helped. All glad enough to turn in again this time, and with more success, as no accident occurred any more that night.

Up early and two or three sent after the missing camel. He was found some eight or ten miles on the road, going quietly along in his hobbles. He was soon caught and brought back. This little freak of (Mr. Cassim) the camel detained us here all day, as he did not arrive at the camp till nearly 4 P.M.

25*th*. Off in the morning on the road for Maranaric, and camped without tents. The cart, as usual, not up to-night. One of the fellows with a native black went after the camels, just to see where they were, as it was rather scrubby, when the wicked one (Siva) rushed at the two men and made them go for their lives, scrambling over logs and stumps and stones, much to the enjoyment of those in camp, who were watching their eccentric movements. Here it was necessary to walk about four miles to the station for supper—pleasant that after the day's work.

26*th*. Camels this morning not to be found, the horses and cart proceed without them to the camp at Lower Pekuna, a very nice one, there being an old shepherd's hut close by with a good well of water. Turned off the road some way to camp here on account of the water. Began forthwith to demolish the old hut and get logs on the fire, which soon was blazing away in grand style. The pots were quickly on and the supper got ready, to which ample justice was done. The camels did not come in till nearly 9 P.M., the men having been delayed from not finding them for several hours, and from their having had again a good general fight on the road. The two men with them were very nearly done up from fatigue in walking the stage, which was a long one, and running all over the country in the first place to catch these animals. However, a good supper and a sound sleep recruited them, and in the morning they were all right again.

Stayed here all day, Mr. McKinlay trying to buy some bullocks for the cart instead of the horses, the bullocks being more able to tackle the heavy roads. Here all the men took advantage of the spell and fine weather, and a general wash of all the clothes took place.

27th. Off again to-day for Price Morris Place, and camped there on a gentle rise, the weather very cold and wet. Pitched tents and got as cozy as circumstances would permit. This was a very bleak dirty camp. Here Wylde got a tremendous kick on his breast, fortunately rather high, so he did not feel it so much. It was a most wretched night, cold and raining, and the tents all blowing about.

28th. A long day's stage to-day, and after a bad night very trying for all. Nothing of importance occurred to-day, but everything "went merry as the marriage bell."

29th. Start this morning after a good night. And here a new hand in the shape of a native joined the expedition; Frank by name, and not a bad sort of fellow; speaks English well and rides well. He will be of great use. Here at Wirrandery the hostess was very kind to one or two who were in early—tea and cakes, with the invariable damper and mutton of every Australian sheep-station, being the order of the day.

30th. Left here for a very pretty place called Willow Creek. The camp was really picturesque. Did not arrive here till late, and off again very early in the morning. There are some copper mines here, and report speaks well of them. And here another black fellow was added to the store; one of the roughest specimens of the genus *homo* you would see in a day's march, even in Australia; hair long and matted. The miners had rigged him out with some old clothes much too large for him, and a wild-looking specimen "Jack" presented. The good people at Wirrandery call it eleven miles to Willow Creek; it is twenty-three good English miles, as all tried the distance when in camp. Supper as usual, *al fresco.*

31st. Left Willow Creek early in the morning

for Warcowei, under the superintendence of Mr. John Roe, a jolly good fellow. As usual, the cart in a fix, and could not be extricated; the driver rode into Warcowie about 4 P.M. for assistance; so immediately some of the party mounted, and rode out for that purpose. The business took a long time to do; it was quite dark when finished, so determined to camp there for the night, and proceed to the station in the morning. Middleton, however, rode in for something to eat and drink, and returned about 8 P.M., when three or four remained in charge of the cart, and Middleton and Davis returned to the station with all the horses, leaving the bullocks. Mr. McKinlay did not accompany the party to the station, as he was away in another direction to buy some bullocks.

Sept. 1st and 2nd. Remained at Warcowie, waiting for McKinlay. Pitched tents and did not trouble the good people at the station any more. McKinlay arrived, and was unsuccessful in his attempt to get more bullocks.

3rd. Again on the move this morning; the horses were not to be found; the camels, however, led the way to Mr. George Marchant's station, Perriwallia. Found him and several neighbours mustering cattle. All hospitality; gave us anything he had. As the camels were in long before the rest, and all the grub was with the horses, and they did not arrive till late at night, after this first arrival I had turned in for the night. Mr. Marchant let McKinlay have what bullocks he required.

4th. Start this morning for another out-station of Mr. Marchant's, Yudnapunda; a long delay on the way occasioned again by the cart. The men with the camels stop several times, and once three or four hours, much to their annoyance; and when they did come up they brought word that one of the camels was to return to the cart with Mr. McKinlay's blankets, as, *horribile dictu*, the cart had both shafts broken and could come no further, and Mr. McKinlay had determined to fit it with a pole for bullocks. This, of course, would take some time, as he had to send a considerable distance, to Mr. Frank Marchant's station, Arcola, for the iron-work for the cart. Hodgkinson started with the camel, and Davis took on the other three. The devil's own work to get the wild one packed; he kept rolling off his load. Had they not managed to get the "Rarey strap" on him, and so keep him down, he never would have been packed, and very likely some accident would have happened. He is a real varmint. Arrived, however, with the three, after a good deal of trouble, at Yudnapunda hut, where all the horsemen were regaling themselves with mutton and damper. Quickly unloaded, and joined them.

Stopped here till the morning of the 10th,

when Mr. McKinlay arrived with the cart all put to rights, and here we first met Mr. Jacobs, of Parallanah, a station some way farther up, and where he has invited the party to call *en route*.

10*th*. Off this night to Belcrackna Creek; rather pretty some part of the way; had to sleep for the first time without water; turned in about 10 o'clock, after a long stirring march.

11*th*. Proceed now to Willielpa, one of Mr. Chambers' stations, over which reigns supreme a certain Mr. Tom Coffin, quite a character in his way, and quite a curiosity to look at, with very long yellow hair, and nose to match. Fell in with a native well on the march, in which was a dead dog, but we drank the water, and thought it splendid. Who was that general of old who said that the river in which hundreds of the enemy were floating about was the best water he ever tasted? Tom produced milk, bread, and butter, things we had not tasted for some time.

12*th*. The next stage was Chambers' Creek, some twenty-five miles from Tom Coffin's, which we left the following morning for John's Creek; thence to McTaggart's station, passing through Mr. McCullum's on the way.

13*th*. At Mr. McCullum's station Mr. McKinlay procured the services of a bullock-driver, and bought his team from him. Ned Palmer was the *beau ideal* of a bullock-driver; hardy, devil-may-care, good-tempered, could swear as none but bullock-drivers can, and a very pleasant little fellow he was during the rest of the journey, and could spin his yarn with the best, and it lost nothing by his telling it. But to return to the track, McTaggart was very hospitable, and welcomed the party heartily.

15th. Made tracks now for Jacob's station, the gentleman last seen at Yudnapunda station. At this station, Parallanah, are many Aborigines about half-tamed. Here you might see a man with a cap on, and *nothing else*, or perhaps a tail-coat only, the women with a blanket or piece of cloth just thrown over their shoulders. But this is only just at the station; as soon as they arrive at their whirlies, off goes everything, and they appear strictly in a state of nature—unadorned, but whether it may be considered adorned the most in this case, I leave for abler hands to decide. This tribe is ugly in the extreme, and badly made.

Stopped here till the morning of the 20th, making, mending, and repairing, etc.; and about 10 P.M. started on course. To-day Hodgkinson killed a fine kangaroo with Davis's revolver (a very fine weapon by Colt); it was certainly forty yards off. Distance travelled to-day about twenty-two miles.

21st. Arrived at Parabandara. Fine water,

which was procured from some rocks above the camp. Left this camp tolerably early, but could not find the camels for some time; Davis found them, and returned just in time to find every pot and pan packed, and the cook oblivious of his existence. Pleasant, with a fourteen miles' stretch before you. I am afraid he made use of some colloquial expletives.

22nd. Now off for Blanchewater. This station is the last, or was last year, where the white man dwells permanently; here also were some of the Aborigines—ugly enough, and of anything but a sweet-smelling savour; the men have their front teeth knocked out, denoting that they have arrived at the age of manhood.

Here are taken in the stores—tobacco, sugar, tea, flour, horseshoes, soap, etc., etc., etc., too numerous to mention, enough for six months. Here Hodgkinson takes his place as second in command, as he appeared shortly after on his charger; it was the general opinion that he should have booked an inside place. Middleton takes his place with the camels. The stores had been sent up to Port Augusta, and thence per bullock dray to Blanchewater. Some of the flour had been spoiled by coming in contact with some paraffine oil. This flour was left behind, and Mr. Dean, the overseer, kindly provided us with some instead.

CHAPTER II.

BLANCHEWATER TO THE DEPOT, LAKE BUCHANAN.

Editor's Remarks—Start from Blanchewater—The Outfit—A Desert: Two of the Party nearly Lost—Arrival and Halt at Lake Hope or Pando—Many Natives, Friendly—Lakes Camel, Poole, and Siva, or Perigundi—Rumours of a White Man having died at Cooper's Creek—Lake Buchanan, or Cudgeecudgeena—October 18th, McKinlay starts for Cooper's Creek.

THE expedition now quits the furthest of the pastoral stations, Mr. Baker's, called Blanchewater. The travellers do not immediately enter upon uninhabited wilds, for after two days' march and twenty-seven miles of progress, they are only at one of Mr. Baker's out-stations, thus giving us some idea of the extent occasionally necessary to an Australian squattage in parts where the country is poor, and subject for most of the summer to those excessive droughts that altogether suspend the growth of pasture. From Blanchewater, for about fifty miles to Pando or Lake Hope, the country was so sterile and water so scarce, that all the animals suffered more or less, and ten days were spent at the lake in recruiting.

PANDO OR 'LAKE HOPE'

About Lake Hope commences a country of a different and rather remarkable kind. We may call it the lake district. The soil is generally clayey, hard and baked in hot dry weather, but only requiring rain to cover it with grass, which in many parts is most luxuriant. This is particularly the case with hollow parts of the surface, natural indentations apparently, which, with adequate rains, are converted into temporary lakes, and at other times are so many natural meadows luxuriant with long grass. Occasionally the soil is impregnated with saline or bitter particles, which are not tasted when the lakes are fresh filled by the rain, but which after a large evaporation render the diminished waters quite undrinkable. The rate of evaporation in these open plains, under a hot sun, and in the strong winds that often sweep the surface, is almost incredible. The party go on to Lake Buchanan, where a depôt is formed for some time, until some additional provisions are brought up by a detachment sent back for that purpose, and Mr. McKinlay has made his proposed search for Burke's missing expedition. Here he is already in the latitude of Cooper's Creek, and about sixty miles to the westward of it.

They are now in a region that seems full of the aboriginal natives, and in fact full of life of every kind, where water, that great and precariously supplied requisite of Australia, is abundant. The lakes seem full of fish, even when from their shallow appearance they can hardly be supposed to have water permanently. Mr. McKinlay subsequently alludes to the natives catching in these lakes or the creeks connected with them, the cat-fish of the Murray and the nombre of the Darling, as well as the brown perch, and what he thought a small cod. The natives were generally friendly, excepting on the occasion of Mr. McKinlay's search excursion to Lake Massacre, which we shall come to in another chapter. We leave Mr. Davis to tell of the everlasting troubles with the quadrupeds of the expedition's diversified menagerie.

Sept. 24th, 1861. Left Blanchewater this morning, and proceeded to a small creek some few miles further on. And now we are fairly off; no more haunts of civilized man! Let the gentle and I trust patient reader take his parallel ruler, scale, and protractor, and accompany us to the Leichhardt River. Down it also for 100 miles if he pleases, then *through* or *over*—or by any other means he chooses to adopt—the Burdekin ranges, including a swim through waters where alligators most do congregate, and on to Port Denison; thence in that terrible smack, "Ben Bolt," twenty-five days to Rockhampton, 300 miles only, with nothing to eat but bottled porter. Those gentlemen from "Heligo's Isle," had a cheerful trip, in point of fact a yachting excursion, in comparison, Hyperion to a satyr; but as Sairey Gamp justly observes, "I never likes to protigipate," so I will now my round unvarnished tale deliver.

25*th*. Our stock consists of twenty-four horses, twelve bullocks, one hundred sheep, and last, though not least, four camels: had we taken the sage advice of our clerical friend who left us for the Burra, our stock would also have been added to, in the shape of fowls, which he told Mr. McKinlay would add greatly to our comfort, as we should then be able to obtain new laid eggs for breakfast. Of course we must wait in the desert while the said fowls were nidifying, horses and camels already packed. Fancy explorers who expect to meet with no end of difficulties, bothering themselves with fowls!

Accompanied now by Mr. Elder and Mr. Stuckey, who was the first to explore beyond this as far as Lake Hope, to which lake we are now bound. Cracks of the stock whip, and clouds of dust denote a mob of cattle for the station; no doubt some of the men who were driving them looked on us as for the last time. It was a dreary walk for the men with the camels, a great part of the way through sand. Mr. McKinlay, with camels and sheep, arrived at a small creek with some large water-holes in it at 5·30. The horses were nowhere to be seen, which is very annoying. They had mistaken the creek that Mr. McKinlay intended camping at, and continued travelling until nightfall, when they came to a halt, and had some difficulty in unpacking one or two of the horses, and the night dark. Start and arrive at Mr. Baker's out-station, Toonkitchen. Mr. McKinlay with the camels, arrived also about 4 P.M., the cart at nightfall.

26th. On the following morning two horses got into a deep creek and hobbled they were at the time; got them out however, and packed and proceeded to the last hut in the settled districts, Manawankanina, distance about sixteen miles.

27th. Made an early start across the Fifty Miles' Desert, and there certainly could not have been found a more appropriate name. We travelled twenty-five miles the first day. Each man one quart of water, which we had in leather bags and tin canteens on the camels and horses, the remainder we buried for the bullocks when they came up next morning. Our leader remained behind with the bullocks, their driver, and two blacks. Had to watch the horses all night, or they would certainly have rambled in search of water. When at length they did see it, in they went, packs and all, and we were all parched with thirst travelling over nothing but hot sand. The sheep came in the morning early, and shortly after Mr. McKinlay came in with the bullocks, minus one, who went mad and rushed at Peter, a native, and had it not been for the canteen on his back, his doom was sealed. We were obliged to leave the bullock in the desert, but whether he ever returned to the settled districts or no, remains in obscurity. After the bullocks had refreshed themselves with a good long drink and plenty to eat, they, with Bell and Peter, returned to join the cart, which they came up with early the following morning.

28th. We had filled the mussocks ready for a start at daylight, and the four camels laden with water started at 5 A.M., Middleton and Hodgkinson in charge. They delivered their loads, and intended returning again, but unfortunately lost the tracks; and, after wandering about for two days, became so much exhausted, and the weather so frightfully hot, not having had a taste of water during that time, that death seemed inevitable. They took some loads off the camels which they had taken from the cart to lighten the beasts, and lashed themselves on their backs, which eventually turned out to be the means of saving their lives; for when these animals found themselves free, they immediately turned their tails southward, and after travelling all night our two companions' eyes were greeted with the sight of a beautiful sheet of water. They unlashed themselves, and when the camels arrived at the lake they jumped off and rolled into the water. After they had quenched their thirst, some natives came and brought them some fish, and treated them very kindly, and one accompanied them to our camp, about six or seven miles, and very happy indeed we were to see them return, for great doubts were entertained of ever seeing them again. Very weak and ill they looked; McKinlay out all the morning in search of them, and rejoiced he was to find them stretched out in the tent, and gradually improving.

We had meanwhile safely found our way to this water, Lake Hope, where we halted some time to recruit. Hodgkinson found himself so much improved that he and Davis started after the stores that had been left behind, and returned in the evening, having succeeded in finding the camel tracks. Had these stores been lost, we should have missed them very much—some 200 lb. of bacon, etc., which came in very handy afterwards. The natives who showed our missing comrades the way to the camp were rewarded—tomahawk, blanket, etc. Middleton slowly recovering.

Oct. 8th. Lake Hope abounds in fish, and any quantity of wild fowl. Took the shoes off the horses, and stuffed pack-saddles afresh, started from Pando Lake Camp, at 9·20, and found another

LAKE CAMEL.

beautiful lake (Camel, see illustration), named by Mr. McKinlay.

9th. Went round the western side of the lake. Peter and Sambo absconded after getting shirts, etc.; had to retrace our steps, having mistaken the dry top of a creek for a lake. Started about 7 A.M. and crossed creek.

11th. Mr. McKinlay started on the 11th with two camels, Mr. Middleton, and a native, with provisions and water, for whites said to be in the interior; they saw about 200 natives, apparently friendly. Horses rambled away about ten miles but were brought back again in the afternoon. Short hobbled them and went to roost. Shifted camp in the morning to better water, which the leader has named Poole's Pond, after Bobby Poole, one of the party. Plenty of natives about, but quite friendly. Wild ducks in numbers. Sewed a couple of sheepskins on the packs to prevent them from chafing. The skins, as we killed the sheep, came in very useful.

12th. Two of the bullocks missing; the driver went after them, and did not return till late the following day; they had gone back as far as Lake Hope. The water at the lake Mr. McKinlay found while he was out scouring the country is very bad indeed, in fact almost undrinkable; fortunately we had some other in our canteens. Water the horses from a canvas trough, as the sides of the lake were too boggy for them to go in. We did not finish till 9 P.M.

13th. Bullocks having again strayed we spelled on the 13th. Mr. McKinlay and Mr. Hodgkinson went out scouting, and returned about 4 P.M.

14th. Lake "Siva," named after the fierce camel, or "Perigundi" Lake, the native name. In the afternoon natives, both men and women, came to our camp, and were curious to see anything there; but on their departure we discovered that an axe was missing.

15th. This evening the watch (which was regularly kept) was surprised by a native coming to the camp *alone;* and what, reader, would you imagine was the cause of his midnight trip? Only to bring back the axe that one of his tribe had stolen. The old man then quietly took leave, saying he would return in the morning. His name was Mooticlina, *esto perpetua!* Henceforth we must not say that there is no honour among the aborigines.

16th. In the morning some natives came near the camp, and presently the old man arrived. Mr. McKinlay gave the women some beads and fish-hooks, which pleased them much; to the old man for his honesty a tomahawk, a thing more prized by these children of the desert than any other. Started, passing north-west of lake. Cleared the timber that surrounds it and commenced ascending sand hills very soft, high, and steep, then through flooded flats with box and polygonum. Distance travelled about eight and a half miles to Kierie Creek, and camped at water-hole. (Name "Wantula Depôt.")

17*th*. Remained here to-day, preparing for Mr. McKinlay's start for Cooper's Creek, where, as the black fellows say, "white man *sit down*" (*die*). They take with them stores, and some little creature comforts, in case they find the poor fellow alive, such as arrowroot, coffee, chocolate, etc. Mr. McKinlay takes the four camels with him, also two men and a native, who seems to know all about the "white fellow." Here we opened the store of recuperated sausages, 200 lb., and found them, to our sorrow, nearly all bad, one tin quite rotten and had to be thrown away there and then. We missed them much, as the sequel will show. The remainder we have hung on lines, hoping they might improve by the process. Thermometer to-day 122°.

18*th*. Mr. McKinlay and party before-mentioned off this morning, to find the truth of the report of the native, and whether the white man was still alive; and they take with them our best wishes for their success of course.

We must take from McKinlay's journal as the writer was not personally with him (be it known that it is with his permission), but the book would not be complete were we to omit any incident that occurred during the journey. We will now leave the detachment under McKinlay and proceed with a short detail of what took place in the interim.

After the party left us, we remained at Kierie Creek, expecting to remain there as a depôt camp till Mr. McKinlay's return. Lots of natives camped here on our arrival, but left with the detachment, and we saw no more of them till the following afternoon, when a "*lubra*" (English, a *wife*) arrived with a letter from the leader, ordering us to go to a lake about nine or ten miles further on. She was accompanied by three or four lubras and several men, and appeared as friendly as possible.

Being too late to proceed there to-night, got everything ready for an early start in the morning; and glad we were of it, for McKinlay had ordered us to clear all the bushes away round the camp for the space of two or three hundred yards, and with the thermometer at 124°, I think, dear reader, you will coincide with me, when I say we were delighted to have to move camp to a fine lake, as the next intended depôt was represented to be.

A magnificent night, the moon shining as if she were idle, or had nothing else to do, and the clear blue of the Australian sky; all Nature

VIEW OF KIEBI.

seemed to be at rest except ourselves. We woke the echoes of the night with many a song of home, and love, and *blighted hopes.*

20*th.* Strike camp, with the natives for our guides, at 5 A.M., thermometer 59° in the tent. We started at 7.30 A.M.; we crossed a succession of sand hills, afterwards well-grassed, flooded flats, and arrived at Cudgeecudgeena, about 10 A.M., passing a dry lake in our way. Mr. McKinlay has called this Lake Cudgeecudgeena, "Lake Buchanan," after Mr. Buchanan, of Anlaby, the gentleman who showed us such kindness on the way out, and a small hill, on the south-west side of it, he has named "Anlaby," after Mr. Buchanan's station.

The day was fearfully hot, the dry, hot sand piercing the boots of those who were obliged to walk; it was fearful, and made one and all of us unfit for work: nevertheless we were obliged to build a sheep-yard, and, the timber not being very close, it proved a much longer job than we approved of. Quite knocked up, and too tired to put the tents up, slept with mother earth for our bed, and the canopy of heaven for our tent. We kept watch, however, but each man was right glad when his two hours' guard was over.

Lake Cudgeecudgeena is very pretty from our camp, the water beautifully clear, with belts of timber all round; the pelican, ducks, geese, and other water-fowls, are here in thousands on its bosom. Rising above the timber, opposite our tents, are seen sand hills covered with salt-bushes. On the south-west rises Anlaby Hill; it is a pretty spot. Perhaps, reader, it appears pretty to us after so much desert, and only a little pool or so. Here is an immense sheet of water, ten to fifteen miles round; place yourself in our position, and perhaps then you would appreciate it as we did.

This is to be our depôt camp, and we shall remain here some time, how long we cannot say, till Mr. McKinlay comes back from his trip to find the "White fellow what sit down *along* water." This word the natives use almost indiscriminately.

CHAPTER III.

CAMP LIFE AT THE DEPOT.

Editor's *précis*—October 22nd, Shooting Sports—23rd, Extreme Heat and Cold—24th, McKinlay's Return from Cooper's Creek—28th, Party sent back for more Supplies—30th, Wild Dogs and Poisoned Baits—November 1st, Visits of Natives—10th, Jerking Mutton—17th, Rumours of White People at Cooper's Creek—27th, Well-digging—29th, Return of Party with Supplies—Bring News of Burke and Wills' Fate.—December 2nd, McKinlay goes to Cooper's Creek—11th, McKinlay's Return—16th, Ready for start Northward.

Mr. McKinlay had been on the look-out for a site suitable for a camp or depôt, with the view of the expedition making a halt for a considerable time, while he went in search of the missing party of Burke and Wills. The banks of Perigundi or Lake Siva, which they had passed were not suitable, owing to their boggy character. "One of the camels got bogged, and narrowly escaped." Cudgeecudgeena, or Lake Buchanan, was more promising, and in the prospect of a long stay, presented abundance of grass and clover. The water, however, was all but dried up, a few inches only being around the margin. After some search they came to a water-hole called Wantula, and there established the Wantula Depôt, where our author and others of the party enjoyed themselves with such resources as were within reach, and to such limited extent as a very chequered climate would permit.

The high temperatures recorded by Mr. Davis were occasionally those "in the sun," which of course are not much of a guide to the actual heat of the air, but in general they are "shade temperatures" to all intents and purposes to those who endured them either within the tent or outside under the scanty shelter, but where the air near the ground was heated by the baked and burning soil. There was cold too as well as heat. For example, "13*th* Nov. Weather quite cool and pleasant to-day, and in the afternoon cold." And again the next day, "Thermometer at 5 A.M. only 54°. Rather cold in the night watch. Greatcoats in request."

Mr. McKinlay's expeditions to Lake Massacre and Cooper's Creek, we shall give in the next chapter, as taken from his report made to the Colonial Government. Mr. Davis continues:—

Oct. 21*st.* Here is most splendid feed for our horses, bullocks, and all the stock, and from the quantity of wild fowl, we may say also for men; and many a goose, duck, etc., will lose the members of *his* mess to add to the comfort of *ours*.

I must here digress a little, and tell the reader what rations were allowed us per week, so that as we go on he may see how we go down in the scale (I don't wish to pun on such a serious subject) as we proceeded on our journey. Each man per week: sugar 2 lb., tea 4 oz., flour 8 lb., mutton and bacon as much as we liked. Saved flour, but nothing else; sugar was gone before the week was out often.

22*nd*. We shot sixteen ducks fit for an alderman's table (he is proverbially a good judge). They were of several kinds, the common, the wood duck, and various descriptions of teal. If it was not a jolly supper, I don't know what constitutes one; but oh! for a glass or a dozen of "Arthur," or Byass, or Alsopp, or Bass, for the ducks to swim in. Notwithstanding this *hiatus valde deflensus* in the repast, I don't think that just then any one had a care, or wished for a more jovial evening than this, for we sung ourselves to roost.

23*rd*. Awfully hot day, and no wind to help us. We read to-day the story of poor Kennedy's sad exploring expedition. Poor fellow! perhaps we may all of us share the same fate as his companions, who all died or were killed, like himself, on their perilous journey, with the exception of a black fellow. Watch kept all night; natives close at hand.

24th. Very cool the first part of to-day. Mr. McKinlay returned about 2·30 from Lake Kadhiberri, called by him "Lake Massacre." (His account of this expedition will be found in the next chapter.)

25th. Camp Lake Buchanan. General orders to-day for a party to proceed to Blanchewater with the despatches for government and home. Small remains of the dead, hair, etc., taken from the grave at Kadhiberri.

26th. All to-day in camp; some reading, others writing to their friends letters to be posted at Blanchewater by the party now preparing to start.

27th. Preparing for the departure of our lads for Blanchewater—Wylde, Bell, and Hodgkinson, with a native ("Jack"); they will start to-morrow, carrying despatches, and also to bring up some more stores.

28th. Our party off for another look at the settled districts; they go with twelve pack-horses and four saddle, sixteen in all. The weather very sultry and close. Mr. McKinlay says there will be a storm. About 7 P.M., it was as black as midnight; at 9 P.M. a regular westerly gale. All hands turned out; but our little canvas camp was soon flying in all directions. The tents we tried to peg down as fast as a peg drew, but all to no use,

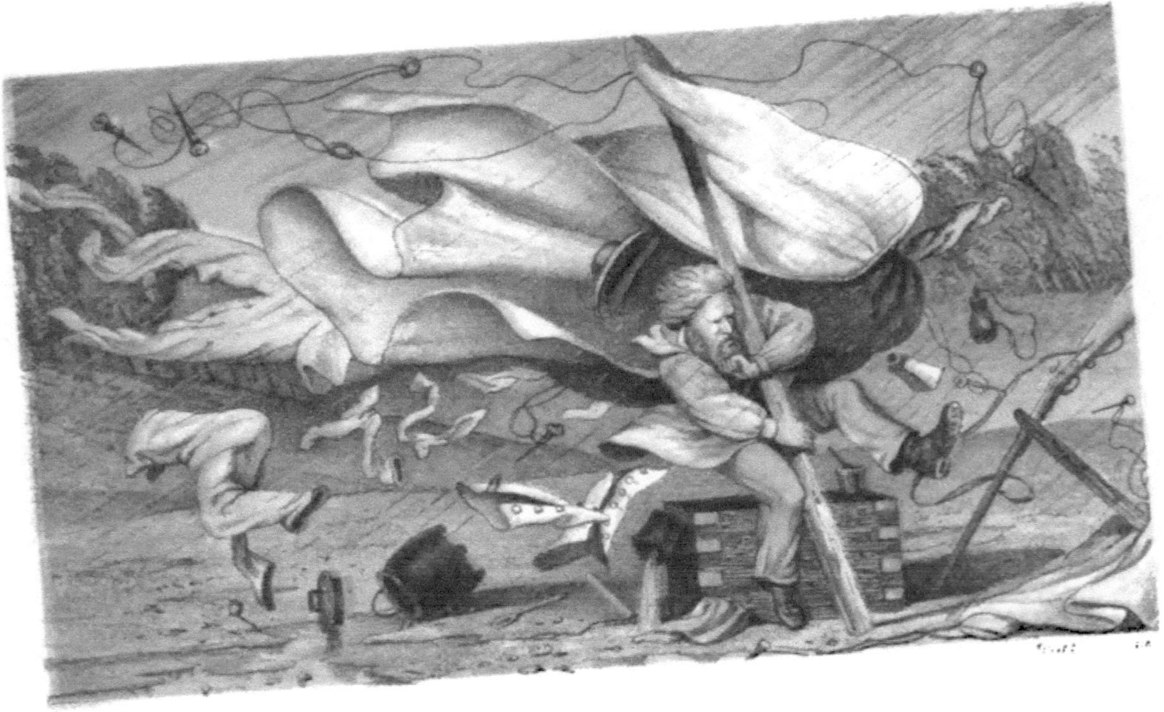

"Our little canvas camp flying in all directions"

they were soon blown down; then came lightning and thunder, and during the flashes could be descried hats, trousers, gaiters, shirts, taking their private airing by themselves, and McKinlay holding on by his tent-pole, "There go my trousers!" "There goes my hat!" sings out another, and so on. Had I the pencil of "Crowquill," or the world-known "George," I might scratch that scene; and although shivering with cold and wet we could not help laughing, the picture was too ludicrous. It soon came to an end, then we tried to settle ourselves somehow or [illegible], but, oh, so wet!

It was of no use trying [illegible] they were rent to [illegible] we could [illegible] so we [illegible] from the [illegible] the lee of the [illegible] our damp beds, [illegible] till 12 o'clock.

[illegible] Called by [illegible] to loose [illegible] [illegible]

they were soon blown down; then came lightning and thunder, and during the flashes could be descried hats, trousers, gaiters, shirts, taking their private airing by themselves, and McKinlay holding on by his tent-pole, "There go my trousers!" "There goes my hat!" sings out another, and so on. Had I the pencil of "Crowquill," or the world-known "George," I might scratch that scene; and although shivering with cold and wet we could not help laughing, the picture was too ludicrous. It soon came to an end, then we tried to settle ourselves somehow or other, but, oh, so wet!

It was of no use trying to put up the tents, for they were rent to atoms, and so dark was it that we could not have found a peg for the life of us; so we got out our blankets as well as we could from the *débris*, and made a camp outside, under the lee of the sheep pen. We were soon asleep in our damp beds, and it continued to rain nearly till 12 o'clock.

29th. Called by Mr. McKinlay to loose camels, when we managed to get some blankets from the camp, feeling rather miserable. However the morning was beautifully fine, and soon put life into us. Oh! for some thing or other said each of us; rum, shrub, or whiskey, brandy-spider or sherry-cobbler. We remained cleaning arms, for they were in a frightful state from last night's storm.

30th. Plenty of work to-day, mending and

repairing the damaged tents, putting them up, and drying all our goods, etc. The only thing dry was the nest of stores covered with tarpaulin. Laid some poisoned baits for the wild dogs. Flies here by thousands, ants millions; flies in soup and the ants in the tea. It is too bad, I was going to say terrible; in a spoonful of soup you would get, I will not say how many—for fear the reader might think I was telling a traveller's tale—but this I must and will say, that if you stopped you would get no soup at all, for they (the flies) came in as fast as you could take them out.

31*st.* All of us employed in various ways to make our stay here comfortable, as we shall remain till the party returns from Blanchewater, probably more than six weeks. Three of the poisoned baits taken, and found two wild dogs quite dead, and we also lost our own dog Wallace; he must have got hold of one of the baits which had not been taken up, or else one must have fallen from the stump of the tree where they were placed for safety; he died about 5 P.M., and was buried in a clump of trees a little south of our camp, the *first*, and I trust the *last*, of Mr. McKinlay's party.

To-day we plant a lot of seeds—melon, peach, plum, and apricot, also some pumpkin. I hope they will grow, as they will be a boon to any poor fellows who may follow us.

Nov. 1st. Our old native friend came into camp to-day quite unexpectedly; he did not know how he would be received, but being a useful fellow, Mr. McKinlay spoke to him in rather a jocular way, and he was himself again very shortly. A westerly wind to-day, and very cold; we thought perhaps Mr. Bullenjani would be up to some of his sly tricks, and be only a spy to see if he could catch us napping, but if he did come with malice aforethought, he was done, as the watch has strict orders to note all the movements of this chap.

2nd. Mr. McKinlay left us to-day for a short time, and went out on horseback to see if he could make out any water to the east or west of our present position. He came on a fine creek north-west. Mr. Bullenjani left us again to-day, with promises to be back again to-morrow; we shall see if he keeps his word. On Mr. McKinlay's return he reported having seen fresh tracks of natives within 300 or 400 yards of our camp, showing that there had been something in the wind with the sable gentry; the good watch kept over our ally, however, prevented his giving the signal for attack, which I now think they had thought feasible. Had such a thing occurred, I fear they would have had to sing the "Darkey's Lament," for our little Terry's breech-loaders would have told on them, and many would have been food for the crows. Mr. McKinlay found on his travels to-day some horse-dung, very old, some little distance from our camp. Who has been here with horses? And one of our fellows, the cook, getting wood, found a bottle-strap very old and rotten. No signs, however, of any camp of white men here.

5th. Guy's day in the wilds of Australia! How we talked of what would be done at home, of rockets, crackers, and pocketsful of squibs; and visions of Vauxhall and Cremorne appeared to our mental vision, an agreeable relief to the eternal gum trees.

Many natives visited us to-day, all having their front teeth knocked out. Two of our men shot twelve birds—ducks and waterfowls. The natives who came over had an invitation from our chief to dine, which they accepted with seeming pleasure, and did ample justice to roast mutton, damper, and blood pudding. The blood of every sheep was caught and made into a pudding with rice, pepper, and salt, and very good they are; it is also used by us to put into the soup, it thickens it and gives it a good colour.

6th. Fearfully dull to-day; nothing doing after 8 A.M.; worse than a soldier's life in barracks, there you can get books from the regimental library. Mr. McKinlay has a few books, such as the "Travels of Leichhardt," and "Stokes' Discoveries in the Rattlesnake." We had also a few pictorial newspapers; had we the courage perhaps we might have been able to put up a small library, but as it is we are all thrown on our own resources. Wind east. Out after ducks this afternoon, but could not get near them. We all weighed ourselves, having nothing better to do, and found that most of us had lost considerably. Mr. McKinlay lost two stones, Davis twenty pounds, Kirby sixteen pounds, Wylde eight pounds, Middleton four pounds, but strange to say the bullock-driver had gained four pounds; perhaps this may be accounted for by his having done the duty of cook for some time, as cooks generally do get fat; and another thing, he had been on the roads for years, and was able to stand the hard life we were leading.

7th. To-day we got up a revolver match, Poole *v.* Middleton, distance fifty yards, Mr. McKinlay umpire, who did all in his power to keep us employed, lending us his books and getting up rifle matches to pass the time pleasantly, keeping away blue devils; three shots each this match, at 10*s.* a shot. The shooting would pass muster, but Middleton proving himself the best man, Poole was not satisfied, but challenged him to a second contest, when Middleton again was the winner; when Mr. McKinlay took his revolver, and put all three bullets within an inch of the bull's eye, clearly showing that he was the best shot of the lot, and he commenced chaffing Middleton and Poole until they were glad when the cook called out "Supper." No sport to-day, nothing shot. Every appearance of rain.

8th. Mr. McKinlay left us this morning to look at the country to the east. We were visited during his absence by a lot of natives, old friends from Lake Siva; did not let them come into the camp, but gave them a fire-stick to make their own fire some 300 yards away. One or two got talking to them by signs, for it is impossible for us to understand a word they say, nor could they understand us. We surprised them much with a revolver, firing off the six barrels one after another as fast as possible. They looked at it when offered them, but would not touch it; what they thought of it of course we could not tell, but they talked very fast among themselves, and by their actions seemed to look upon the pistol as a wonderful machine. It reminded me of some of the hill tribes in India, who for the first time saw a steam-engine at work, and after they had danced round the place for some time, they fell down and worshipped it.

9th. Many natives coming about our camp and very friendly with our black fellow, who is taking care of the sheep on the other side of the lake.

Mr. McKinlay returned to-day very much

knocked up, having had no water or food since he left (twenty-four hours); his horse failed him, and I certainly never saw one so done up and so fallen away in so short a time. He was seventeen hands high, and from his appearance you would have imagined he would have held out much longer. Mr. McKinlay was looking very ill, his cheeks hollow, and his eyes sunk; he turned in after some breakfast, and drinking citric acid and water. He suffers also from a slight attack of dysentery. Weather very hot and disagreeable. Got two new natives to go to Cooper's Creek.

10*th*. Mr. McKinlay very unwell to-day; however, there is plenty of medicine. Some of us also suffering from sore eyes, caused by those pests of Australia, the flies.

We jerked some mutton yesterday, that is cut it in strips and dried it in the sun, and it is very nice; we tasted it to-day at dinner; it reminds one of the "Tasso" of the Orinoco prepared from beef, only it is well rubbed with salt before drying. A day of rest to-day. Our native ally seems very comfortable; he requested leave to go for a net to the lake, and promised to return shortly.

11*th*. Fearfully hot; thermometer 135°. Mr. McKinlay still continues very unwell. It is so very hot in the sun that most of the animals are in the lake, some even rolling in the water. Mr. McKinlay rather worse to-day.

12th. The wind very high last night, and nearly sent the tents all flying again. Mr. McKinlay still very unwell, but rather better. The flies bother the animals very much, and what with them and the excessive heat, they are falling off visibly. Obliged to throw away all the remainder of the sausages, and very sorry we are. We boiled them, fried them, and tried them in rolls, but they were too bad; so we put them in a hole by the side of the lake. The bacon we got from Mr. Poole is first-rate; pity there is only such a little, as it is a good stand-by; and fancy bringing all the sausages this long way only to bury them!

13th. Weather quite cool and pleasant to-day, and in the afternoon cold. Quite glad to get into the blankets when off guard at midnight. Beautiful night; sky without a cloud. Still at Lake Buchanan, with little or nothing to occupy the mind. Mr. McKinlay gradually getting better. Very cold; blue shirts over Crimean. Flies still teasing animals. Bullocks looking better than the horses; feed round this lake splendid.

14th. Thermometer at 5 A.M. only 54°. Fine weather lately; rather cold in the night-watch. Greatcoats in request. It is rather dreary, that two hours; nothing to be heard but curlews and wild dogs, and your own measured tread. And then in fancy you go home to scenes never to be enacted again, and conjure up happy faces never to be seen any more, and old associations—till you get lost in thought, and so the night slips, or rather glides, away, till I rouse my relief and let him take a spell. But enough of this, and I should not have written it, only that it is very hot, and I am in a queer temper.

15*th*. Our native friend, with two women, came into camp to-day, and brought another male native; very friendly. They got their dinners, and slept at the camp—rather cold, I should think, as neither man nor woman had the slightest covering; the men, perhaps, with a belt of hair plaited round their waists. These are from Lake Perigundi, or Lake Siva. This new chap has a most hang-dog look about him; the other native is not so bad-looking. The ladies, of course, quite nude. If they went as the Turkish women do, faces and all covered, it would be an improvement. One of them, say sixteen; the other quite a girl, scarcely twelve years old. I dare say, as they have their lubras with them, that the men may remain in camp some time.

16*th*. At daylight the thermometer was 63°; at 2 P.M. it was up to 140°; heat intense; no breeze. Some natives fishing this afternoon on the opposite side of the lake. One is with us, making a net of the rushes that abound round us. They use no mesh, but the first two fingers of their left hand answer the purpose, and they make a neat, tidy net.

17*th*. Quite calm this morning. Read aloud Galton's "Art of Travel." The thermometer at noon was 130°; at 12·20 it was up to 164°! The heat was so great we could do nothing. We tried to sleep, but the flies prevented our burying our troubles in that way. Everything was hot, the water in the lake even. I think it was about the worst day any poor devils ever spent.

A number of natives on the other side of the lake. Frank, our nigger, got a story out of Mr. Bullenjani, that there was only one white man killed at Kadhiberri. He says that four fellows came there with camels and horses, and attacked the blacks first; that several were killed and wounded, but only one white, and he was buried by his comrades, who then went away in the direction of Cooper's Creek; that afterwards the natives dug him up, and eat the sinewy part of his legs and arms, and then reburied him, but not in the same grave. This seems a true tale, as Mr. McKinlay only found one skull, and that had old marks of sabre-cuts. This, in all probability, is Grey, who is reported to have died, in Burke's journal, on his way down; but there is no mention of any encounter with the natives; he seems silent on this point. There must, however, have been a scrimmage there some time or other, as a smashed tin pot was found, some empty "Eley" cartridges, and also some "Terry" rifle cartridges, empty too; so I don't think there can be much doubt on the subject after these indications of a fight.

18*th*. This day opened fine, with very little wind; the highest temperature 160° in the sun. We are anxiously expecting the detachment from Blanchewater. Any quantity of natives on the opposite side of the lake. We read to-day poor Wills' journal—or rather, that part of it up to Cooper's Creek; also Wright's journal, the officer Mr. Burke left in charge at a place called "Bulla." They were interesting to us, we being one of the relief-parties sent out in search of Burke. Let us hope we may succeed better. At all events, we have every confidence in our leader; for it is a well-admitted fact that the colonies cannot produce a BETTER, if as good, a bushman as McKinlay, and having been here so long, he is up to all the dodges of the natives, and knows their general character well. The Government could not have found a better man; in fact, for a wonder, it was "the right man in the right place."

19*th*. The weather still hot, with fine south-east breeze. Thunder and lightning to the north-west; looks as if there was rain in that quarter.

20*th*. Last night the heat was insufferable;

most of us forsook the tent and took our blankets into the open air, which was an improvement. Rain brewing all round. Some heavy drops falling. To the west and north it seems to be raining heavily. Thermometer, 6 A.M., 86°; wind strong; perhaps when it lulls we may have some rain. The wind as hot as if it came out of a furnace. Our Blanchewater fellows ought to be close at hand, as they have now been away some twenty-four days. Very boisterous indeed—looks like rain.

The wind was so high to-day that it actually drove back the water in the lake some five or six hundred yards. We could not make out what was up at first, when we discovered the water receding so fast from our camp. It looked very curious.

21*st*. This morning calm and sultry, and no rain to disturb us last night, but the sentry in the middle watch called us, as he was afraid the wind would take the tents away again. We were all soon out, but the tents were too well pegged down, and we turned in, "all standing," in case we might be wanted in a hurry.

The water in the lake has returned to its old mark. Thermometer at daylight 85°. Mr. McKinlay got a long yarn out of a native who came into camp yesterday, about Burke and his companions. He seems to have been up to

Cooper's Creek with him, or followed him, as he tells McKinlay every water they passed, and every place they halted at. They had been seen by this fellow gathering the "adoo" (or, as Burke calls it, "nardoo"), grinding it and preparing it for food; also baking it in the ashes, as we do the damper. The seed is procured in almost any quantities in the flooded flats, by sweeping it up into heaps. When cooked it is not very nice, leaving a nasty sensation in the throat; but it will sustain life for a long time.

We had a visit from the natives to-day, some from the north-west, and others from west-north-west, from about the Stony Desert, as they speak of nothing but stones in that quarter. Mr. McKinlay distributed to them necklaces of glass beads; to one set he gave white beads, to the others necklaces of different colours, so as to distinguish one tribe from another. He also showed them some *papier maché* figures of Tom Sayers, Uncle Tom, monkeys, etc., with which they were highly delighted; and when the strings were pulled, and the legs and arms set in motion, nothing could exceed their astonishment: it was quite childish. Several of the men had their hair and beard dyed red, and the hair of the head was all brought up to the top and tied in a knot quite on the very top. To see Mr. McKinlay with his white hair blowing from under his Scotch cap, surrounded by some 150 niggers—men, women, and children of all ages—with some of us hovering round with rifles all ready in case of a rise—was quite a pretty picture. The expression of the faces, and the positions they were in, was very pleasing. Had we brought a photographic machine to have taken their likenesses, it would have been first-rate; but, alas! no such thing was thought of till it was too late. Mr. McKinlay and all of us often regretted that we had not brought one.

Some of these men are very like those at Aden, with their red heads and beards, whom I dare say many of my readers may have seen on the overland trip to India or the colonies, as the steamer lies coaling in Aden harbour, diving for coins that the passengers throw over the side into the water, so clear that they often catch the sixpence before it gets to the bottom. A great many of these birds of the wilds had only one eye, and many also at the time they came to see us were suffering from ophthalmia or some other disease of the eye. Some were awful looking rascals, as if nothing were too hot or too heavy for them. The majority, however, were fine looking fellows, jolly, sleek, and healthy; and had they only known their strength, I fear we poor fellows would have come off second best. They don't seem to understand the proverb about unity. I suspect the little shindy at Kadhiberri gave them a wholesome dread of

Mr. McKinlay and party. They won't forget us in a hurry in that quarter. These chaps are easily managed, and Mr. McKinlay knows how to do it.

The heat very great to-day—no air to speak of; looks like rain, only I fear it will blow over as before. The Blanchewater party not in yet. Mr. McKinlay very anxious about them. They could not have been able to get the quantity of provisions there, and must have gone down lower to Mr. Jacob's station for the stores required, or they would have been back by this time.

A circumstance happened to-day which put us all on the *qui vive*. Mr. Bullenjani bolted off all of a sudden, and the other niggers would have gone but we saw him in time and collared him, and kept him in conversation till dark, and then watched him. Why he started we could not make out. Towards dark a lot of lubras and children crossed the lake and came into our camp, as if there was something very formidable up with them, but Mr. McKinlay made them go back where they came from. They were evidently in a great fright about something, but what it was we could not find out.

22nd. Many native watch fires on other side of lake, and last night we had to keep a bright look-out on our watches, as something uncommon was certainly stirring. We all slept with our arms by our side, and some slept in their clothes, ready to turn out at a moment's warning; and knowing that there were two or three hundred natives camped on the other side of the lake, it looked like an attack. We all expected it, and I don't think anything would have pleased some of us better than to have had a brush if they meant mischief, though five or six whites to that mob of natives. I should like to have known what really was in the wind. Our native bolting first, then all the women and children coming up to our camp for protection. We tried to fathom it, but, alas, it was no use. They could not understand us, and we, on the other hand, could not make out what they were talking about, so we were obliged to give it up as hopeless. No Blanchewater detachment yet, McKinlay very uneasy about them, though he does not say much.

23*rd*. Fine and cool to-day, the highest temperature 94°, every appearance of rain, clouds heavy and low, and the wind rising. There was rather a row to-day between two of our fellows, all about a whip. It was thought there would have been a stand-up fight, the odds being about three to one on the little one; but they both thought that discretion was the better part of valour, and let it alone after a good deal of wrangling. I should not have mentioned this incident were it not that I can add that this was the only serious row during the whole of our wanderings except one that occurred at a place called Broad-sound, on the East Coast. This speaks a great deal for the *morale* of the party. I think that considering all things, and that not one of us knew a single mate till we met at the place of "*enlistment*," I might say Mr. McKinlay could not have had a much better selection. At all events he has expressed himself in almost the same terms, and therefore I suppose it is a fact.

More natives down to-day. McKinlay held a *levée*, and presented certain individuals not exactly with the Cross of the Legion of Honour, but what they valued perhaps more, some necklaces. They are simple beings indeed, and I believe would, if well treated, be docile and tractable. There is a great feeling against them. I do not like them, in fact I was going to say that I hate any black after the horrible atrocities and massacres in India, and having been present one almost takes a dislike to the whole of the "black family;" and even here there have been several horrible murders committed by the natives; but perhaps they were occasioned by some aggression on the part of the whites at some time or other, and the law of reprisals here is not well defined, revenge being their motto.

24th. We are out now 102 days, but the time has slipped away quickly and pleasantly, and we are all in good health here at the depôt camp, Lake Buchanan, and we hope that our absent men are as well and hearty. They ought to be with us now with the extra rations. To-day we had nothing to do but the usual routine, seeing all the animals right and safe. The weather cool and fine, the thermometer only 84° in the shade.

25th. Fine cool breeze from south-south-east. All hands mending boots, clothes, etc. Some one or two went out with McKinlay after ducks, and shot a few—a great treat, as we had lived on mutton only so long. Anything for a change. After dinner we turned into washerwomen—a transformation none of us like.

26th. There is not much doing in a camp like this. Unless the niggers attack us, or some other game of the same harmless nature occurs, there is hardly anything to put down in a journal; in fact, in McKinlay's there is nothing save the state of the weather and the range of the thermometer. The wind from south-east and beautifully cool, which, as you may imagine, dear reader, is a luxury in an Australian summer. Highest range of thermometer to-day, 120°.

27th. McKinlay gone out to-day to the eastward on horseback; passed a lake with not much water in it; passed a dry one, "Pal-coor-a-ganny," with very fine feed in it, consisting of clover and various grasses. There is a well here dug by the natives, about twelve feet deep. East of the lake there is also a small encampment of blacks close to us. Before leaving McKinlay started us to dig a well, although there is a fine lake within thirty yards of our tents. What in the world he wants with a well no one knows, unless it is to keep us from brooding over our cares, and just keep the cerulean imps away. Nothing like active employment to do that. We of course commented on the propriety of working like navvies, and apparently for nothing, in a temperature of 117° in the sun, and we came to the conclusion that it was insanity, or bordering close on it, while so many black chaps were to be had for a stick or two of tobacco. So we set them to work; they did it *well*, too, and struck water at about nine to ten feet. Then we went to work, and finished the job, and most beautiful water it was, clear as crystal, and splendidly cool. This water was so hard that the soap would not lather, but floated on the top. On Mr. McKinlay's return he had a bucket poured over his head, and it made his hair stand up as stiff as wire, and he was obliged to send to the lake for some, which is very soft indeed, to wash it, before he could get it into its usual state. It was, however, first-rate for drinking, as we could always get it cold. McKinlay returned about 6.30 P.M., and was glad we had found it. The well is to be deepened to-morrow, and made larger altogether. No rest for the wicked, "*Ora pro nobis*." Very uneasy, all of us, about Blanchewater detachment.

28th. At daylight set to work after breakfast at the well; had to do all the work ourselves, governor being in camp; wished him away. We set to, however, with a will, and soon accomplished the feat, making it full ten feet deep, and about three times the size, the water rising from south-east corner, and almost too fast for us to bale out and work too. The soil through which we dug before obtaining water was partly a mixture of light-coloured yellow clay and sand, next three and a half feet gypsum and blue clay, and at the bottom fine sand, through which the water pours in from all sides now it is finished.

29th. News this morning at daylight of the Blanchewater detachment brought in by some blacks. They were at a creek called "Karadinti." They arrived at 9·30, all well, and we were very happy to see them; they brought us news that Howitt and party had found the remains of Burke and Wills at Cooper's Creek; also that they had found the only survivor of that ill-fated expedition (King) living with blacks on Cooper's Creek. There is no necessity to mention here what they told us on their return, or what we read in the Adelaide newspapers they brought us; the circumstances are now so well known. It certainly was a most unfortunate expedition, equalled only by poor Kennedy's. Where is Gray? He must be the poor fellow whose bones were found at Lake Massacre; but then how are the different coloured hairs to be accounted for? Perhaps the mystery will be cleared up when King gets to Melbourne, or when Burke's journal is published.*

"Jack," the black fellow who went with the detachment to Blanchewater, has bolted, not much liking the service. He was an obliging fellow, and good-natured. Instead of him they have brought a white man from Mr. Jacob's station, to act as cook. Of him more anon.

30th. Highest temperature to-day 120°; wind this morning south-south-east. Mr. McKinlay and party, composed of Middleton, Poole, and two natives, preparing to start for Cooper's Creek, and to look at some water reported to the south-east.

I wonder where we shall be off to, now that the fate of the Melbourne explorers has been determined. I hope the governor will go to the Gulf of Carpentaria, that is, if he can do so without leaving behind him half his crew; although, perhaps, if he does, the difficulties and dangers passed will be thought little of should he fail, even if he leaves his bones and those of most of us in this hitherto unexplored country. Should any

* The next chapter alludes to this subject.

return, they will doubtless get all the glory of the exploit; at least, so it is with the world generally. Eighteen inches of water in well; temperature only 99° at noon.

Poor Burke and Wills! it is sad to think that those intrepid fellows should have been the first to cross this great continent, the vast deserts of the interior, and supposed to have arrived within almost a "cooey" of the settled districts, to have only arrived at their depôt some few hours after the depôt party had left there, under Mr. Brahe —who remained there until he could do so no longer from the illness of his men,—and to have there laid down and died; it was hard just as they had the laurel wreath almost within their grasp, and that so hardly won. I can fancy these poor fellows, after digging, finding the note stating that Brahe had only left that morning. It must have been a fearful disappointment to them; fancy, reader, just place yourself in their situation, seeing the date of that note after arriving from such an expedition, weary and faint with hunger and exhaustion, clothes in rags, and perhaps hardly a boot to your foot; fancy, I say, arriving a few hours after your friends had gone, who you fully expected would be there to give you help and succour, and finding yourself too feeble to follow in their track. They, as it afterwards turned out, were only fourteen miles away.

Dec 1. Kept holy the Sabbath-day; all very quiet reading newspapers, and those who had any, their letters. Good news from home. How pleasant it is to receive a little cheerful tidings from anywhere, but from those we love doubly so! I was not troubled with anything of the sort, but one of the party had enough for the lot, so he told us anything he thought we might like to hear—lucky dog, to have friends to write to him! Temperature to-day 139°, and rather hot, as you may suppose.

McKinlay and party start to-morrow for the south-east and Cooper's Creek. I wish I was going with them. To-day a few natives came into camp, and round the neck of one of them was found suspended the side-spring of a Terry's breech-loading rifle, and tells McKinlay that the rest of the rifle is out to the north-east. I suspect it must be one of Burke's, who left it behind at the fight, or else it got disabled, and was of no further use: a little bit of mystery again. "I wonder whose rifle it was," or, "Who left it, I wonder," you hear from mouth to mouth, and divers opinions on the subject. I suppose it will be all cleared up by the publishing of Burke's journal.

110 days out to-day. All well, but much thinner, at least the majority. I wish we had some Bass or Alsopp, or any other good beer.

You, reader, will perhaps ask why we did not tako some. The answer is simple—we had no carriage for it.

2nd. Mr. McKinlay and party started this morning with two camels and four horses, about 9 A.M. Bullenjani is left in charge of sheep. Frank, our native shepherd, going with McKinlay.

Again we must trespass on McKinlay's journal for the narrative of his trip, as I was not with him to Cooper's Creek and back. Meantime I will just jot down what happened during his absence at the depôt camp, Lake Buchanan, where the remainder of us are staying.

Wind very light to-day. A squall, accompanied with rain, passed over the camp about 3 P.M., and the wind continued blowing hard till midnight. We had a jolly evening notwithstanding, singing songs and telling stories of bygone days. To-day the last tobacco served out—twenty-eight sticks for each man; not much certainly, so we must husband it. Two of the party tossed up who should have the two allowances. Ned Palmer won the toss, and immediately put them up to auction, and they were bought by Davis for £1 4*s*., so he has three. Ned knocks off smoking at once.

3rd. The morning broke fine and clear, wind west. Our rations reduced to-day—flour, from

8 lb. to 7 lb.; sugar, from 2 lb. to 1½ lb.; and tea, from 4 oz. to 3 oz., a man per week. Our sugar never held out before, what will it do now? We may have to go without presently, which I think very likely to occur if we are out any length of time, and so it is as well to begin to live on short commons by degrees.

4th. Blew very hard this morning and during the night, and very cold during the middle part. Could not see the thermometer, the night was too dark; the two camels on being let loose this morning started away round the lake, and took it into their heads to explore a trifle on their own account. A fine walk I had after them, seven or eight miles. I got on their tracks, but could see nothing of them for a long time, the sand hills being so many and close together. At last I saw one on the top of rather a high sand hill, just going over, then in a short time discovered the other; they were hobbled still; they went along at a good stiff walk, and kept me for an hour or so till I could come upon them, a stern chase being always a long one. I at last headed them, and turned them to go home.

Arrived at 11·30, and found that Bell and a black had gone out after me, thinking that I had lost the tracks returning, or could not find the animals; it certainly was rather difficult tracking them, as they leave so little marks behind them, and then the sand was blowing so much that in many places the marks were quite obliterated, and having no compass I steered by the sun, knowing pretty well where the camp was.

I missed Bell as he followed the outward tracks, and I had come a shorter way home. He arrived about 1·30, and found us just getting our dinners. It was a weary and lonely walk, and I was tired when I got home, the sand being in some places very deep and soft. One of our men had got a severe kick from a horse to-day, which placed him *hors de combat* for two days. The well was sounded to-day, and had two feet eight inches water in it. Temperature cool; rather windy.

5th. This morning delightfully cool and pleasant. 113 days out from Adelaide to-day. On going after the animals to see if they were all right, the bullocks were not to be seen. Ned and the driver went after them, and found their tracks to the eastward, and also our faithful (?) native Bullenjani on the track, which circumstance created the suspicion that they had been driven off by some of the natives.

6th to 10th. For the last week I find nothing in the journal but the temperature; extreme variation, 54° to 122°. Making trousers and repairing wardrobes generally, which by this time were rather the worse for wear, seeing we were only allowed to take two shirts, two pairs of boots, two pairs of trousers, and half a dozen pairs of socks, one coat, etc.; some did infringe a little, and took three or four shirts. We sang songs, and made ourselves as jolly as circumstances would permit. The water in the well has risen to 3 ft. 10 in., although we are constantly using it for drinking.

11*th*. To-day, about noon, McKinlay returned, having succeeded in finding Burke's and Wills' graves.

13*th*. Mr. McKinlay is going out to-morrow to the stony desert of *Sturt*. The party consists of two white men, two blacks, five horses, and two camels. At 11·30 A.M. to 12 o'clock the thermometer was up to 165°. Reader, how would you like that style?

14*th*. This morning the party started at 7·30, crossed sand hills and flooded flats, thirty or forty miles, to a small creek, where they camped; there is little or no water in it, and from the report of the natives there seems to be no likelihood to be any further on; so McKinlay determined to return to camp to-morrow, and to go no further, as the natives' report seems correct from the appearance of this creek, and from what we could see of the country from off the top of a very high stony hill. Had a first-rate supper—chocolate and jerked mutton.

15*th*. Up very early; got breakfast, and started

for depôt at 8 A.M. We went another route home. Soon got out of the stones. At 12 A.M. came to a native well, where we camped under some trees; unloaded the animals for a couple of hours; gave them some water from the well, and let them browse about while we got a fire under way, and our pots on for some tea. By the time the horses had been watered, our *impromptu* snack was ready, consisting of tea and jerked mutton. We then had a smoke, till McKinlay gave the word to saddle, which was soon done; and we started for Lake Buchanan, and arrived about 6·30, tired and hungry. Country undulating, and not very promising.

16th. Up very early this morning to get all ready for a start northward, packing the dray. We shall be off to-morrow if all goes on well, at least that is the leader's intention. Many natives about. Cut on a large tree at the back of the camp, after nicely squaring a place on it about 2 ft. by 1 ft. 3 in.

MK
fm. Oct. 20th to Dec. 17th,
1861.
Dig.

The arrow points to the spot where McKinlay buried some letters in an air-tight tin case, for any parties who might come there; also some memoranda for the Commissioner of Crown Lands.

We are all very happy that we are to be on the road again, although we were very comfortable here under all circumstances. Still we got tired of the awful monotony of the same humdrum life; same niggers, same trees, same pelicans. Everything ready for a start the first thing to-morrow morning.

CHAPTER IV.

THE SEARCH FOR BURKE AND WILLS.

Editor's Remarks: Contradictory Accounts of Burke's Party reconciled; Peculiarities of Climate of the Lake District —October 18th, McKinlay starts on the search—Fish of the Lakes and Creeks—20th, Kadhiberri or Lake Massacre—21st, The White Man's Grave and the Skeleton—Other Signs—Conjectures—22nd, Meet Natives—Keri Keri; His Character and Doings—23rd, Collision with Natives—24th, Return to Depôt—November 29th, Return of Party sent for Supplies—December 2nd, Start for Cooper's Creek—3rd–5th, More of the Lake District —6th, 7th, The Graves of Wills and of Burke—11th, Return to Camp.

HAVING settled the camp at Lake Buchanan, Mr. McKinlay the following day, 18th October, sets off with a section of his party, with the view of prosecuting a search for the missing expedition. Various reports had been heard on the route from the settled parts, and a native of this neighbourhood, called Bullenjani, who seemed to know a great deal of the matter, accompanies the party. The reports point chiefly in a north-easterly direction, where it is said there was a fight between the whites and the blacks, and where one or more

Vincent Brooks lith.

LAKE BUCHANAN,

by moonlight.

of the former lie buried. There were also reports of some of the whites being still alive, and living on the Cooper. Some difficulty in reconciling these reports made by the natives of fights and massacres, as well as the actual data supplied by McKinlay, with the narratives of Burke's party, led to the idea that there must have been some other party of colonists on the scene, about whom we know nothing beyond these lamentable rumours and traces of their extinction. It is, however, quite unlikely that any such party could have proceeded from any of the adjacent colonies thus entirely unheard of; the accounts, besides, are not really irreconcileable when critically examined by the aid of the reliable facts given by McKinlay. The following short statement is the probable clearing up of the fog.

A report from a distance of four white persons killed seems, as the distance narrowed, to settle down with increasing clearness to one person—at least, there was but one body alluded to as McKinlay neared the scene; and report went on to say that he was buried by his comrades, but that after their departure the natives had dug him up, and cut off the fleshy parts and eaten them. Close to a small lake, which, in the face of such reports McKinlay could not do less than name Lake Massacre, a grave was pointed out—not that of a native, evidently, from the slight care bestowed upon it. A little below the surface soil, which was removed by aid of a stick, was a body; or, rather, a skeleton, which seemed that of a white man. Further on another grave is pointed out; this grave has the marks of having been dug with a spade or shovel; no body, however, is found in it. Near the spot is a camping-ground, with the marks as of camels and horses that had been tied up.

The accounts we possess of Burke's expedition enable us readily to interpret all this, and to ascertain with some probability how much of the natives' reports are true. Burke's party of four arrived entire thus far on their return, but all weary and exhausted from travel and want of food, and one of them, Gray, so much so, that he lay down and expired. Dutifully his comrades sacrificed a day in order that, with their feeble strength, they might make a grave and bury him —a fatal day to them, for otherwise they would have reached the depôt at Cooper's Creek the day before Brahe and his party had left. This duty over, the three survivors pass on to the Cooper.

And now comes a probable part of the reports of the natives; they had dug up the body after Burke had left; and, most probably, had feasted on the flesh, re-interring the skeleton in another place, and in the careless way alluded to. There are no allusions to actual hostilities to be found in the accounts of Burke's party, but on at least one occasion he ordered King to fire upon the natives when they were pressing threateningly upon him. As to the rest of the reports, adjacent alien tribes may not be supposed to catch up news from one another very accurately. The ball-ridden and shot-ridden system of the native Keri Keri, whom McKinlay's party caught near the scene, and whom Bullenjani immediately pointed out as the murderer of the white man, and who himself seemed to admit the occurrence of the massacre, may be a little perplexing. But Keri evidently indulged a most intense hostility towards these white intruders, and, as with his four "lubras," or wives, he seems to have been a chief man, it is probable that most of whatever firing did take place took a direction towards him. He had plainly been at the bottom of the determined attack made on McKinlay's party when at this scene of his old doings; although, in this one instance, at least, he seems to have kept out of harm's way, supposing, perhaps, that his share of the cold lead on such occasions had already been beyond average. Our illustration, showing his marked physiognomy, and Mr. Hodgkinson's paragraph describing his qualities, give together a good notion of this sworn enemy of our people.

Mr. McKinlay returned to the depôt from this

excursion on 24th October. It was not until the 29th November that the party sent back to Blanchewater for more provisions had returned, bringing the news that Howitt had learned the fate of Burke's party, and had rescued the solitary survivor, King. Howitt arrived at the Cooper in the middle of September, just a month prior to McKinlay's arrival at Lake Buchanan, so that the reports of the natives as to some surviving remnant of the whites being at the Cooper were accurate enough. He still resolves to visit the Cooper, however, in the hope of observing its lower course towards the south, should the preceding rains have filled its bed with a running stream. After being detained above a month in the hope of rain to enable him to get over the parched country, he reaches the Cooper, and conjectures that it discharges its waters partly by Strzelecki Creek, running south towards the Torrens and Spencer Gulf, and partly by another branch taking at first a north-westerly course, but eventually turning in the southerly direction. He was successful in finding also the graves of both Burke and Wills. The remains of the unfortunate travellers were, as we have already stated elsewhere, conveyed to Melbourne by a party under Howitt, sent a second time and specially for the purpose by the Government of Victoria, and publicly re-interred in the cemetery outside that city.

The reports of the natives as to many sheets of water in this part of the country induced McKinlay to spend considerable time in making explorations, and rendered necessary the addition to his stock of provisions which he has just received. The country presented in striking contrast the remarkable features we alluded to in our opening remarks in a preceding chapter. Long continued absence of rain had completely dessicated the higher surface of the plains, where the vegetation was so crisp and dry that it would have burned like so much tinder. On the other hand the creek banks and the lake beds, some with, others without water, were generally luxuriantly grassed. In most parts the country only wanted rain to present vegetation throughout; from the numbers of the natives and the crowd of animated nature generally, McKinlay inferred that there must be supplies of permanent water, thus rendering the country valuable for pastoral purposes. There were opportunities to explore some of these numerous lakes, but others spoken of by the natives could not be visited, as time pressed for the onward march.

In a country possessing these characteristics the climate was remarkable for its extremes, being one day cool and delightful, although now near the middle of summer, and another day unbearably hot. Strong winds swept the open country, on one occasion causing the waters of the depôt lake to recede for the time six hundred yards. The evaporative power of these winds was quite marvellous; owing to the comparatively small water area which they blew over they were usually imperfectly supplied with moisture, and had therefore a hot and dry feeling. On the other hand, after abundant rains the cold produced by the extended surface of evaporation greatly modified the climate. By thermometric observations taken between 15th November and 20th December, the latter date being towards the middle of the antipodean summer, the temperature varied as follows, premising that the party were in south latitude 27° and 28° in the midst of this lake district: at sunrise or daylight it varied from 54° to 85°; at sunset the temperature was usually a good deal higher, as high sometimes as 90° and 100°. In the daytime with the powerful sun, the burning ground, and the imperfect shelter, the heat was sometimes, of course, much more extreme. We now turn to Mr. McKinlay's journal.

Oct. 17th. At depôt making arrangements for a start; out in search of the water the whites are supposed to be at. I will take with me Mr. Hodgkinson, Middleton, and a native of this country, Bullenjani (who seems to say he knows something of the whites), four camels, three horses, 160 lb. flour, 32 lb. sugar, 4 lb. tea, 11 lb. bacon, and some little necessaries, etc., for persons likely to be in a weak state. Leave Bell in charge of the arrangements of the camp, Davis in charge of the stores. About twenty natives are encamped within pistol shot; but have made a fold for the sheep, and put everything in such a shape that I may find things all right on my return. Opened the sausages, and found them all less or more damaged; one tin, in fact, as nearly rotten as possible, which had to be thrown away; the others are now drying in the sun in the hope we may be able to use them. We would have been in a sad fix without the sheep.

18*th*. At 8 A.M., started; crossed well-grassed flooded polygonum flats or plains, for an hour, crossing Kiradinte in the Careri Creek; then left the creek on the left, and passed over a succession of sand ridges. At 9·15 arrived at Lake Cudgeecudgeena, at about nine miles. It was quite a treat, abundance of good water, and any quantity of grass of various kinds, and plenty of clover. It bears 345°, is about six miles long, and fully half a mile wide, well timbered. On a bearing from this southern end of lake (now called Lake Buchanan, after Mr. Buchanan, of Anlaby, from whom the whole party experienced the utmost kindness), Lake Bulpaner, now all but dry (and what was mistaken by me the other day, when in search of a good depôt, for this lake—very dissimilar indeed), bears 158°, distant about two miles, along almost a valley. Saw some of the natives on the way here, and sent Mr. Hodgkinson and Bullenjani back for one of them to forward a letter to Camp Depôt, to desire them to move on to this place, so much more desirable for a depôt than where they now are. Turned out the animals, to await their return. In the meantime, three lubras arrived on the opposite side of the lake, and we called them over. Shortly after, Mr. Hodgkinson and the black came back: we had some luncheon, started the lubras back to the cart at the depôt with a note requesting them to advance to this lake, and, at 1·25 P.M., started on a bearing of 345° along the side of the lake, and, at 2·45, left the north-east sweep of the lake; then, on a bearing of 32°, over sand ridges and salt-bush flats. Very open country till within one mile of camp at Gunany, a large creek, about sixty to eighty yards wide, and from twenty to thirty deep, on which we found a number of natives just finishing their day's fishing. They had been successful, and had three or four different sorts of fish, viz., the catfish of the Murray, the nombre of the Darling, and the brown perch, and I think I observed a small cod. They offered, and I took several, which were very good; they promised to bring more in the morning. We came upon and crossed a large flooded wooded polygonum flat, which continued close to the camp. Distance travelled, twenty-five and three-quarters miles.

19*th*. Early this morning, about eighty natives of all sorts, healthy and strong, visited the camp, and could not be coaxed or driven away. I think they would have tried to help themselves were it not from fear of the arms; how they came to know their deadliness, I cannot say. Altering one of the camel-saddles that has hurt one of their backs, and caused us to be late in starting. Started 8·40 A.M. Immediately crossed creek to Toorabinganee, a succession of reaches of water in a broad creek, some apparently deep; spelled half an hour, crossed creek, and went over very high sand hills, pretty well grassed, with a little salt-bush of various kinds, with some flooded and salt-bush flats, and arrived at Luncheon Place, an island often, now partly dry on south-eastern side, in an extensive irregular lake of about eight and a half to nine miles long, by an average of one and three-quarters to two miles. Very hot. Name of lake, Canna Canta-jandide. Thought I might be able to cross it at the narrowest place with the horses and camels, instead of going all round, as it put me out of my course. Sent Mr. Hodgkinson to ascertain its depth, and found it too deep, so had to go round. Arrived at Luncheon Place at

12·10, and started again 3·40, and travelled to east end of lake, bearing 202°, till 4·17; then course of 27°, over exceedingly high and abrupt sand hills, with poor miserable flats between them; towards the end of our day's journey, over a rather more flat country, with large dry beds of lakes or swamps, as dry as ashes, with a salt-like appearance, the only vegetation being a few scattered bushes of samphire, and an occasional salt-bush—a more dreary country you could not well imagine. Arrived at Lake Moolion-dhurunnie, a nice little lake, nearly circular, and nearly woodless, about one and a-half miles diameter, at 6·55 P.M. Abundance of good water, and plenty of feed—clover, and some grass. Bearing of creek that fills lake, 350°; east end, 87°; west end, 303°; north side, 15°. Distance travelled, twenty-eight miles. On arrival at lake, saw several native fires, which, on our lighting ours, were immediately put out. Saw nothing of them.

Sunday, 20th. At daylight about ninety to a hundred natives, of all sorts, visited us; they were not so unruly as those of the morning before, having evidently had some communication with whites—using the word "Yanaman" for horse, as in Sydney, and one or two other words familiar to me. Plenty of fish of all sorts in the lake, although not very deep. Cuddibaieni bears 100°. The natives here say that the whites have left above place, and are now at Undaganie. I observed several portions of European clothing about their camps as on our course we passed them. At the camp we found twenty to thirty more natives, principally aged and children; and on the opposite side of the lake there was another encampment, in all numbering about 150 souls. The sand hills in our course were exceedingly high on the western side, but pretty hard; but on the eastern side almost precipitous, and soft drift-sand; a dray or cart might get east, but I cannot fancy it possible it could return. An exceedingly hot day, wind north. On our way, the natives informed us that the natives we had left in the morning had murdered the man said to be at the end of our day's stage. On some of the ridges, and on crossing a large flat creek, I observed two new trees or shrubs (they are both); from one I obtained some seeds like beans, and rather a nice tree; the other, when large, at a distance looks like a shea-oak, having a very dark butt, and long, drooping, dark-green, narrow leaves, and did not appear to have any seeds at present. Started at 7·17. Till 9·38 nine miles, on a bearing of from 100° to 105°. At 8·18 sighted a large timbered creek, distant one mile, for about seven miles, 360° to 140°. At 9·38 observed a large, dry, salt lake, bearing 341°, north-west arm 330°, north arm 355°, distance to extreme point of north bank nine miles. Bullenjani informed us that a large lake lay on a bearing of 110°, some distance off, named Murri Murri Ando. At 10·15 started on a fresh course of 64°, crossing, 11·15, a small salt lake, rapidly drying up. At 11·30 altered course to 100°. At 11·35 to 12·50 spelled on sand hill, waiting for the camels, they feeling the effects of the steep sand hill. At 1·9 altered course to 116°; at 1·15 altered course to 161°; at 1·53 changed to 47°; and at 2·20 reached Lake Kadhiberri. Found plenty of water, and watered the horses (the camels some distance behind quite unable to keep up), and at once proceeded northward along the side of a large, beautifully-timbered, grassed, and clovered swamp (or creek, about one and a half miles across), to ascertain the fact as to the presence of a European, dead or alive, and there found a grave rudely formed by the natives; evidently not one of themselves, sufficient pains not having been taken, and from other appearances, at once set it down as the grave of a white, be he who he may. Returned to lake to await the coming of the camels, which was not till about 5 P.M. Determined in the morning to have the grave opened and ascertain its contents. Whilst I went to top of sand hills, looking round me, Mr. Hodgkinson strayed a short distance to some old deserted native huts, a short distance off, and

KADHI BIBRI, OR MASSACRE LAKE.

by and by returned, bearing with him an old flattened pint pot, no marks upon it—further evidence that it was a white, and felt convinced that the grave we saw was that of a white man. Plenty of clover and grasses the whole distance travelled, about eighteen miles. Kept watch as usual, but did not intend doing so; but just as we were retiring a fire suddenly struck up, and we thought some of the natives had followed us, or some others had come to the lake, rather a strange matter after dark. The fire soon after disappeared, which made us more certain still that it was natives. Intend spelling the camels for a few days to recruit them; one on arrival was completely done up, and none of the others looking very sprightly.

21*st*. Up in good time. Before starting for the grave, went round the lake, taking Mr. Hodgkinson with me, to see if natives were really on the lake, as I did not intend saddling the camels to-day if there were no natives here, intending to leave our camp unprotected; rather unwise, but being so short of hands could not help it, the grave being much out of sight. Found no natives round the lake, nor any very recent traces, saving that some of the trees were still burning that they, when here last, had lighted. We started at once for the grave, taking a canteen of water with us, and all the arms. On arrival removed the earth carefully, and close to the top of the ground found the body of a European, enveloped in a flannel shirt with short sleeves, a piece of the breast of which I have taken; the flesh, I may say, completely cleared from the bones, and very little hair but what must have been decomposed; what little there was I have taken. Description of body, skull, etc.:—Marked with slight sabre cuts, apparently two in number, one immediately over the left eye, the other on the right temple, inclining over right ear, more deep than the left. Decayed teeth existed on both sides of lower jaw, and right of upper; the other teeth were entire and sound. In the lower jaw were two teeth, one on each side (four between in front) rather projecting, as is sometimes called, in the upper jaw, "back teeth." I have measured the bones of the thigh and leg, as well as the arm, with a cord, not having any other method of doing it. Gathered all the bones together and buried them again, cutting a lot of boughs and other wood, and putting over top of the earth. Body lies with head south, feet north, lying on face, head severed from body. On a small tree, immediately south, we marked—"MK. Oct. 21, 1861." Immediately this was over we questioned the native further on the subject of his death. He says he was killed by a stroke from what the natives use as a sword (an instrument of semicircular form), five to eight feet long, and very formidable. He showed us where the whites had been in camp when attacked. We saw lots of fish-bones, but no evidence then on the trees to suppose whites had been there. They had certainly chosen a very bad camp, in the centre of a box shrub, with native huts within 150 to 200 yards of them. On further examination, we found the dung of camels and horse or horses, evidently tied up a long time ago. Between that and the grave we found another grave, evidently dug with a spade or shovel, and a lot of human hair of two colours, that had become decomposed on the skin of the skull, and fallen off in flakes—some of which I have also taken. I fancy they must all have been murdered here; dug out the new formed grave with a stick (the only instrument we had), but found no remains of bodies save one little bone. The black accounted for this in this manner, he says they had eaten them. Found in an old fire-place, immediately adjoining, what appeared to be bones very well burned, but not in any quantity. In and about the last grave named, a piece of light blue tweed, and fragments of paper, and small pieces of a nautical almanack were found, and an exploded "Eley's cartridge." No appearance on any of the trees of bullet marks, as if a struggle had taken place. On a further examination of the blacks' camp, where the pint pot was found, there was also found a tin canteen, similar to what is used for keeping naphtha in, or some such stuff, both of which we keep. The native says that any memos. the whites had are back on the last camp we were at on the lake, with the natives, as well as the iron-work of saddles, which, on our return, we mean to endeavour to recover if the blacks can be found; it may be rash, but there is necessity for it. I intend, before returning, to have a further search. No natives yet seen here.

22nd. Breakfasted, and are just about to get in the horses to have a further search, when the natives make their appearance within half a mile of us, making for some of their old huts. Immediately on observing us, made off at full speed. Mounted the horses and soon overtook one fellow in much fear. In the pursuit, the black fellow with us was thrown from his horse; the horse followed, and came up with us just as we pulled the frightened fellow up. Immediately after, our black fellow came up, mounted his horse, and requested us at once to shoot the savage, as he knew him to be one of the murderers of the man or party; but we declined, thinking we might be able to glean something of the others from him. On taking him back from where we caught him to the camp, he brought us to a camp (old) of the natives, and there dug up a quantity of baked horsehair, for saddle stuffing. He says everything of the saddlery was burned, the iron-work kept, and the other bodies eaten—a sad end of the poor fellows. He stated that there is a pistol north-east of us, at a creek, which I have sent him to fetch; and a rifle or gun at the lake we last passed, which, with the other articles, we will endeavour to recover. Exceedingly hot; windy, and looks as if it would rain. The natives describe the country from south to north of east as being destitute of water or creeks, which I afterwards found cause to doubt. I have marked a tree here on north side—"MK, Oct. 22-61; west side, Dig 1ft.;" where I will bury a memo., in case anyone should see my tracks, that they may know the fate of the party we are in search of. There are tens of thousands of the flock pigeon here; in fact, since we came north of Lake Torrens, they have been very numerous, and at the same time very wary. Mr. Hodgkinson has been very successful in killing as many of them as we can use, mixed with a little bacon. Before the native went to fetch the pistol he displayed on his body, both before and behind, the marks of ball and shot wounds now quite healed. One ball, inside of left knee, so disabled him that he had to be carried about (as he states) for some considerable time; he has also the mark of a pistol bullet on right collar bone; and on his breast a number of shot—some now in the flesh, but healed. His family, consisting of four lubras and two boys, remained close to our camp awaiting his return, which he said (from pointing to the sun) would be 10 or 11 o'clock next day. When called at 10·40 P.M. to take my watch, I had not been on duty ten minutes when I observed a signal fire in the direction he had gone, about six miles distant, and wondered he did not make his appearance but all was quiet for the rest of the night, excepting that at intervals the fire was replenished.

23*rd*, 4 A.M. Just as we were getting up, not very clear yet, headed by the fellow I yesterday sent for the pistol, came about forty others bearing torches, shields, etc., etc., etc., shouting and kicking up a great noise, and evidently endeavouring to surround us. I immediately ordered them back, also telling the native that was with me to tell them that if they did not keep back I would fire upon them, which they one and all disregarded—some were then within a few paces of us, the others at various other distances. I requested Hodgkinson and Middleton to be ready with their arms and fire when desired. Seeing nothing else left but to be butchered ourselves, I gave the word "Fire!" A few of those closest retired a few paces, and were being encouraged on to the attack, when we repeated our fire; and until several rounds were fired into them (and, no doubt, many felt the effects) they did not wholly retire. I am afraid the "messenger," the greatest vagabond of the lot, escaped scathless. They then took to the lake, and a few came round the western side of it, southward, whom we favoured with a few dropping shots to show the danger they were in, by the distance the rifles would carry on the water. They then cleared off, and we finished with them. I then buried the memo., for any person that might happen to follow my footsteps, at the same time informing them to beware of the natives as we had, in self-defence, to fire upon them. I have no doubt, from the manner they came up, that they at once considered us an easy prey; but I fancy they miscalculated, and I hope it may prove a useful lesson to them in future.

We here transfer from Mr. Hodgkinson's journal a description of this "messenger," who was no other than the Keri Keri, already alluded to.

"*Oct.* 22*nd.*, Kadhiberri. We had just saddled the horses this morning, purposing to ride some few miles beyond Burke Swamp, when our attention was attracted by some natives walking from the north towards the whirlies where I had found the pannican and canteen. They were five in number, a man and four lubras (women), and did not at first perceive our presence on the lake. The flutter of our blankets, which were hanging on the branch of a tree, at length attracted their pursuit, and away they posted in the direction from which they had come. Mr. McKinlay, Bullenjani (a native), and I were after them at full gallop in an instant, but Bullenjani, unaccustomed to such rapid motion, parted with his horse, which still continued the pursuit. In about a mile we two riders with our three horses pulled up the dark individual, and certainly a more expressive subject of mingled fear and rage could not be found. With hanging jaw to show his fear, dis-

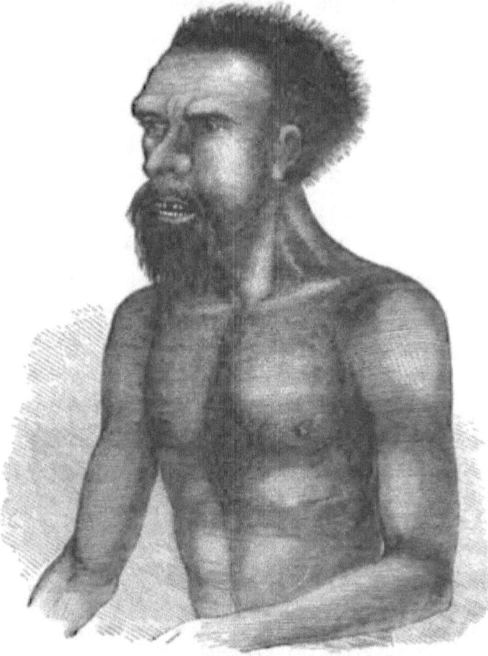

KERI KERI, A NATIVE OF KADHIBERRI, CENTRAL AUSTRALIA.

tended nostrils his surprise, and glaring eye his hate, there he stood, covered by my gun, convulsively twitching his waddy, as if meditating to hurl it at one or other. Bellenjani coming up, however, somewhat assuaged his fears, and ultimately forced a maniacal laugh from him. With a few shrill cries he let his lubras know no immediate harm was intended, and forth from their place of concealment came these hideous objects of his solicitude. On being questioned as to the white fellows, he led us to an adjacent sand hill, and without hesitation commenced scratching on a spot from which he brought to view a quantity of burnt horsehair, used for the stuffing of saddles. He was then taken to our camp, fed, and more closely examined. A wound on his knee attracting our attention, he showed how he had been shot, by pointing to my gun, and carried from the spot on another native's back. Besides the wound on his knee, there was another bullet-mark on his chest, re-issuing between the shoulders, and four buckshot still protruding from the centre of his back. He corroborated all Bullenjani had said relative to the massacre and its cannibalistic dénouement, distinctly stated that four whites were killed, and ultimately departed, leaving his lubras as a hostage, for the purpose of fetching a pistol in the possession of his tribe. . . . He said his name was Keri Keri."

Got breakfast ready and over without further molestation, and started at 10·30, on a bearing of 197°. At 11·15 reached a recently-flooded richly-grassed flat, surrounded by a margin of trees; the main bulk of it lying south of our course; thence, bearing 202°, stopping twenty minutes for camels, and proceeding, and at 12·30, crossing north-west end of another dry lake or grassed and clovered flat, similar to the other. At 1·20, made a large box creek, with occasional gums, about from fifty to sixty yards wide, and eighteen to twenty feet deep, sandy bottom, where we struck it perfectly dry, where a stream flows to west of north, with immense side creeks (I fancy Cooper's Creek is a branch of it). Followed its bed in its course northward, and at 2 P.M. reached a water-hole with no very considerable quantity of water. Watered the camels and horses. This creek is named Werridi Marara. From thence, Lake Buchanan bears 232° 30′; Kadhiberri 41°; Lake Moolion-dhurunnie, 296°. Crossed the creek and went on a bearing of 215° 30 till 6 P.M., striking same creek and following its bed (dry) for about two miles, and reached Dharannie Creek; a little indifferent water in its bed, very steep banks, about thirty feet high and sixty yards broad. The bed of the creek, from where we struck it at 6 P.M., was chiefly rocky or conglomerate stone, resembling burned limestone.

24th. Left at 7·15, bearing 215°; travelling one hour and twenty minutes over splendid grassy flats with low intervening sand-ridges. At 9·55 made Arannie, a recently-dried lake (abundance of clover and grasses), three miles long by one broad, at right angles to our course, and struck it quarter of a mile from its northern extremity. At 10·22 made Ity-a-mudkie, another recently-dried lake; plenty of luxuriant feed. At 10·50 reached its western border, at a creek called Anti-wocarra, with no great quantity of water, flowing from 320°. At 1 P.M. left Anti-wocarra. At 1.55 made a large flooded flat, recently under water, with a great abundance of clover and grasses reaching as far as the eye can trace. At right angles to our course, at 2·15, reached its western border, and at 2·25 reached the depôt at Lake Buchanan, or Cudgeecudgeena—the place where I directed the camp to be shifted to,—and found everything in good order, much to my satisfaction. My black female messengers it appears did not go back at once to our camp with the note I gave them, and consequently they did not get here till Sunday.

25th. At camp very much the appearance of rain, but none has fallen. Clearing off any heavy trees round our camp that could be used by natives as places of concealment. Have made up my mind to send a party into the settled districts, as far as Blanchewater, with such information regarding the object of my search and as much general information as is in my power, with copy of journal and tracing showing our route, which Mr. Hodgkinson will be better able to do neatly at Blanchewater than here in the tents; although he has made here on the spot such a one as would give a very good idea of all that is necessary. No part of this country has had any rain for very many months; the grasses and herbage, generally, on the hilly ground, being like tinder. If it had an ordinary share it would be an excellent healthy stock country. From the number of natives, and their excellent condition, I am satisfied that many lakes and creeks in this part are permanent; and as I mean to give it a good look over I have come to the conclusion that I will require a further supply of flour, tea, sugar, and a few little *et ceteras*, and will therefore send horses with the party that goes to Blanchewater, under the guidance of Mr. Hodgkinson, to bring up additional supplies, trusting to get them there, and at the same time hoping this course may meet the approbation of the Government; for in so doing I adopt the course I would pursue on my own account, and therefore do it on theirs. The men are in excellent health and good spirits, and the animals, except the camels (they cannot stand the heavy hills of sand if at all hot, which it was on our last trip), are all in good condition—many of them much better than when we left Adelaide. The wind is blowing from all parts of the compass, but rather cool. For days previous it kept from the north, and generally very hot indeed. As yet no rare specimens obtained of birds, animals, or anything else.

COPY OF LETTER BURIED AT LAKE MASSACRE.

S. A. B. R. Expedition.

"To the Leader of any Expedition seeking tidings of Burke and party.

"SIR,—I reached this water on the 19th inst., and by means of a native guide discovered a European camp one mile north, on west side of flat. At or near this camp traces of horses, camels, and whites were found. Hair, apparently belonging to Mr. Wills, Charles Gray, and Mr. Burke or King was picked from the surface of a grave dug by a spade, and from the skull of a European buried by the natives. Other less important traces—such as a pannican, oil can, saddle stuffing, etc., have been found. Beware of the natives; upon whom we have had to fire. We do not intend to return to Adelaide, but proceed to west of north. From information, all Burke's party were killed and eaten.

I have, etc., JNO. McKINLAY.

P.S.—All the party in good health. If you had any difficulty in reaching this spot, and wish to return to Adelaide by a more practicable route, you may do so for at least three months to come by driving west for eighteen miles, then south of west, cutting our dray track within thirty miles. Abundance of water and feed at easy stages.

Mr. McKinlay gives some of his views and plans after the return of the party sent south to Blanchewater for additional supplies.

29th. At 7·30 two natives arrived on opposite side of the lake, bringing the joyous tidings that the party under charge of Mr. Hodgkinson had camped at a creek called Keradinte, about eight miles from this, last night, so that I expect them every hour. I was heartily glad to hear of them. At 9·30 A.M. Mr. Hodgkinson and party arrived safe, for which I was truly thankful. I was afraid something had happened to them, from their apparent long absence. I am sorry that the native, Jack, that accompanied them from this, deserted about the inner stations, having heard some idle report of something having happened to the party here. Mr. Hodgkinson has brought back with him nearly everything I required. By him I also received some Adelaide papers, in which were some Melbourne telegrams, one of which announced the rescue by Mr. Howitt of one of Burke's party, King; so that I have been deceived as to appearances at Lake Kadhiberri respecting the different colours of hair found. Still I am under the impression that when Burke's diary is published that it will show of some affray with the natives about that place, or they would not have acted towards us when there as they did. By receipt of such intelligence, and that now the whole of the unfortunate party are accounted for, it renders my journey to Cooper's Creek as I intended, useless for any purpose of relief. Had they on their arrival from the north coast at Cooper's Creek depôt only pushed westward this length, they could, with the greatest ease to themselves, have made the Adelaide stations. I am quite surprised that they could not get south by Strzelecki's Creek, being under the impression that two-thirds of the water of Cooper's Creek was drained off by that watercourse southward. My impression from observation here is, that a very great portion of the waters of Cooper's Creek is drained northwards from this. Before leaving this it is my intention to push eastward some distance to ascertain the character of the country, and on my return to push westward for some distance to ascertain if the

Stony Desert exists so far southward as this. I will then proceed northward and examine the waters reported by the natives to exist in that quarter, and ascertain if they are likely to be of permanent use to South Australia. From them, I shall be entirely guided by the appearance of the country there as to my future movements. I am now satisfied that water can be had by digging. By the time I return from the east and westward the horses that have been down to the settled districts will have so far recovered from their fatigue, and be again able to proceed northward.

[The indefatigable leader now gets ready for Cooper's Creek, rain or no rain.]

Sunday, Dec. 1. A little rain during the night, but not enough to wet a sheet of paper. At sunrise temperature 70°, calm. At noon slight breeze, southerly; temperature 110°. Found suspended the spring of one of Terry's breech-loading rifles round the neck of a native. He describes the remaining portions of the rifle out to the north-east, which will be nearly in our north course. Highest temperature during the afternoon in the sun, 129°; at sunset, 90°.

2*nd.* Wind south-south-east, temperature at sunrise 77°, sky completely overcast. Start out eastward to examine the country, with two camels, five horses, and sufficient food for one and a half weeks, taking with me Middleton, Poole, Frank (native), and a native of this place. My main object in going out now is—firstly, to ascertain if there is a likelihood of a flood down Cooper's Creek this season, after all the rain that has fallen along the eastern side of the continent some months back, and which I thought possible might have fallen as well on and to west of coast range, so to secure to us an open retreat in the event of our being able to make some considerable advance northward, and being detained some time; and secondly, to ascertain if any one was as yet stationed on Cooper's Creek, in order to intimate to such my intentions of proceeding northward for some distance, and the almost certainty of my crossing any track which either of the search parties from the northern coast could possibly make *en route* to Cooper's Creek or even Eyre's Creek. Started at 9·15 A.M., and passed through nothing but sandhill and flooded flat country till 3 P.M., and arrived at Tac Wilten Creek, containing little water, but drinkable. For the first few miles the sand hills were further apart, with, in the interval, salt-bush and grassy flats. Watered the horses and camels, crossed the creek, passed up the south side, crossed a sand hill, crossed the creek, went a short distance on north side of creek, recrossed it, and went up south side to water. This is a long narrow strip of water, not deep, and drying up fast. A number of natives here. Crossed creek again and went to Aunrinnie, arrived at north-east end of water, and crossed creek 4·30 P.M. Distance about twenty-five miles. The water here, although enough, is quite unfit for use, the horses and camels refusing it, but there is good green feed in the flat.

3rd. Started at 8 A.M., passed over sand hills till 8·43 and made large lake, dry, Cullamun by name, destitute of vegetation, and no margin of trees; passed over sand hills and flooded flat to a creek very broad, deep, and well defined by timber, and trending northward; not much water at present, good here, but unfit for use above and below, like that of last night. Creek called A-ga-boog-ana. Distance, about eight miles. I went there rather out of my course to water the camels, being the nearest in going anything like the course I wished; passed sand hills through south end of large dry lake at 11·22, and again sand hills; then through large flooded swamp, Narrogoonnoo Mooku, with no marginal trees; southern end a good deal of cane grass; then again sand hills till 12·46; then large cracked flooded plain, Wandra-brin-nannie, till arrived at a creek with no water; crossed and rode up creek on south side to east of north to Barka Water, no feed. Got down into the bed of the creek and rode up about three-quarters of a mile to a water called Moollaney, pretty good; no great quantity, and but little feed. Total distance, about twenty-five miles. A lot of stones of a fruit found here of a very ornamental little tree, from six to fifteen feet high, which I have secured.

4th. At or rather before daylight Middleton, in attending to the camels, unfortunately got his foot seriously injured by a considerable sized stick which was stuck in the ground, its end penetrating deeply into the foot as he was returning to the camp down the steep bank. I am afraid I will have to return with him. I have pulled out several ragged pieces of wood from the wound; a lot of small tendons protrude. I will try one day up the creek, and see if he can stand it. Started at 9·40 leaving creek on right, crossed small flooded flat to sand hill, then good low sand hills, firm travelling; passed a water called Appo-more-millia, about one and a half miles to our right in the creek. Crossed creek in the centre of a cracked flooded flat, bearing to the north by west; passed over sand hills and a heavy flooded, cracked, and timbered flat, in which is a creek bearing north-east, with sandy hillocks and native whirlies. Bore south to creek Goonnooboorroo, with little water. Distance, about sixteen miles to-day. Middleton's foot pains him much.

5th. Obliged to camp with Middleton. On a large gum tree marked "MK Dec. 4, 5, 1861." One large creek comes in here from the south, and immediately below this, about 100 yards, another from same quarter. Bronze wing and crested pigeons here; also some beautiful parrots, black ducks, teal, whistlers, painted widgeons, and wood-duck in small number, also parroquets and quail. Some dry grass here on top of banks up to my waist, further out there is some good tussocky grasses, and there has been plenty of oats. Secured seeds from the bean tree, and the stones of the fruit before alluded to. Fish in water here, although there is only a small quantity and drying up fast. In looking for the horses in the morning up the main creek, found about three-quarters of a mile from this where Burke had camped in the bed, and had dug for water. From the appearance of their camp and quantity of camel dung, he slept more than one night here. I think when they camped there, there was water both below and above; it is now quite dry, however. A small quantity of sewing twine was found at this camp.

6th. Middleton's foot a little easier. Thought of returning, as he is quite unfit for work, but have made up my mind now to go on and ascertain the facts I went out to obtain. I therefore started at 8·25 A.M. for the upper waters of the creek, keeping on the south bank; crossed several creeks until 12 o'clock, when we found in the camp a little above Pardulli a gum tree marked "W.I.Wills, N.N.W., xlv. yds., A.H." Turned out our horses here for some time; between the last crossing of the creek and this I got a view of a couple of red sand bluffs, and distant sand hills or hills of some kind to north-west. Started from Wills' grave at 4·10 and crossed creek, struck the creek again at 5·35 with plenty of water to Howitt's camp, xxxii.; thence on to Burke's grave, striking dry creek, and following it to Yarrowanda; arrived here at 7·10 P.M.

7th. Started at 7·7 A.M. and came to Burke's grave, about two miles on south bank of creek. On the north-east side of a box tree, at upper end of water-hole, native name Yae-ni-mem-gi, found marked on tree, "R.O'H.B., 21-9-61., A.H." Deposited a document, in case of the return of any party. Saw a cobby horse on arrival here last night; tried to catch him. Saw the tracks of cattle up the creek short distance from him, they had gone further up the creek to a water, Culli-muno. Spelled to-day.

8th. Started back for camp; passed large numbers of natives; marked small gum sapling "MK" roughly; made for heavy creek that joins another at Strzelecki's Creek, and camped at a water called Tac-durrie, a small water about two miles from Goone-borrow in the main creek. Distance travelled to-day about twenty-seven and a half miles.

COPY OF DOCUMENT LEFT AT COOPER'S CREEK, DATED 7TH DECEMBER, 1861.

"To the Leader of the Party out for the remains of the lost Burke and Wills, but more especially to the Officer in charge of the Depôt likely to be formed on this creek.

"SIR,—I beg to state that I have had communication with Adelaide, and have received papers from there intimating the relief of King, the only survivor of the Melbourne Gulf of Carpentaria party, and an announcement that the Melbourne Government were likely to have the remains of the late gentlemen removed from this creek to Melbourne to receive a public burial and monument to their memory; and at the same time stating their intention of establishing a depôt somewhere on this creek to await the arrival of one or other of the parties (in search of the late Burke and Wills) from Rockhampton, or the Albert, on the Gulf of Carpentaria.

"I beg to state I am with my party stationed on a lake about eighty-five miles westerly of this, and immediately on my return there I start northward; and for the first part of my journey a little to east of north, and will at every suitable camp on my route bury documents conveying the intelligence meant to be conveyed to either of the parties by the depôt party likely to be formed here of the fate of the late party, by which means they will be put in possession of the facts, and can return to the Albert or go on through to Adelaide. There is at present, and will be for some time to come, easy access to Adelaide by my route, which the wheel tracts of my cart have clearly defined.

"By this means of intimation to the parties in question, it will relieve the party about to be stationed here from the necessity of passing a summer in this hot region. My course will intersect any course either of the parties out from the northward can make between Eyre's Creek and the late Burke's depôt on this creek.

"I beg to remain, sir,

"Your most obedient servant,

"JOHN McKINLAY,

"Leader of the S. A. B. R. Expedition."

9th. Started 7·25 A.M., followed creek down, and passed Goonooboorroo water-hole; passed flooded cracked flats and sand hills to Molanny Creek. Distance travelled to-day, seventeen miles.

10*th*. Started and crossed creek at 7·30 A.M. over sand hills, then through bed of large dry lake or swamp; name of swamp Wando Binannie, a good deal cracked, and bad travelling. From thence through low sand hills, flooded box flats, steep sand hills; crossed Narro Dhaerrie swamp, crossed creek at east end of main water, this drying up fast, crossed creek twice, and camped on south side of lower end of Tac Wilten.

11*th*. Started at 6·30, crossed creek and flat, over sand hills and flooded flat, with large salt-bush and polygonum; timber to the right, and some samphire bushes; crossed my old single track with alternate sand hills and cracked flooded flats, and arrived at our depôt camp on Lake Buchanan at 11 A.M. Distance, about nineteen miles.

CHAPTER V.

LAKE BUCHANAN TO LAKE HODGKINSON.

Editor's *précis* of subject—December 17th, Start from Depôt—Natives and Reciprocal Adieux—A Local Newspaper—20th, Lake McKinlay, deep water—23rd, Lake Jeannie—Christmas Day, and what is done for it in the Wilds—28th, Lake Hodgkinson—Presents of Necklaces to Natives—January 2nd, Suspicious Conduct of Natives—Excursion to Explore Lake District: Browne Creek, Lakes Blanche, Sir Richard, Strangways, and Ellar.

The expedition breaks up at length from Lake Buchanan, after a two months' camping, and takes a course about north-north-east, to a fine sheet of water about sixteen miles in circumference, named after the second in command, Lake Hodgkinson. We are now in the very heart of the summer, and our travellers experience all the defects of this remarkable country. The heat is frequently intense, almost beyond the endurance of either man or beast, and aggravated by the total want of shelter of any kind, which was most commonly their lot in camping or marching over such an open country. The country was not without attractions, especially those of a utilitarian character. The principal lakes, some of which, from their extent and depth, seemed to be permanent, were fringed with luxuriant grass, and fed by fine deep, broad creeks, whose cool and shaded waters afforded delightful bathing for the party.

And yet the precarious climate of all this lake region, variegated as it now is by well supplied lakes and creeks, and in many parts waving with long grass, holds us in suspense as to its practical value for colonization. The great question is the permanency of the water—or at least of some portion of it here and there, even although that portion be reduced, during unusually dry seasons, merely to the deeper corner of some lake, or an occasional water-hole in the bed of a creek. The live-stock can readily put up with the dried-up tinder-looking vegetation. Indeed this natural hay is greatly relished by them, and during very hot dry weather, when the grass-growing quite ceases, a very small supply may suffice for the animals. But water is indispensable for daily wants, and cannot conveniently be very far distant. We have already alluded to the rapidity of evaporation over the open area of this lake district. A very striking instance occurs further on in the case of the very promising Lake Hodgkinson itself, "a splendid sheet of water," as Mr. McKinlay calls it, but which, during a brief absent interval, on one occasion, of but twelve days, the party found had changed its level to a very ominous extent, and what was still more discouraging, had in that short time changed the quality of its waters, from being quite drinkable and good, to a state entirely unfit for use by either the men or the quadrupeds. The bitter or other qualities imparted by the soil had not previously been detected unpleasantly in the larger body of water, but as the volume diminished by evaporation, these qualities gradually predominated to the extent of thus rendering the water useless. This alternation did not, however, seem to be a characteristic of all these natural water reservoirs.

The teeming life of the country seemed, as Mr. McKinlay thought, to supply the best assurance as to the permanency of the water. And yet, in alluding to the great numbers of the Aborigines he saw hereabouts, he remarks that Sturt in passing this neighbourhood seventeen years before, had met no such multitude. On the contrary, he states that few natives were seen. And with respect to this fine lake country, it must have presented quite a different appearance to Sturt, for, as Mr. Davis observes, he does not allude to any such promising features as were now seen, although he must have passed at no great distance from McKinlay's line of march. Had the unusually dry season, then, during which, as we know, Sturt went upon his central expedition, dried up everything—creek and lake, high plain and "clay-pan hollow," and left the crisp and brittle grass to be swept away by the hot wind? Mr. McKinlay dilates upon creeks winding their devious course alternately through flooded flats and grassy hollows; one in particular running "principally through what was recently a large lake, now a splendidly grassed plain of vast extent." A month or two more perhaps, and the retrospect would class the grassy plain, with the lakes, as among the things that are not. If so, what a country of contrasts! The sheep grew so fat, says the journal, that one in a condition fit for "jerking" could hardly be found in the flock.

The Aborigines seemed to pour out from every "nook and corner" where there was water. They were in companies of fifty or a hundred, and sometimes in considerably greater bodies. They were mostly an athletic, hearty, well-conditioned people. There were few children among them, and the most of these, as Mr. McKinlay states, were females. Both sexes of adults had the custom of knocking out the four front teeth of the upper jaw, but a good many preserved the perfect set. With one or two suspicious exceptions, they generally were quite inoffensively disposed, and Mr. McKinlay delighted the simple creatures by distributions of bead necklaces, and on one occasion by the welcome feast of a sheep.

17th. The cart is off, and we are only waiting till it gets a certain distance ahead, so that it may not be too late in coming into camp after us, as the cart carries the commissariat, and it won't do to let that be much behind in arriving after us poor famished mortals.

At 10·45 all off; horses and camels with their attendants. Blacks all around us to say "Good-bye;" they lined the side of the lake, jabbering their farewells; but there was no cambric fluttering in the breeze, there was no fair one who had lost her heart taking a last fond look of the gay deceiver. I can assure you, gentle reader, we all left free and unencumbered with the sins consequent on civilization. There is an encampment of 300 or 400 up the creek; they could soon make short work of us if they knew how we travelled. Twelve to fourteen miles to-day, nothing but sand hills and flooded flats all sandy.

Here during our long stay we got up a newspaper called the "Dakoo Review"—Mr. Hodgkinson editor,—the leading article of which I give with one or two other contributions.

"CHRISTMAS DAY.

"No snowdrift hides from view the face of the earth, no frost holds in its adamantine chain the waters; while bright as may be the stars, and deeply blue the sky, their splendour is not derived from stern winter's power. As with nature, so with mankind, the eye in vain seeks those pitiable objects of charity abounding in more northern lands; no wretched outcast parades his barely-covered and famine-stricken form, while the hand idly retains the ready dole. Still, though in lieu of this, we are now beneath a sultry sun, and seek relief in densest shade, though the myriad, busy ant swarms on the ill-protected plate, and the rapacious fly devours our luscious plums, yet the cherished recollections of the season hedge round us, repelling all incongruity, and demanding all effort for enjoyment. It must not, however, be forgotten that Christmas comprehends other duties besides those of feasting, and that our presence among the unenlightened of the earth affords to us a particular opportunity of discharging them; the good sense of the community will enable them to effect this. No one will attempt to give the savage a desire for an article of luxury incapable of an entire gratification on our limited stock of currants. No one will sigh for roast beef when only our toiling bullocks meet the gaze; but all doubtless will raise the deadly gun, bringing down the swift pigeon and obese ducks, or extend commerce by a traffic for the scaly 'parro' (a kind of fish). Should the dusky savage chaunt his wild corroboree on these southern shores, let the north resound in reply with the good old Anglo-Saxon cry of a 'Merry Christmas and a happy new year to all.'"

"IMPROMPTU BY THE COOK.

"Roast, boil, and bake,
Throughout the livelong day;
Alas! why did I take
The *billet* and the pay?"

"NEWS OF THE DAY.

"As some of our female correspondents, including many ladies of the *haut ton*, having expressed a desire to learn the costume worn on state occasions by the grand hereditary Albeena of Cudgeecudgeena, the Lady Kinbella, we re-insert the following:—"Coiffure à la Centrale Australie; bust, au naturel; arms, bracelet pure; neck, necklace à la Birmingham, the whole forming a very novel *tout ensemble*, and extremely adapted for hot weather."

"TO MARJARA,

A NATIVE LADY OF CUDGEECUDGEENA.

I.

"She wore no wreath. No braided locks
Told Art was busy there;
No dress, no gem, no shoes, no socks,
Concealed from view the fair.

II.

"No marring touch had ever sought
To hide her lithesome form
With fabrics from the Indies brought,
Or of the silkworm born.

III.

"Ah, no! a purer taste had reigned
Upon her natal hour,
And Nature's simple rule retained
Her beauty in its power.

IV.

"Swept by the breeze, each darkened tress
To lover oft revealed
The beauties that a jealous dress
Too surely had concealed.

V.

"The swelling orbs of ebon hue,
That from her bosom sprung,
Left unconfined the ravished view
The gazer oftimes flung.

VI.

"No more shall meretricious charms
Win homage from my soul,
Since, in this lovely maiden's arms,
Love reigns without control."

Several more literary efforts might be added, but *perhaps* the above will be sufficient.

18*th*. Two black fellows came into camp last night, one our own "Friday," (Milmilly), the other a stranger, who was ordered off the premises; ours remained and slept in camp, and we kept a strict watch over him during the night. Orders this morning for Wylde and Davis to go to the cart with water on two camels. Bell is cook to-day, the cook being left behind with Kirby and Ned to take care of the cart. We left for the cart at 8 A.M., Wylde to remain to strengthen the detachment. I return by myself with some things from the cart. Ned and Hodgkinson found the bullocks that had strayed this morning, and brought them into camp about 3·30 P.M. They will proceed to the cart this afternoon with the stick that it may be fitted; we shall wait here till it comes.

19th. Remained in camp all day. Cut "MK., Dec. 17th, 18th, 19th, 1861," on a tree under which we camped. A native dog came into camp last night, and tried to get at the sheep in the fold (for at every camp we have to build a brush fold), but was shot by our native "Frank." The natives in the encampment close by, already mentioned, took fright at the report, and cleared out sharp, and not one was to be heard a quarter of an hour after. With them Bullenjani—he was a useful fellow in his way; I don't suppose we shall see him again. One of them returned in the morning. Temperature during the afternoon, 145°—very hot; indeed, no air hardly. The cart arrived all right; the men worked all night at it by the light of a fire, and, consequently, came up some hours before they were expected—too late for a start, but to-morrow we shall be on the road again.

20th. Up very early, and left "Gunani" Creek

at 8 A.M.; passed over some fearful country, the horses and camels up to their knees in the rotten flats, over which our course lay, the horses quite in a lather; the camels even sweated, the first time they ever did so during the journey; it was awful work for the bullocks; the cart, when we passed it, was up to the naves of the wheels in the rotten earth, and the bullocks up to their knees. I don't know when they will get into camp to-night.

One of the finest bullocks died from the heat of the sun to-day; he was very fat, and it is a pity we could not save any of the meat, as it would have helped out our sheep considerably; Mr. McKinlay did not know anything of it till the cart came in the evening, too late to send out.

On our journey to-day, after passing these rotten flats, we came to a small creek, where we spelled for a short time, and crossed this creek to a lake, where we camped on the north-east shore at about 1 P.M., where the water seemed deepest. Mr. Hodgkinson went out to try the depth, and found at some 300 yards from the shore 10½ feet. It is certainly the deepest lake we have yet come to. This lake I should say is permanent, and from its depth must be a great resort of the natives far and near in great droughts. The native name of it is "Goonaidranganni," but called after our worthy leader, "Lake McKinlay." Splendid bathing in this lake, the water being so

LAKE M^c KINLAY

deep enabled those who could swim to indulge in that healthy exercise.

Orders to-night for three of the party to go after the dead bullock and get his hide, it being so very useful for hobbles or ropes; and in the event of being very hard up for grub, what can be better than bullock's hide well boiled!

A good deal of thunder, with indications of rain; hope it may come and cool the air. Hot wind blowing to-day, and very disagreeable. McKinlay found Frank, the native, asleep on his watch last night, for which he got severely reprimanded. He became impudent and sulky. It would have served him right had the governor given him a good tanning for his insolence. He said he would go no further, so McKinlay discharged him, giving him an order on the Commissioner of Crown Lands for his money. He has gone back to Perigundi, where is a young female, rejoicing in the name "Kintullah" (Anglice, "she-dog") with whom this fellow had fallen deeply in love, as he told us some time before at Lake Buchanan. He said that he should when he returned marry this Kintullah—a nice name for a man's wife. I expect that she is the chief cause of his leaving; so wishing him a happy honeymoon, if they have moons of that description here, we will leave him to his own devices. Only a few drops of rain after all our expectations.

21*st*. This morning three started off about 4 A.M. to skin the dead ox and bring in his hide; they returned at 8·30 A.M. The bullocks were left unhobbled last night, as they were very much distressed; consequently, they rambled away, and were not found till 11 A.M. We started about 1 P.M. This was a day indeed; the horses before they were packed were in a perfect lather, and the perspiration pouring off us like water; the camels also suffered much, the loading and saddling the beasts was quite a task from the intense heat. We were nearly done up before we started; in fact, it was a mercy none of us had a sun-stroke. We arrived after a start at 3 P.M., at Moolionboorrana, hot, tired, and nothing to eat, the cart, as usual, not having arrived. We had a great loss to-day, the thermometer got broken, so from this time we shall be unable to record the temperature.

Passed over flooded flats and sandhills, then made the bed of a dry lake, with splendid grass, looking very park-like and pretty. All the rest of the way was over low sandhills and flats. We arrived with the horses and camels about 3·30 P.M. Not a tree hardly to be seen at Lake Moolionboorrana, so we had to camp without the slightest shade; reflection from the water and sand very trying, the latter burning the feet as we walked. The cart and sheep not up to time. Wylde and Bell went in search of the missing party with a pack-horse to bring some food, if the dray could not come on; it became so dark, however, they could not follow the tracks, and returned unsuccessful at 10 P.M. Innumerable pelicans, ducks, gulls, waders, cormorants, and pigeons, plenty of fish also. Small quantities of rain in the clay-pans. A little flour and water mixed, on the coals, and to bed.

22*nd.* We remained at this camp all day, awfully hot, no covering, the pegs of the tents having no hold in the sand, so we had to make a sort of an impromptu one with blankets, pack-bags, and camel saddles; water very brackish, and containing soda. Hodgkinson, Bell, and a native were off very early to see what had become of the cart. It appeared that it got turned over crossing a sand hill; sheep all right, and nothing the matter. The men with the sheep and cart had to be up all night to watch the natives, they being numerous, and moving about close by all the time. This lake is about three miles long by two wide. The bullocks very much jaded to-day from the last two days' work, and persist in remaining in the water, sometimes lying at full length in it; they are all off their feed.

23*rd.* We left this morning with no regret, and came to a creek about seven miles off. The water shocking, so bad that neither horses nor camels would touch it, *quite bitter*—the name of it Gadbung-oonie; fortunately, we had a little in the canteens, or we should have felt the heat more. We, with the horses and camels, came up to Mr. McKinlay, who was waiting for us here. He started, after getting a drink of water, very much disappointed, as he intended to stop here to give the bullocks a short stage. We soon followed on his track to a second creek, "Watthie-gurkie," which fills Lake Abberangainie. This is quite dry, and the water in the creek salt and bad, so had to go on to Lake Cann-boog-o-nannie; passed two or three salt lakes on our way, also another quite dry, well timbered, with lots of feed. We arrived at this fine lake, Cann-boog-o-nannie, at about 4 P.M.; splendid feed and water.

This is a fine lake, but not so deep by any means as Lake McKinlay. Pelican, ducks, and fish here. We shall spend Christmas-day here, so that the bullocks will have a rest; they will not arrive here till to-morrow, as they will not be able to travel this long stage (twenty-five miles) to-day, in this fearful heat, after the last two hard days' work. This lake is some nine or ten miles round, perhaps more. We passed through some of the best country for grazing to-day since we left Adelaide. The female camel gave us some trouble to-day; she did not seem to like the long day's march, and kept breaking her nose-string. We arrived here rather tired, but the cart, as usual, not being up with the pots, kettles, and meat, we were obliged to sup off scons* baked on the coals, and a pot of tea without sugar. The natives came round, as many were old friends who had also visited us at Lake Buchanan. They brought lots of women with them, and among them the only pretty face we have seen, and she is really very pretty, her features regular, and her figure faultless. They provided us with an ample supply of fish. Some of those who had been with us before baked some "adoo" for us, but we did not touch it, having seen the process of the manufacture, which certainly was anything but tempting. They grind it between two stones, then winnow it, put it into a wooden trough, and mix it thus—they don't pour water on it as we should, but take a mouthful at a time, and squirt over this *flour*, if it may bear that name, until they have kneaded it into a paste, which they make into thin cakes, and bake in the ashes, in fact an "adoo" damper. One of our men got some from one of the natives, and made it into a small cake; it had a strong astringent taste, and leaves a hot sensation in the throat. They also brought us water for cooking, wood, etc., and were highly delighted we had come. Not less than 200 or 300 were round us at one time.

Mr. McKinlay has called this "Lake Jeannie,"

* A Scotch term for thin cakes of kneaded flour and water.

after Miss Jane Pile, of Gawler. We called it Lake Christmas, and did not know that he had named it otherwise till we saw it in his journal in Adelaide. Cart only got as far as the last bitter water-hole we passed.

24th. Christmas-eve. We spelled to-day; many natives. Mr. McKinlay started Hodgkinson this morning to the cart with a pack-horse and two large canteens of water for the men, and to find a firmer place to cross the creek than where we did, as it was rather boggy. Any quantity of pelicans, showing that fish is plentiful; in fact, we saw the natives with large strings of fish going to their whirlies; they brought us plenty also. Cart arrived at 12·30 P.M.; they found a little good water last night. Kirby with the sheep got astray to-day, but was found during the afternoon not far from the camp, but going quite past it, by Bell and Wylde. This part of the country is very fine; magnificent feed, indeed, all round about here.

The natives were kicking up a great disturbance in their camp last night, when the governor ordered a rocket to be sent up, when, as if by magic, the noise ceased, and was heard no more this night. What their ideas may be of fireworks I don't know; perhaps they think us some superior beings, making stars and coloured fires in the clouds. It is a pity that we can understand them so little; their ideas on different subjects would be very original and amusing. We made a night of it—singing, throwing weights, etc.—but no grog, or perhaps we should not have gone to bed at all; first time I was ever without it—maybe it is all the better for us.

25th. Christmas-day: a sober and very quiet one it was, but we had a first-rate dinner off roast mutton and plum-pudding, and we made it as jolly as circumstances would allow; we had no cares or Christmas bills. This is, I suspect, the first English plum-pudding made and eaten on this lake, and I shall long remember this day. I have spent Christmas-day in many parts of the world, but this is the quietest I ever did see. I spent one coming down the Red Sea, and I thought that was bad enough, but I find there are worse places in the world to eat your Christmas dinner in than on board a fine Peninsular and Oriental steamer. It does not seem like Christmas, it is so hot, the wind quite a hot blast, and endless myriads of ants and flies teasing us to death—may we never spend another like it, say I. We roused the echoes a bit with songs, and many a cheer for absent friends and the girls we left behind us, drinking their healths in cold tea (if ever it did get cold), and so ended with us Christmas of 1861. Where shall we all be this time next year?

Any number of natives prowling about all round our camp; strict watch kept all night.

26th. This morning broke fine and clear. Mr. McKinlay deposited documents under a tree, against which our tent was pitched—the tree being marked—

MK
Dec. 23, 24, 25,
61.
Dig.

Started about 8 A.M. Going to the north end of lake. We, with the camels, took a short cut, and came on to the cart crossing a creek. McKinlay had gone in a straight course for another lake, and we followed on his tracks, and came up to the cart in a very short time. The horses were long after us. Had they followed us they would have been all right. There are lots of natives on and about this creek; its name, "Appam-barra." Got here about 11 A.M. Plenty of water in the creek, which abounds with fish. We camped on a small tributary of this creek. Feed not very good. Any quantity of crawfish here also.

Country looks very hard and bare; no vegetation to speak of, great numbers of salt, polygonum, samphire, and other kinds of bushes. The natives are a fine, healthy race of men, the women as usual rather small and insipid-looking; they always accompany the men when they visit us. Mr. McKinlay distributed a quantity of necklaces and bracelets to them all. They are as friendly as any one could wish, doing almost anything that is required of them. Their bringing up their lubras is a sign of faith and good will to the "white fellow." They all smell awfully of fish, living as they do principally on the scaly denizens of the lakes about here; you can positively scent them some distance from you.

27th. On sending for the horses this morning up the creek, it was found they had vanished, showing by their tracks that they had gone in the direction of our last camp, on Lake Cann-boog-o-nannie, so some of us had to go after them on two or three that had not wandered. We found them right on the lake. They seem to like the feed there better than on the creek. We did not get back till 4·30 P.M., so were obliged to remain here all night. McKinlay set us to work to clear the polygonum bushes on the side of the creek, to prevent a surprise. It was terribly hot work, but he likes to see the men usefully employed, and quite right too. Had he not found work for us at the different camps we remained at, some would certainly have had the blue-devils. Nothing like employment; at any rate, it keeps the men out of mischief. Something must have frightened the horses, as many of the hobbles were broken; consequently we lost the chains attached to them, which is a serious matter.

From the number of natives here, there will

be a strict watch kept. There was a slight row in the evening, so McKinlay, Bell, and Davis started off. McKinlay fired his revolver, but no natives could we see, so returned to camp, and went to bed with our arms by our sides. We lost a ewe in lamb in the scrub: how she got away is a mystery to us all.

28th. Left the camp about 9 A.M. There was not a breath of wind to stir a leaf, consequently very hot. After a short journey of about five miles struck a most magnificent lake, which Mr. McKinlay has named after Mr. Hodgkinson; in fact it may be called two lakes, as there are two fine sheets of water joined by a narrow strait. We shall remain here a few days, I expect, as Mr. McKinlay is going to look for some more lakes, said to be east and south of our present camp.

More necklaces for the natives, who were highly delighted with their presents; they are all a fine, sleek, fat-looking race: they must live principally on fish, in fact there seems little else for them to eat, unless they can catch the gulls and ducks sailing about the broad and beautiful lake, or bring down some of the pigeons and cockatoos of all kinds that abound here. Occasionally a black may be seen with a solitary bird, but not often.

This is a fearful camp, sand everywhere, gets into all your things, and every mouthful you take is covered. Seven or eight dark houris camped close to us by themselves, in a "mia mia," but no one knew anything of it till the following morning—rather cool that; the morning watch thought he discovered something in the bush, and sure enough there they were, all curled up together. Their intentions were evidently friendly to us poor forlorn travellers of the desert. Native name of this creek is "Watti-widulo." As soon as we arrived here we were beset by natives—young men and maidens, old men and children, and some of the most hideous old crones among them ever seen; they were nearly all to be decorated with beads, and Mr. McKinlay sat down and hung round their jet necks necklaces, and round the arms of the young girls he placed bracelets of multifarious colours. The tribe here is legion. Most of the elderly people have their four front teeth knocked out in the upper jaw; in the younger portion of the community you do not see it so often.

Killed a sheep to be jerked for the coming journey to the east, but all were too fat, and we were obliged to pick out the poorest for the purpose; but they were all fat, fatter, fattest, and not a poor one to be found; however, we picked out the leanest, and soon had him cut up and hung out to dry; the sun being very hot will soon jerk it. The little sheep are holding out well, you will say, and the country not so very bad, when they are too fat to jerk.

29*th*. Remained at Watti-widulo. Weather sultry and uncomfortable in the extreme. A black fellow from our last camp arrived to-day with the news that a party of white fellows, some six or eight, had arrived at Lake Buchanan, and were coming on our tracks to overtake us. Mr. McKinlay and all of us wondered who and what they could be. The only conjecture we could come to was that the Government had heard the same report that our detachment did at Blanchewater, that we had all who were left behind been killed and eaten by the natives. McKinlay does not put much faith in any party being out at all; however, we shall soon see, as we shall remain here some days, and they can be with us in a day or two. If they have come out on account of the story told, they will all be rejoiced to find us both well in body and spirits. It may be also only some *ruse* of the blacks, as they, in common with most savages, are well up in deceit.

Busy jerking for McKinlay and party to-morrow. Hot wind, and the sand blowing in all directions. Pity the thermometer is gone, as we should have noted day by day the changes in the temperature, which are very great and sudden out here.

30*th*. McKinlay and party started this morning to explore the lakes talked of by the natives. Wind very high from south-west. Middleton, Hodgkinson, and Wylde accompanied the leader in this expedition, and a native calling himself Dilbilly. It is very odd that Sturt did not discover these lakes, as he went within a few miles of them. McKinlay takes with him two camels and horses, with a week's provisions.

31*st.* Sky heavy, and looking very much for rain. Remained in camp, certainly the most uncomfortable one we have had; no green to shelter us, and not much grass or other green to counteract the fierce glare from the white sand. We all hope the party will soon return, so that we may escape out of this. Mr. McKinlay left orders to see that the wants of the white men, should they arrive, were properly attended to; and they shall be if they can be satisfied with roast mutton, bread, rice, and a pot of good tea out in the desert. A feed like this makes you forget weariness, and instills new life into you. This afternoon as we were cleaning our arms, etc., a whirlwind took our tent completely away, leaving it a wreck some yards off. The other tent, some fifty yards away, was not touched.

We shall see the old year out, and bid him farewell with one hand, while with the other we welcome the new face of his successor. Farewell then, 1861! Could we but recall thee, and just look over the days and nights we have spent and wasted thoughtlessly, we might, perhaps, like to blot out the remembrance! but it is idle regretting. This wont bring back the days gone by; but we may, by "overhauling" a little our faults and failings, benefit somewhat, and render a better account at the close of 1862, by avoiding the follies of the past year.

Jan. 1*st*, 1862. All hail to the new year! May we have a more jolly and a happier one than the last, and may it also prove more profitable to us all than the last! This year opens bright and fair—the sky without a cloud, and millions of stars out. I sit at 1 A.M. ruminating on the past, and hoping for the future, for it is my sentry from 12 to 2.

The blacks had annoyed us much during the first part of the night, numerous fire-sticks being seen in various parts, through the bushes and scrub, which kept us on the alert, in case they had intended anything in a hostile way. I believe they had some notion that way, as our black came into camp, and slept by the fire all night. Nothing happened, and the others turned in at 12 o'clock, having fired once or twice into the bushes at the sight of the fire-sticks. Nothing, however, was seen between 12 and 2, not a stick. Another very significant thing occurred. The fair deceivers decamped from their domicile, where they had been since our arrival, and did not return till the next morning early.

2nd. Two of our men going out for the horses were told by the native to "take their saddles with them" (we always carried revolvers, so did not require any other aids), and it was a long time before they would; but he was so urgent that they eventually did. They caught the two first horses, and got on them, to go quickly after the others, and head them, when to their astonishment, they disturbed a hundred or more of these black brutes, armed for war, with boomerangs and spears, etc., cowering and hiding in the bushes. They appeared not to notice them, but went after their other horses. At last they began to move, when the horsemen gave chase, and drove them across the creek. Poole and I, who were superintending the jerking of some mutton, were surprised to see some black fellows running from a sand hill, seemingly in a great hurry, and appearing to show us by their gestures that the whites were coming round the lake. The women also joined them, and it was evident that they had some plan in their heads to surprise the camp, and rob it, if not murder us, as well. We did not see the force of their arrangements, so did not move. They wanted us away, and the fellows that Bell and Ned drove across the creek would have come down and done for the few in camp, and murdered us in detail; pleasant, kind creatures, certainly! I confess I should not like to be eaten by very ugly savages. The idea is not agreeable; bad enough if you were *sure* two or three pretty young females of the wild tribes had the picking of your bones; and even then, living a little longer is preferable; and "so said all of us." So they were frustrated this time. Had they come in for a good fight, I should have more to write about. They have a wholesome dislike and dread of fire-arms; moreover, essentially cowards. If they can catch you "on the hop," well and good; but for anything like a fair stand-up fight, they don't believe in it.

Washing clothes to-day—a job which everybody detests, though it must be done. Cutting down and burning scrub behind our camp, as it affords too good an ambush for our sable friends; and it is not worth while giving them a chance of surprising us, which they might have done easily from behind. About 5 P.M. Mr. McKinlay and party returned from the eastward, having ascertained that there are lakes there, for which you will search HIS journal; or, rather, the following extract:—

"*Dec. 30th.* Sky very much overcast and very sultry; wind from north-east. Started at 8·10 with two camels and five horses, and a week's provisions. At four and a half miles got to Appam-barra, near old camp, at the dray crossing. At 8·45 arrived at about one mile west of dry lake Toondow-low-annie; centre bearing of lake, north and south, three miles, by a width, east and west, of one and a half miles; well grassed. At ten and a quarter miles passed south end of lake, and travelled on flooded ground on west side of Cariderro Creek, in which there is water, to where we cut the Cariderro Creek, about sixteen miles, at a place in the creek where a large creek branches off east, and fills a large lake, now dry; abundance of feed. Lake called Mar-cour-gannie, and found water in creek—a short distance south, from which quarter it appears to come. It is a splendid gum creek, from 80 to 100 yards wide, and fifteen to twenty feet deep, and flows a northward course. Started after spelling a time, and went one and a quarter mile, on bearing of 239° to Appa-dar-annie, now a dry lake with abundance of good feed in its bed; then went south by east, eight miles, along the Cariderro Creek. It is a splendid one, and well lined with fine gum trees; and as far as we went, I may say, was one continuous sheet of water, and with not less than from 200 to 300 natives. I have named it Browne Creek, after W. H. Browne, Esq. Many of the natives have, apparently, quite white hair and beards; they were particularly anxious that we should encamp with them; they were the first tribe that we fell in with so fully armed, every man with a shield and a lot of boomerangs, and some with spears. I thought it better not to camp there, as they had a good deal of sneaking, and concealing themselves from bush to bush, and might have brought about a disturbance, which I did not desire. Took some water in air bags, and started out from the creek, one and a quarter mile; then on a bearing of 5° for Appacal-ra-dillie Lake, seven miles fully. Crossed, and camped on east corner of dry lake Mar-cour-gannie, and on the margin of the dry lake Merrada-booda-boo; the bulk of this last lake bearing north from this, and splendidly grassed.

"31*st*. Started at 6·30 A.M. to Appacal-ra-dillie Lake, through side of Lake Merrada-booda-boo; passed several flooded flats proceeding east from last-named dry lake—the first of which was an extensive one, passing on our course from left round to the right, and apparently round to south as far as visible, then over alternate and indifferent flats and large sand hills—a considerable deal of flooded land to the westward. At fifteen miles, arrived on top of a very prominent sand hill, which I have named Mount MacDonnell, from which hill opens out to our view two beautiful lakes, which, in honour of her ladyship and his Excellency the present governor of South Australia, I have named respectively Lake Blanche and Lake Sir Richard, separated by a small sandy rise, through which passes a small channel that connects them, and which I have named New Year's Straits.

"*Jan. 1st*, 1862. Started at 6·45 round the first lake, Blanche (Lady MacDonnell), to where the creek passes through a low sand hill and connects it with the other lake, Sir Richard (his Excellency the Governor). The first-named of these lakes is, where it was tried, between five and six feet deep, and seven and three-quarter miles in circumference, nearly circular, bare of timber, and tens of thousands of pelicans on it, one solitary swan, with innumerable other birds, gulls and ducks of various kinds (one new and one dark-brown large winged), cormorants, avocats, white spoonbills, crows, kites, pigeons and magpies of various kinds, and plenty of fish. The other lake immediately adjoins, and its south-east end is more to the eastward than Lake Blanche, it is nearly circular, and is six and three-quarter miles in circumference, but when casually tried was not quite five feet deep; pelicans, birds of all kinds, fish, etc., as the other. Between forty and fifty men (natives) came to meet us as we were passing round the lakes at the creek, which they had all to swim; and from the appearance of the camp, some short distance off, there could not have been less than about 150, all apparently friendly. Started from north-west end of Lake Sir Richard, and went along the course of the creek that fills these lakes on a bearing of 305°; then south-south-west half a mile, to a fine basin of water in the valley of the creek, three-quarters of a mile wide and more than that in length, and opening again and contracting alternately up to Lake Blanche, which in honour of the veteran explorer I have named Sturt's Ponds; abundance of fish and fowls. From this point, course 308° up the creek for four miles; at two miles a creek went off to the right through a flooded flat, thence on a course varying from 224° to 239°, principally through what was recently a large lake—now a splendidly-grassed plain of vast extent, and at the latter part a few small sand hills. Distance to-day, thirty-six miles."

3rd. Shift camp to-day from this side of the lake to the north-east side. Mr. McKinlay goes out to-day with two camels, five horses, and the same party as before, Middleton, Hodgkinson, Wylde, and black fellows, to see some lakes reported to be to the south-west, but returned soon after we had finished the sheepfold and pitched tents. They found a fine creek with deep water, well timbered, with plenty of fish. Also they came on the lake to the south, called "Wattigaroony," which Mr. McKinlay has called Lake Strangways, after the Hon. the Commissioner of Crown Lands. It is a fine deep one, but not well timbered.

We keep New Year's Day to-day with plum-pudding and roast mutton, as we were not all together yesterday. I sat in the water yesterday for a long time with only my shirt on, and the consequence is my legs, from the intense heat of the sun, are so burnt I cannot wear any trousers, and feel very unwell. Applied glycerine and they got better. The lake literally covered with waterfowl.

4th. Very monotonous to-day. Shoeing horses, repairing pack-bags, jerking mutton, etc.

5th. Mr. McKinlay took a ride out to the north to-day, accompanied by Poole and black fellows. He returned in the evening.

The following is an extract from his journal of this excursion :—

"*Jan. 4th.* Camp, Lake Hodgkinson. Shoeing horses, repairing pack-bags, etc.

"*Sunday, 5th.* I, with Poole and a black, went out north to see what the country was like. On bearing 360°, over sand hills, arrived at and found lake dry; four and a half miles of stones around it, same as in Stony Desert; went through the middle of it, it sweeps round from north-east to south-west; passed through it where it was two miles broad, it is fed from Lake Goonalcarae (now dry); the lake passed through has not had a supply of water for years apparently; lots of dead mussels and crayfish in its bed. At two and a half miles further (nine miles in all), over sand hills, changed course to 16° for a large sand hill in the distance, the country to the north being rather low. At two and a half miles on this course came upon a succession of flooded basins, some of great extent, Gnatowullie, and slightly lined with stunted box, some as high up the sides of the sand hills as forty-five to fifty feet, entirely supplied by the rains, but have not had a supply for some time, as there was neither water nor vegetation; which flooded basins continued till I went nine miles on this last course, and from the top of the hill could distinctly see the beds of innumerable others of the same kind. From west round to north-east and east some dark-peaked sand hills, north-east of last course, as far as I could discern with the aid of a glass; turned back on course of 200° to where I saw some shady box trees about two and a half miles, and turned out horses to rest, and went to camp direct. On bearing of 187° at five and a half miles, came to the water-course that supplies the dry lake Marroboothana from Goonalcarae, which I have named the Ellar, and the creek that fills it, in which there is at present water, Ellar's Creek."

A terrible row with the horses and bullocks. They went off in scores to-night, either driven off by the natives, or frightened in some manner by them. Several of the party went after them, and a nice night's walk they had of it, as they could not head them for a long time. They did at last, and turned them. Saw no natives about the horses. They were very wild after they were brought in, and must have been terrified by something or other. Still very busy jerking mutton.

CHAPTER VI.

LAKE HODGKINSON TO THE STONY DESERT.

Editor's *précis*—January 6th, Lakes Blanche and Sir Richard —Excessive Heat—Mount Wylde—18th, Lake Hodgkinson much evaporated and undrinkable; go on to Hayward's Creek—Bathing; Creek full of Fish—23rd-26th, Excursion into the Desert—27th, 28th, Natives impatient at Party's stay: they report Floods—29th, In great numbers on the Creek—Lake Jeannie drying up and Water bad—February 8th, Rains commence—9th, Preparations for a Start into the Desert.

THE expedition spends nearly four months in this remarkable region of lakes and grass. Mr. McKinlay having procured an additional supply of provisions, has been enabled to devote so much time to the exploration of this particular district, the object of his search being mainly to ascertain if there are creeks and lakes of such depth of water as to give reliance that they may prove permanent under all contingencies of climate. But during the last weeks of this protracted stay, the party had been detained waiting for rain, to enable them to get safely through the "Stony Desert." This very different and not less remarkable tract of country lay to the north, quite close to the lake and its neighbourhood where they had been encamped. We have already alluded more than once to "the Desert." We now know that there is no great central desert, properly speaking. The interior is interspersed with patches of poor soil and of sterile sand and stones, alternating with better country. In the region the party were about to enter, these sterile patches were the prevailing feature, and there seems to be a considerable belt of continuous stony desert sufficiently noticeable to maintain against this particular part, and a good deal of the neighbourhood tinged with its inhospitalities, the title of the Stony Desert. The name has descended from Sturt, but the area of "the enemy" and his terrible associations, have been very much cut down.

But, however circumscribed, the desert must not be despised. McKinlay, while waiting the much desired rain that the passing clouds often promised and as often refused, takes an excursion into this desert. Its hard features, he finds, have not been at all overstated. Stony plains in one direction, bare sand hills in another, water nowhere. Even the hardy and courageous spinifex has disappeared, or is very sparsely limited to the shady side of an occasional sand hill. And yet, with true Australian diversity, "a heavy timbered creek" is seen at some miles distance to come in upon the desert, the timber, however, ceasing as the creek emerges upon the dry open plain. But this pleasant oasis did not run in the right direction for the travellers. After four days' excursion the party return, greatly fatigued, and not less convinced that they must depend upon the clouds for a practicable passage through this considerable desert region. This waiting for rain to make some arid tract passable to the traveller is no uncommon incident of Australian travel. Leichhardt alludes to the vast waterless plains which a timely rain enabled him to get over. The bold explorer must push on, taking the providence of the hour. We may thus in imagination make a good shower into a safe ferry-boat, or a plank thrown across an impassable gorge, without whose aid the traveller must only remain where he is.

As this excursion was in the middle of summer —23rd to 26th January—the desert was certainly seen to all advantage after its own sort. How different the rain made it we shall see in the next chapter. The rain did at length come. On the 8th of February there was "splendid rain and steady," as Mr. McKinlay notes, and forthwith the party prepare to march. The natives, who were hereabouts even more numerous than before, were watching the clouds as well as our travellers, for the rain has a providence for them too. As soon as it began to pour down in earnest, they were off in all directions to the sand hills to catch the lizards and other animals that instinctively make for these higher grounds to avoid the succeeding flood. These natives had already become angry and impatient at the long stay of the expedition in their neighbourhood, and they were fain to get rid of their visitors some days before the rain had begun, by getting up a premature alarm about the coming flood. They seemed to revel in plenty of food. With nets of their own fabricating they dragged the creeks for fish, procuring large quantities. The rains seem to have been most timely for all parties and the country alike, as the waters were fast disappearing. One small lake near the camp was already emitting an unsavoury odour, which it was suspected was the cause of some bad health amongst the party, and the pretty Lake Jeannie, when revisited, was found to be fast drying up, its waters already of unpleasant taste, and giving promise to be quite unfit for use in another month unless restored by fresh rain.

Jan. 6th. We started from Lake Hodgkinson this morning at 6·30 after marking a tree, under which McKinlay had placed some documents for any one of the parties who might come this way. On to lakes "Blanche" and "Sir Richard," twenty-three miles hence. The cart started first, with our little sheep also. We arrived at the lake about 3·30 through some very unprofitable looking country; we shall spell here to-morrow. About one hundred and fifty niggers round the lake. Another very cheerless camp, but there is fine bathing in the creek that runs into the lake. The water is quite clear, with a delightful taste, and makes most excellent tea.

7th. Remain at Lake Blanche. Mr. McKinlay and Hodgkinson, with black, went out to the north. Not the slightest shelter here; the sun scorching and the wind like the blast from a furnace. Mr. McKinlay returned early to-day, and soon after there was a decided attempt to drive off the bullocks by themselves. Some of us were soon in the saddle and after them, but the wily blacks were nowhere to be seen. Got the animals all safe after having been driven nearly round the lake. The bullocks broke from natives once, and they tried ineffectually to turn them, after following them some three miles. When they saw us they instantly took to flight, and easily hid themselves in the bush. Brought bullocks into camp and hobbled them short for to-night, so that they could not very well bolt again. It would be a serious thing if we lost them, or indeed any of them, as if the grub runs out they would stand to us in good stead, and you cannot depend on your gun, as anything like good game is very scarce, in fact I never saw so little in any country I have been in. *Strict watch.*

Mr. McKinlay thus describes in his journal the employments, although not the enjoyments, of this warm region of the world :—

"*Jan. 7th.* At Lake Blanche; went out north with Mr. Hodgkinson and native to examine the creek alluded to, but to my disappointment found that it only formed a large valley, and, at some distance on, a dry lake, Millie Millie, to the eastward of Lake Sir Richard, over some high sand hills; returned very much chagrined, and have made up my mind to stay here a short time, although very poor shelter from the excessive heat of the sun (to-day even it blows as if from a furnace), and endeavour, with the camels, to ascertain the description of country first to the east, and probably also from here, if the camels will stand it, to the north. From the appearance of the country about here I do not expect any water, at least for some distance; the land low, hills between the two lakes, and running northward for some five or six miles, have just the appearance of dirty drift snow heaps with heath bushes protruding; whereas those round to north-east, east, south, and south-east are a glaring red, with coarse grass and shrubs. Shortly after my return to-day a number of natives got the bullocks on the east side of the creek New Year Straits, about two and a half miles from camp, and raced them round Lake Blanche from us in sight; on seeing which, five of the party got mounted and armed, and went after them; they had taken the bullocks two-thirds of the way round the lake, and by some means they broke back from them; they did their best to overtake and turn them again for about two or three miles; when they observed the horsemen, they immediately took to flight, and where shelter was so abundant, of course were immediately out of reach and sight of the horsemen. What their intentions were was difficult to say, but it looked rather suspicious; took the bullocks to camp late and hobbled most of them. The evening before leaving Lake Hodgkinson, about 8·30 P.M., they took both horses and bullocks and raced them round from us for about three miles, but were pursued on foot by three of the party, who succeeded in getting all the bullocks and horses, after having broken three-fourths of their chains, and were in a very excited state, nor could the horses be quieted for more than two hours afterwards, but the wary savage was nowhere to be seen."

8th. Moved our camp this morning three-quarters of a mile to a little wood, and pitched. The wind fearfully hot, and the white sand distressing to the eyes. We were obliged to adopt this plan, as in the other place there was not a stick to boil or bake with. All we got was from the grave of some poor defunct native. They always pile wood over the native graves. The heat is insufferable. We shall surely get baked or cooked somehow alive, if this goes on much longer. McKinlay and party preparing to start for the east for the purpose of finding water, if he can, in that direction. The four camels to go and no horses, that is the arrangement at the present.

9th. Camp, Lake Blanche. It looks as if we should have a terrible storm, but as usual I suppose it will blow over. A heavy gale last night demolished the tents and made us all very uncomfortable; it would be all the better for us if these blows would come in the daytime, when we could see what we were about; but *no*, these accidents seem generally to happen in the night, when it is more difficult to get to rights again. Plenty of thunder and lightning. The gale lasted two hours or more.

10th. We had hoped that the tempest would have cooled the air a little, but it is clear we are to be cooked. All done up. No energy left hardly. The animals are all under what little shade there is; poor things, they feel the weather greatly. There is plenty of fish here, with lots of "adoo." The sunset to-night was magnificent.

11th. My legs very painful from the effects of the sun. Heat fearful.

12th. Thunder and lightning; no rain. Heat not abated one iota. If it does not get cooler soon and we don't have some rain, some of us will be getting ill I fear.

13th. A little cooler to-day than it has been. Mr. McKinlay going out to-morrow; the heat had hitherto prevented him; he goes eastward to prospect the country generally.

14th. Mr. McKinlay starts this morning, and takes three horses part of the way; Ned brings them back. The reason why they go is that Mr. McKinlay wishes to put as little on the camels to-day as possible. Bell taken very ill with cramp in the stomach. We thought he was going to die right off. He was quite doubled up and could not speak. I gave him some medicine which restored him in a short time. At one time we really thought it was all up with him.

15th. Bell and I very ill from dysentery. Found some dogs dead from poisoned baits placed for the purpose. They are very numerous here, and from the small quantity of wood we could not get enough to build a good yard for the sheep, and we feared they might be getting at them.

Ned with the horses returned last night about 11·30 P.M. The heat did not contribute to our recovery. The sun comes through these American drill tents (I was about to say "*like*") *without* winking.

16th. We are still very ill, and yesterday another of the party, Maitland the cook, was taken with the same disease. He suffered very much at first. It must be the weather, or the water, or perhaps both combined. Mr. McKinlay and party returned about 1 P.M., and found us on our beam ends. The sooner we are out of this nasty hot and sickly camp the better.

Mr. McKinlay, upon another of his excursions, remarks in his journal :—

"*Jan.* 14*th.* Eastward to-day, over undulations, sand hills, clay pans, and flats, for nineteen miles, till we reached a very prominent high hill, which I have called Mount Wylde. A considerable range is visible to east, and south of east. Went on for seven miles further, over sand ridges, covered with spinifex, successive box-covered flooded flats, formed by heavy rains, through which were innumerable small creeks, no doubt, in heavy rains, forming source or tributaries to Cooper's Creek. Took the horses out this morning to make the work lighter for the camels on the march. Sent the horses back again this afternoon; gave the camels from three to four gallons of water each—they appeared as if they could have drunk all that we possessed. Distance travelled to-day about twenty-six miles. East, in the far distance, I can trace the continuance of the range.

"15*th*. Every appearance of a hot day. Followed over hard sand undulations, well-grassed, with some little spinifex intermixed, with a creek on our left, and crossed it at eight miles, going south-east, then apparently south—gum and box on creek, and a sandy bed. We then passed over some good grassed country, with stony flats, and latterly a stony sand hill, the ascent difficult for the camels on account of the sharp stones for ten miles; distance, making in all eighteen miles. Low hills about six or seven miles ahead, running north and south; nothing very marked about them. The heat fearful; camels not doing so well as I could wish, so will give them all the water that is to spare, and proceed toward camp this evening in the cool; they won't feed, nor stay without constant watching. Started back at 8·30 P.M. Went first to the south of west, to avoid a stony hill by going round a valley, then went on for about fifteen miles.

"16*th*. Started at 6 A.M., then bore for Mount Wylde. The greater portion of last night's and to-day's journey was over spinifex country. Passed, immediately after starting, a couple of creeks; drainage to the north—whether they continued that course, and gradually swerved to the east and joined a larger one under the main range to east, and formed one, and passed on to the southward to Cooper's Creek, or formed rain water lakes (vast numbers of them here, and well timbered, and often visited by natives), I cannot pretend to say. From Mount Wylde came in, on the lakes, on our outward track, and arrived at camp at 2 P.M. Found some of the party, viz., Bell, Davis, and Maitland, laid up with dysentery, the former seriously. Have made up my mind to leave this, after one day's spell for the camels, and go back to different water, as this must contain some medicinal properties that I am ignorant of, and affects all of us more or less—no doubt the weather has a good deal to do with it; the heat is fearful."

17th. Intensely hot and oppressive, with the wind east of north. Not very good for the sick fellows. I (Davis) am better, but the others are not. It is the general opinion that there must be something in the water that makes us all so unwell. Thank goodness we leave this lake to-morrow for Ellar's Creek, which has been represented by Hodgkinson to have some fine water in it, distance about fifteen miles. The native name of this place is "Appocoldarinnie." Prepare for a start to-morrow, as we none of us like this place. Hurrah!

18th. We are off from this infernal sickly hole. The cart preceding the cavalry and camel corps as usual. Very sultry, with tempest last night, and about 2·30 this morning we arrived at the creek. The country passed through much as usual, sandy and unprofitable; and just fancy our disappointment, more especially the poor fellows who were so ill, finding that instead of camping under the fine shade, and their day's work being done, they had to leave it and go on some ten miles further to Lake Hodgkinson, as the water was so very bad that neither man nor horse could touch it.

This was a dreadful blow for the poor fellows, but those who go out on expeditions of this sort ought not to know how to spell "*grumble,*" for who can tell what will occur, or what sort of country they shall see next, or whether they will find water at the camping place, even if they tried till 12 o'clock at night? Yes, such is the lot of an explorer, and a hard life and a jolly one, no care for the morrow, no duns to fear and no debts incurred. It is a primitive life, but as before said a jolly one; but there is one thing wanting, it is the smile and solace of gentle woman!

> "Oh! woman in our hours of ease,
> Uncertain, coy, and hard to please,
> And variable as the shade,
> By the light quivering aspen made;
> When pain and anguish wring the brow,
> A ministering angel thou."

After that I must take a cooler before dinner.

This would have been a pleasant, cool, and pretty camp, but fate and bad water conspired against us, so now after stopping a short time to rest, proceed to Lake Hodgkinson. The water had gone bad since it was visited by Hodgkinson. Very sultry, and looking like rain. I hope we shall not be disappointed. On our way to the creek we passed a fine lake, and to every appearance with water in it. The natives who were with us were even deceived, and McKinlay has called it "Deception Lake," for all of us were regularly sold by its appearance.

We arrived at Lake Hodgkinson, and found it much dried up, and the water quite bitter; so we have now to go on to Hayward's Creek, which flows into this lake, and there we find excellent water, fine feed—in fact, everything that men in our position require, beautiful shelter, almost a necessary in this latitude. The dray did not camp with us, but at the east end of the lake. We had to dig to get water for drinking purposes. A short distance from the edge of the lake, after only about four feet sinking, they found beautifully clear water and well tasted. There is splendid bathing here, the water up to your chin. This luxury will soon drive our illness away. We shall remain here till some change in the weather takes place, and also to recruit the sick. It is too hot at present for a dip, so we must wait patiently till it is cooler. A few friendly natives come into camp. The animals suffering much from the heat, and we were nearly baked in our saddles, but rewarded at last after our disappointments by everything that could gladden our eyes.

19th. Dray came in about noon to-day. Last night heavy rain, and we had to turn out and secure the perishable articles with tarpauling. Lots of rain to north-north-east, indications of more. We bathed to-day. Found crawfish here. As there is plenty of material for the purpose, we begin tomorrow to build "whirlies" with a fine bushy shrub which abounds here. Bell still ill. Bathing will soon set us all right. Many natives higher up the creek. We still keep two "black guards" with us, and very useful we find them.

20th. Hayward Creek Camp. There being a great quantity of light rushes on the creek side of our camp, we cut them down to-day to prevent a surprise, and very good beds they make. Rain to the north-north-east.

21st. Mr. McKinlay gave our two natives a sheep to have a jollification with their friends higher up the creek. A novelty to them I should imagine.

22nd. The sick slowly improving. We cut down trees to make a "good" yard for the sheep, so we shall be here some time; also plenty of a small bushy shrub, "whillaroo," to build a house over McKinlay's tent, and improve our own domiciles. We can follow the bent of "our own glad wills," for there is no one here to say anything against it; in fact, the natives absolutely come and ask permission to fish in their own waters! McKinlay goes out for a short journey to-morrow to see what effect the late rains have had on the country towards the north.

23rd. McKinlay leaves to-day, accompanied by Wylde, Hodgkinson, and the two natives. They started about 12, and took with them plenty of provisions; McKinlay says he may be away three weeks, at all events they have taken with them supplies for that time, but I don't think he will be out so long, as the rain has fallen so partially. We were building yesterday, and are still at work at the McKinlay bower, and very comfortable it will be. This is about the nicest camp we ever had, and the bathing, don't mention it. Bell is better, but he has had a stiff time of it. Only about 600 lb. of flour left, no great shakes you will say; we shall soon have reduced rations again; never mind, half a loaf is better than no bread.

24th. The day broke magnificently, and continued so fine that it put me in mind of a spring day in the old country. If we go on as we are, the governor will have a fairy kind of palace instead of a bower, so deliciously cool, the wind finding its way through the boughs. It is to be hoped that he won't get TOO comfortable, and so remain here longer than he intended, although a good spell will be of vast service to the sick and weak, for it is a frightful thing to be on a march, under a broiling sun, feeling as though you could hardly move, and nothing to look forward to in camping but the usual tea, and no chance of a "wet" just to revive you; although tea is a great drink, and I believe never enjoyed by any one of the party so much in their lives, though there is not a man who would not give a quart of it for a "pint o' beer." Some of the men shoeing horses; very cold on the morning watch, and greatcoats called out for active service; the bathing has done us a power of good; the sheep, too, are as fat as possible, and they have turned out little trumps for travelling; they know the voice of old Kirby who has the care of them as well as possible, and well he does take care of them, and no mistake.

25th. Another fine day, and cool, we could never have better; what a blessing for us who are so busy overhauling and repairing tents; large flight of ducks and teal, too high to bag any for the pot, going north-east; do they smell water after the heavy rains in that quarter? Bell much better; a "header" into cold water three times a day has worked wonders with us all; but talk about fish, they knock up against your legs as you are swimming, and one absolutely jumped out of the water and hit Wylde in the eye; he did not black it certainly, but the eye looked rather fishy. Very cold again during the night.

Sunday, 26th. Kept to-day holy, it being Sunday, and read the Bible aloud, just to put us in mind that we were, or ought to be, Christians, though in a heathen land.

2 P.M. McKinlay and party returned, having failed to cross the Stony Desert for want of water, the horses looking very badly on that account, having hardly had a drink since they left this on Thursday; the men, too, did not look well, having had very little themselves.

We here give from McKinlay's journal the account of his excursion into the Stony Desert.

"23*rd*. Started out at 11·30 A.M.; got to the top of a sand hill on north side of Lake Hodgkinson, about six miles from camp; camp bearing about 175°; passed (dry) Lake Marra-boothana; then through flats and basins, a large one cutting our course. Changed course, and came to a dry creek, called Pantyh-wurladgie; then, on a bearing of 284°, over stony desert, for a large sand hill; a little water back about two miles, from whence we shall have to send for it, amongst the stones. Total distance travelled about thirty-three miles; to the north-east and south all stones, but sand hills bound the two latter quarters; beyond the termination of large sand hill there is nothing visible. To the west is a succession of sand hills, running north and south; and terminating in desert and stony plains. Round to 348° in the distance are to be seen some terminations of inconsiderable sand hills.

"24*th*. The country being short of water, I merely go out to-day to return to-morrow; leaving here all the rations I intended for our journey northward, which, for the present I had abandoned, with the intention, at a more suitable time, to try it. Natives are with me, but they declare it to be all dry; but I cannot rely on their statements at all times. The water: our supply for to-day, is about two miles off in the desert; our journey being over a succession of very high sand hills, and stony flooded flats; skirting, for the first three-quarters of an hour, the desert, to this spot, with a large, red-topped sand hill on our right, which terminates close by; have not seen a drop of water during the day, and camp without it. I return to-morrow early for the last water, which will be nearly dried up by the time I reach it. Distance travelled to-day twenty-four miles. Tops of all the hills to north-east and east are very red, quite free from vegetation on tops, and some with spinifix on their sides. To north, termination of sand hills with stony flats; north-west, unbroken horizon; from west-north-west round towards south-west, a sand hill in the distance; altogether a dreary spot. A heavy timbered creek comes in from south-west into the desert, and appears in the distance to have a tributary from east-south-east; the timber ceases as it comes on to the open desert plain, between four and five miles from this. Quite an unbroken horizon to the west of north-west for some distance. The sand hills that are in view are small and detached.

"25*th*. Started back, and got to water just in time to give the horses about half as much as they could drink, and a little for ourselves; rapid evaporation has taken place since we left yesterday, for then there was enough for a hundred horses, now there is not half enough for our eight, so must make for one of the permanent waters south of this to-morrow; have to close-hobble our horses and tie their heads down to them to prevent them straying too far; strong breeze from the southward.

"*Sunday*, 26*th*. Started at 7 A.M. for Coonhadie, a rain-water watering-place in desert, but found it quite dry; start for camp, Hayward's Creek, and arrived at 1 P.M.; distance about twenty-nine and a quarter miles direct from place to place, but we made it more, being obliged to go round to avoid sand hills and rounding Lake Hodgkinson. The horses stood much in need of water, and seemed to enjoy it much from quantity they drank, and the time they took about it. It was fortunate for us that the weather was cool for the season of the year. Wind south and east; found all right at the camp, and the men that were ailing much improved. The water in the creek is diminishing gradually, about three-quarters of an inch per day."

27*th*. Still at Hayward's Creek; we are employed to-day, merely to keep us in working order, in putting up a verandah to McKinlay's palace. Nice work, very, with thermometer 120° or 130°. A great argument at dinner to-day, Middleton and Palmer *v.* Wylde, as to distance to a certain spot;

to be chained to-morrow for deciding the bets; it will be a close shave.

The natives are very much displeased at our remaining here; they are trying all they can for us to go, as no doubt we are disturbing their fishing arrangements, for we are close to the creek from our tent—one, two, three, and into the water. McKinlay is very little troubled about it, as he says in his journal, "Natives very much displeased at our remaining here, but until the weather suits my purpose better than it has done at present they must put up with it."

28th. The natives still at us to-day to decamp; they have got a fine story to-day that the floods are coming down, and that if we remain here much longer we shall be drowned, as the "arimitha," or native name for flood, is coming down, and has reached a certain place which McKinlay knows well; so he is off to-morrow to see if there be any truth in the assertion, and if there is to shift camp to some higher ground. We all hope not, as this is a jolly place, and we shall lose our splendid bath in the morning. We went out early this morning to decide the important bet of yesterday; the distance was 1376 yards, so Wylde loses £2, which never will be paid until we reach the settled districts once again.

29th. McKinlay and Middleton go out to see if there be any appearance of the said flood; it will take some time to get there from the north on account of the many lakes and creeks it will have to fill on its way. They returned about 5 P.M., very hungry, as they generally were after a trip, and had seen no signs of a flood. There is seven or eight feet of water in this creek now, and first-rate water it is, but it is receding fast, for every morning we look to the gauge, a stick stuck in the mud graduated to inches, so that it is easily determined how much it recedes per diem; it is going at the rate of three-quarters of an inch a day.

I wonder if McKinlay will order us to dig a well here also; I should not be surprised, but there is enough water, provided it does not go bad, to last us for years; never mind if he does, there is nothing like healthy exercise, is there, reader? Talk of the old English game of cricket, it is nothing to digging wells when there is water close to camp; it keeps us from mischief and growling, and that is a great desideratum.

There are, McKinlay says, any number of natives up this creek, which is five or six miles long; he saw between 400 and 500. He did not go up to their whirlies, but from the number he saw he computed them as numerous as stated. There was a small camp close by, but they were gone to join the main body, for what reason deponent knoweth not, as we have never molested them. They pass our camp with their nets to drag the creek; they ask McKinlay always before they do so, and he of course grants permission, and they return loaded with the scaly "paroo," or "multa multa" galover (native names of the fish generally caught); but they are not very generous with them, and should we get into a fix like poor Burke and party, we should fare but badly had we to trust to their hospitality.

30*th*. We gave our camels a good washing with soap and water to-day, and bathed them well, and are making little bags for seeds, as everybody is collecting the unknown productions of the north, and curiosities of all sorts. The flies are very troublesome, they are in *millions*, you may say; they bite, too, just a little nip; had we only a mosquito net large enough to get under at meal times! I have some net certainly, but not large enough to get under for protection from these pestilent little varmints. They come on your meat, and it is with difficulty that you can help eating numbers of them; but we are getting used to it now, like eels to skinning; should you happen to bite one—but, no, I will not say anything on that painful subject.

All the party, McKinlay included, with the exception of myself and Middleton, have been attacked with vomiting and griping after meals. They can keep nothing on their stomachs. Why it should be so no one can tell, as we all eat from the same meat, and live precisely alike.

As I before mentioned that I thought the rations would soon be reduced it has come to pass, and next week they will be reduced to 5 lb. of flour a week, and I dare say very soon to 4 lb. It is better than having none. There are rations waiting for us at Finnis' Springs, to south-west, about 300 miles from our present position. Water is getting scarce below. I hope we shall not be locked up for the want of it. However, McKinlay Lake will be a good stand by, as I don't think that can ever go dry, on account of its depth, though it might go bad like the others, and we should be in a fix with bad water and reduced rations.

McKinlay says: "I wish it would rain, that I could start through the desert out of this, and get on to the waters north and west of this, and be doing something, as this sort of life is worse than hard work on the constitution." There is one thing, this detention here has enabled us to have the backs of the working animals attended to better than we otherwise could have done, and they are on splendid feed; but the flies and the excessive heat of the sun are two things against them, on account of the sores and wounds some of them have, and they will not readily heal. Several of the horses have been bled, but from the heat and flies the necks of the animals have swollen much. This is the devil's own country for insects.

31*st*. Went out after camels, to see how they were getting on, and also to see that they had not rambled far from the feeding ground. On my return found McKinlay, Middleton, and "Nelmilly," native, gone off to "Cann-boog-o-nannie" Lake (Lake Jeannie), to see how the water was, and also to find an easier road for the cart to go towards "Moolionboorrana" Lake. They found a pretty good road, but the water quite unfit for use. The horses would not touch it, so they dug a little hole about eighteen inches from the water's edge, found most excellent water, and made some tea. What is it that turns the water bad? When we were there before it was first-rate. Is it the accumulated dung of the wild fowl, and the excessive heat of the sun, or what is it? This I leave to more scientific men than myself. Lots of natives round this lake. Found innumerable small fish, of the "parro" kind, washed up by the ripple of the lake; perhaps they are killed by the effect the water had on them.

Feb. 1*st*. Had a long walk with Ned this morning, and brought in the camels to get another cooling. Yes; orders are issued, the mandate has gone forth! a well is to be sunk to-day. Sunk it about five or six feet deep; awfully hard the ground. The fellows still sick after their meals; Ned very bad, also Maitland, but I have escaped the infliction. Betting going on to-day on all kinds of events; weather continues awfully hot, but the bathing is delicious; it cools us in the evening, and sets us up for the next day.

A circumstance occurred to-day that highly amused us all; our second in command had often said that the natives had real respect for him, and I believe he thought so; he was, however, doomed to be undeceived; he was ordered to tell some of the hangers-on to decamp. They certainly went, but jabbering something and applying the polinar face of the dexter hand sharply over the region of the glutus. I wonder what they said to him—a high compliment, I dare say. This may be a custom of the country and a mark of respect; I don't think he will put any more trust in the blacks, or spin yarns about their great respect for him. He must have felt very small when the roar of laughter from the camp reached his ears.

Feb. 2nd. Camp Hayward's Creek. Wylde ill to-day. The sickness still sticking to some of them. Camels washed again to-day. Hodgkinson and Middleton shot 27 pigeons to-day. They were in flocks of 100, feeding on the seeds of the grass, and rose the moment you got close to them; consequently the slaughter was greater than if they had been frightened. They made a nice change for our dinner and supper; some done on the ashes, some stewed, and some put into a pie. They were exceedingly nice, and very fat. The water in the creek decreasing fast, bathed as usual. Of course did not work at the well, being Sunday.

3rd. When bringing in the camels to-day saw a flock of geese; had two shots at them with ball, but they were very shy, and we could not get near enough to them.

At the well to-day. Hard and hot work. Came to water; although only a few yards from the creek, which was fine, nice water, that in the well was as salt as brine; so much so that you could not touch it, so all our labour is thrown away. McKinlay thinks that if all the water be baled out in the morning it may come fresh afterwards. I don't expect any such result, but seeing is believing; perhaps he may be right. The only motive for digging a well was that a change of water was desirable, as McKinlay fancied it was the water in the creek that had something to do with the sickness; but we must still stick to the creek, and make the best of it. I rather think a change of diet would do some good; constantly eating the same thing day after day is bad, I know. No vegetables. The greater part of our food is flesh, with a small modicum of bread. No wonder we get indisposed.

4th. We baled out the water this morning.

This well is now some fifteen feet deep, layers of sand chiefly, so it is continually caving in. The water flows in fast, but as salt as ever, though, strange to say, it lathers well with soap. Men mending their shirts; some of us have variegated ones already with the different coloured patches; no one was ill to-day after meals.

McKinlay went off on a ramble to-day to look up the niggers and see where they had gone. As they all seem to have left our vicinity, he fancies that it may be a ruse to lull us into a feeling of security, and so put us off our guard, and some night come down and give us a dressing. Poor deluded gentlemen of colour! if such be your notions, believe me, you have the wrong man to deal with if you think to catch our leader napping. Just after McKinlay started some five or six came down to fish in the creek.

5th. I drew a bucket of water from the well this morning, and it was as salt, if not more so, than before. Mending clothes and cribbage the order of the day. The weather warm towards six; hot indeed.

6th. Wind warm to-day, with thunder and lightning. It appears to be raining in various places, though it does not appear likely we shall get any. We have been so often deceived that it is no use going by appearances any longer up here. The wind chopped round to the south, and it became very hot and oppressive.

Middleton and Hodgkinson are to start off to-morrow morning for Lake McKinlay, to ascertain for certain if that lake still continues to hold abundance of water, and also if it be good; and also on their way, *en passant*, to see if Lake "Moolion-boorrana" will suit for a stage to camp at on the way to Lake McKinlay, should we go there, as it did not contain much water when we were there last, and he has his (McKinlay's) doubts on the subject. McKinlay is quite certain that the water here is affecting us, and he wishes to go to the lake for a change, and remain there till it rains, so as to be able to cross the desert. Natives that come into camp to-day report that lots of rain has fallen to the east and north-east beyond Lake Sir Richard and Lake Blanche.

7th. Mr. Hodgkinson and native started at 7·30 this morning for Lake McKinlay, to see, as before mentioned, the supply of water there. Weather on the change, I think; it blew very strong from the south-east last night. Very cloudy, but no rain to speak of all day; it has been cloudy and cool, and there is really now some chance, I think, of our getting some rain. Plenty of thunder and lightning to-day.

8th. Raining splendidly; steady down-pour last night, with strong wind from south-east; some thunder. Everything looks refreshed; the little birds are chirping merrily, and the old crows pleading their own cause vociferously. The flies, however, are worse, being driven into the tents and whirlies by the rain. The walking this morning was anything but pleasant, the mud being up and over our ankles, and it stuck so to our boots that it was with difficulty we could get ahead at all; and having to go three miles to bring up the camels, it became a very tiring job. The camels themselves could hardly make a walk of it at all, and were more like cats in walnut-shells on ice than anything I recollect having seen.

I expect we shall be able to start for the Desert to-morrow or the next day, as there must be abundance of water now in the claypans and holes, more than sufficient for our purpose. McKinlay has ordered all horses that require it to be shod, so I suppose the Stony Desert is the trip before us, and then on to Finnis' Springs to get our rations. Some of the flour we have been eating lately has had a very peculiar taste; indeed, some of it had got a touch of the naphtha or paraffine that was put on top of it, in its transit from Port Augusta to Blanchewater, and perhaps that has been the cause of the illness, and not the water. Middleton, Hodgkinson, and native returned. They report lots of rain-water this side of Lake McKinlay, and plenty in the lake itself, and good, with lots of natives on the banks; but as the rain has fallen so well and abundantly, we shall not go there, but proceed at once to the Desert.

9th. It is still raining, and the ground as soft as possible—in fact, too soft to travel over, so we shall not go to-day. The blacks are all away over the sand hills to catch lizards and other things to eat. The rain has proved a godsend to them, as well as to us. No holiday to-day, for we have had to work like coolies to get all ready for to-morrow, as we shall certainly start in the morning if it does not rain. McKinlay thinks there will be abundance of water to take us across this time. I hope he will not be disappointed. We shall all miss our nice bathing, which I am sure has been the means of keeping us all much better than if we had been without it. All ready for a start by tea-time, so there will be nothing to delay us in the morning that we know of at present. Hurrah for the road once again!

CHAPTER VII.

THE GREAT STONY DESERT.

Editor's Remarks on the features of the Desert—Repeated Traces of Burke's Party — February 15th, McKinlay seriously ill; and, 19th, also Middleton—25th, Burke's Creek — 27th, 28th, Very heavy Rains — March 1st, Around Camp all Flooded; Difficult Extrication—8th, Named "Escape Camp" — Fine Weather and extraordinary Vegetation—Features of the Country—13th, Elliott's Knob — 16th, McKinlay's description of the Country; Browne Creek; Ellar's and Warren's tiers of Tabletops — Goat's hair Head-ornament and part of a Greatcoat in a Native Whirlie—Diminishing Rations and sorry Substitutes.

The reader, in entering upon this long chapter, may conjecture that there is nothing before him but a wearying uniformity of arid wastes. The account we have given in the last chapter, extracted from Mr. McKinlay's journal, of his four days' excursion into the Desert, will have done nothing to prevent such a conjecture. The description given by the travellers of a scene so wonderfully different in its character when they had entered this Desert. is most striking, and is well worthy of the attention of those who would know of all the peculiarities and vicissitudes by which Australia is distinguished. The expedition waits for rain to enable it to cross the "Desert." We have already gathered some experience of what all the country hereabouts may be reduced to when for a long time deprived of rain. Now the party are to see what are the effects of the rain, when it does at length pour down, upon even the most sterile parts—the stony plains and sand hills.

Heavy rains fall, which appear to be general over a large area, especially northwards in the line of the expedition's subsequent march. In a fortnight the capacious creek-beds, previously quite dry, or interspersed with only a few water-holes, are the channels of great bodies of water, rising momentarily in their level to overflow upon the plains, while the plains themselves are in some parts already shallow lakes. The most of these creeks seemed to have been dry for some time before. "The running of the creek" is quite an event in many parts of colonized Australia, where the creek is, perhaps, for nearly all the year, or for several years together, merely a chain of ponds or natural cisterns. The creek may not "run" at any particular station, after even weeks of pouring rain, because all the waters are being meantime absorbed in filling up the successive natural cisterns of its upper course. But with a roar they come at last, sweeping all before them with the flood. Our travellers experienced such a flood in the midst of the Desert, which this chapter finds them entering upon, and Mr. Davis's journal graphically describes its incidents.

The dangers experienced by the expedition from these recurring floods, suggest to Mr. Davis that Leichhardt's party may have been lost in one of them some fourteen years before, and Mr. McKinlay is disposed to the same view. The head-ornament made of goat's hair, found in a "whirlie," or temporary shelter of the wandering natives, seems, as Davis thinks, to confirm this view, for where could these natives have procured goat's hair except from the flock of goats taken by Leichhardt on his second and fatal expedition? We are doubtful, however, of an Australian *belle* (if indeed she claimed the ornament) bestowing such long lasting care upon any of her *bijouterie*, especially when she leaves it at last in what seems a deserted whirlie. Leichhardt's party were long since reported to have been all killed by natives. Perhaps this is the least likely of the several alternatives, as Leichhardt, an experienced traveller, had a force adequate to resist any attack the usually timid natives were capable of. Starvation was one probable fate; the other we see in our travellers' experience of sudden and tumultuous floods.

Under the genial rain, the dry surface promptly

changes its aspect. The ground, where it is not sand and stones, is mud, impeding the march at every step. For a short time the well-moistened surface exhibits no trace of life. "Nothing green," says McKinlay's journal of 13th February, the third day after starting, "except in the bed of the creek and the trees. The whole country looks as if it had been carefully ploughed, harrowed, and finally rolled, the farmer having omitted the seed." This naked, lifeless aspect soon, however, disappears beneath the verdure called forth by the moisture and the warm air. The plains become covered with pasture. Even "the stony hills and slopes," says McKinlay, on 8th March, "where, from their bronzed and desert appearance a few days ago, one would suppose grass never grew, are now being clothed in many places with a nice green coating, and shortly will give this place quite a lively appearance. When I first saw it, it was as desolate a looking spot as one could picture." He goes on to say, on 19th March, "passed through some magnificent country—one plain extending several miles, and well grassed. The weather, magnificent and quite tropical; the perfume of the flowers quite refreshing." Mr. Davis's account, further on in this chapter, is even more striking. The reader must remember that we are here still in the great Stony Desert, a fact of which the leader's journal keeps us well in mind, for it is stated, after two days' progress beyond this gay, luxuriant scene, "our journey to-day (21st March) was over nothing but red sand hills."

How, then, are we to know when we are in and when we are out of the Desert? Is it when we quit the fragrant region of flowers, and emerge into more ordinary scenery, that we know we have left the region of sand and stones? But the Desert has still its recognizable features throughout. The red sand hills protrude everywhere, varied by stony plains. Hill ranges appear on the horizon, but they are soilless and treeless masses of rock. Timber, if there is any, is confined to the beds of creeks, and there too, in protected spots, may be permanent, or comparatively permanent, grass; but the surface generally is bare under the scorching of sun and drought, excepting on those fitful occasions when the rain, as with a magician's wand, covers the country with beauty—a beauty, however, that may disappear almost as promptly as it came. These are the features of our Australian desert, and let us watch when they cease. On 23rd March there are some ameliorative symptoms. A white gum-tree flat is passed over; the trees are not very large, but the stony character is less conspicuous. The next day the wooded hills of Scott's Range appear in the distance. This last symptom coming upon the others preceding, we take to be decisive, so we close the Desert, and the chapter that describes it, with the 23rd March. Just six weeks had been spent in traversing it.

The Desert was the place of trial for the merits of the camels, and they appear to have come off quite triumphant. Mr. McKinlay says, under date 10th March, "The camels travelled over the stones with their loads apparently quite unconcerned; they are undoubtedly the best of all animals for this kind of work; they eat anything nearly, from the gum-tree down to the smallest herb, and then come and lie down beside you; whereas, horses and bullocks, if there be any lack of food, will wander all over the country." He also greatly commends the sheep. Speaking, on 26th February, of delay and trouble with the other animals, a bullock having dropped down almost dead under the heat, he remarks, "None of our journeys appear to give the sheep the slightest inconvenience, and they are as ready to commence their journey in the morning as the man who attends them; in fact, no party ought ever to go out exploring in the summer months without them."

10th. The cart and sheep started at 7 A.M.; the horses and camels some time after, as usual. Our course lies somewhere about north-west. We passed over sand hills to the other side of the lake, and then over alternate sand hills and flats for nine or ten miles, and passing on our way a salt lake.

"Warma-go-la-dhailie" is its name, and a very pretty one too. The ground is very soft, and, consequently, very heavy travelling. Before leaving, we set fire to our little dwellings, and very soon the "whirlies" were among the things of the past. We shall go a long stage to-day, and hope to find our expectations realized anent the water in the claypans and holes. Some of the water that is caught in the stony hollows is as clear as crystal, while that in the claypans is thick and muddy to a degree; the former is delicious. We camped under a bush, as there is not a tree to be seen. We did not do so till late, having passed the cart and sheep miles back. I do not expect they will be up to-night. There is nothing for the horses to eat, and only a few bushes for the camels. The latter part of the journey over sand-ranges, spinifex, and stony flooded flats, then over sand hill and part of Stony Desert, where we camp on the stones. Hard sleeping to-night. The last part of the way has not so much water as the first. We must do the best we can to-night, and we shall have a nice time of it, watching the animals to prevent them from straying; for, should they do so, it would be almost impossible to track them over the stones, which are quite brown, and look as if they had been packed, and very much water or weather worn. It is a curious sight, such an extent of bronzed surface, without anything but perhaps a small bush to break the view.

The cart not up, so we shall make a few scons of some seconds flour, boil a pot of tea each, and then to bed. I have the first watch, and a nice time it will be, rounding up all the horses, and keeping them together. I am mounted, however, so that I can get after the brutes quicker and better. It is rather dark here, too, which makes it worse.

The camels were brought in and tied up, to prevent their being *non inventi* in the morning. A few natives are seen looking for snakes and lizards, etc.—in fact, anything that has been driven to the hills by the wet. How would you, reader, like to sit down to a snake and lizard supper, served up with that best of all sauces—hunger?

11*th*. At daylight this morning, Mr. McKinlay, by the aid of his binocular, discovered the cart and sheep about two miles off, wending their weary way to camp. They arrived shortly after. The bullocks were taken out and watered, etc., while we got our breakfast. The meal was soon concluded, and away we went to bring up the horses, etc., and prepare for a start. We shall go a short stage to-day, as one of the bullocks got knocked up, and caused the delay on the road yesterday. We start, and continue our journey over the same uninteresting flat of brown stone, with little or no herbage; some high sand hills to our right and left some way off. We then crossed over the one to the left, and camped on the other side where there was some water. No feed here to speak of. We had to kill a sheep, the meat on the cart being unfit for food. We left the old bullock to go by himself to-day, and he was driven into camp some time after we arrived by the man left in charge of him. I fear he won't go much further, as he is so fat, and feels the heat so much. We with the camels picked up the water-keg, which had fallen off the dray, and a sack containing rations. We soon whipped them up on the camels. The bullock-driver was unconscious of his loss.

I never travelled through a more uninteresting country in all my life. As soon as we got to camp, down came the rain, and we had to get such shelter as we could, as it was too windy to put up the tents; the ground being light sand, the pegs would not stand a minute; so we had to grin and bear it. We got tolerably well soaked, as it came down with a will. I had a long and wet walk this evening with the camels to a creek some three miles off, as there was nothing for them to eat but a few bushes, and they wandered in search of something more palatable; and when they do begin that game they will go for miles, even in hobbles. I brought them back, and they were tied up, so I shall not have far to look for them.

In the morning, on crossing the large plain, we found large stones, much larger than any we had seen before, placed side by side, marking out squares, circles, and different kinds of figures as far as the eye could reach; what these were for we could not make out. I suppose the blacks hold merrymakings here, or something of the sort; to-morrow perhaps we shall know all about it, till then it must remain a problem to be solved. Distance to-day nine or ten miles; several sand hills, some distance from them where we are camped, this is called (the large hill where we are camped) "Canna-cannan-thainya." The natives who accompany us are very useful in this way, and point out to the governor the different hills and creeks, and tell him their names. We had a steady rain last night for about three hours, but this morning it is fine and cool. There is plenty of water all along the route, we can see it from the high sand hill.

12*th*. The dray started as usual before us. We crossed a large sand range called "Malla-poorpo-nannie." The country generally is very uninteresting. The greater part of the day's journey we crossed several small creeks, most of them running. The female camel gave us a great deal of trouble to-day, she did not like facing the running water; she detained us most seriously.

Mr. McKinlay thus describes in his journal the country passed through to-day :—

"12*th*. Steady rain for about four hours last night, and this morning breaks fine and clear, with a wind north. Plenty of water lying all over the Desert. Dray started at 7·40 A.M., and at six and three-quarter miles distant got to Malla-poorpo-nannie sand range, the southern end of which is called Coo-korda; about two miles off its northern end dwindles down to nothing in the Desert. To the northern end of Coontarie sand range, a creek and well by the same name; about twelve miles off, a detached sand range in the desert, at the north-west end of which are two waters, named respectively Dhooramoorco and Moongaara; also on north-east side of sand range another water in creek called Cadry-yerra, also a sand range about four to five miles distant. There was a number of small detached sand hills going round to the west-ward, then a perfect blank round to Coontarie well. At about three to four miles struck the flooded flat from the main creek I am now going to. At eleven and a half miles farther came to and crossed a deep creek crossing my course at right angles. At two miles further came to water in Daeragolie Creek, same creek that I crossed before two miles from this; within this last two miles the whole flat is cut up into innumerable channels most difficult to travel over, I must therefore see and get a better road for the cart. Here there is not a green blade of grass to be seen; there are some green shrubs in the bed of the creek that the camels are fond of. I arrived at this camp at 2·5 P.M.; distance travelled to-day, twenty-three and a half miles. This is an immense creek, timbered on its bank with box, bean, and other trees, the water is in detached holes, but good, and apparently plenty of fish and ducks."

The cart not up to-night as usual. Mr. McKinlay talks of abandoning it and packing the bullocks; it has been a great drawback to us and no mistake, still it has been exceedingly useful.

There is very bad feed for the horses here, but capital for the camels. No niggers to be seen, or any signs of them, so we shall have no watch to keep to-night, the first time for some months. Thank goodness we are camped on a fine creek with plenty of water. We had to get our supper of scons baked on the coals, and a pot of tea: we shall not get fat at this rate however.

13th. The cart on its way this morning got upset into a creek close by, no damage done. Bell having been sent to look after it, returned with the above intelligence; it shortly after arrived.

Mr. McKinlay and Hodgkinson go out to look for a good crossing place for it and the animals, as we are to cross this creek, which is very steep, some fifty or sixty feet down almost perpendicular banks. Middleton also goes out to see if he can find a ford close by for the horses, as there is splendid feed here for the camels though bad for horses. The food the camels are so fond of is a tall thin shrub, bearing a very pretty flower, there being three or four varieties, alike in growth and leaf, but differing in the colour of the bloom, some yellow, others white and purple.

Our breakfast was the ditto of last night's supper—a scon and a pot of tea; the cart not coming up, and containing as usual all our commissariat in use. Had a fine bathe in the creek this morning, which quite refreshed all of us.

We shall stay here to-day and rest the bullocks, as they will not be in early, and also that they may get something to eat; the plant in the creek they also are very fond of, and as there is abundance, they will have a good feed to-day, and they want it, for the poor brutes have hardly had anything for two or three days to speak of. We have had no meat to eat since Tuesday morning at 6 o'clock A.M. till to-day at 1 P.M., when we were regaled with a small piece of bacon—hard times—I hope they won't get harder, that's all. We had a jolly good supper, however, of roast mutton and damper to make up for the late short commons; had a good bathe after dinner, and that, reader, is half the battle in these times, although we may not have a change of raiment to put on afterwards. Mr. McKinlay reports the road, from what he saw, as far as he could judge, as better for our next day's journey than it has been for the last few days, so he hopes we shall go ahead better.

The creek we are on is one hundred yards wide, with any number of small creeks flowing into it, draining the flats around. Wind to-day rather hot from south-west. There is another creek not quite so large as the one we are on, that goes away to west and south. There is plenty of limestone seen, and it is heavily timbered; there is nothing green to be seen but the leaves on the trees, and in the creeks the ground is quite black, and looks as if it had been prepared for seed. Two natives came into camp this afternoon and remained with us; they did not appear to be afraid.

14*th*. We went about fifteen miles on the same creek and camped. About three miles from here we came on the bones of a horse and an old saddle. Middleton and self stopped here and examined all the trees to see if we could find any marks, but nothing was to be seen. There was camels' dung found though, plainly showing that this was the spot where poor Burke killed and jerked his horse Billy. We stopped some time to see if we could find anything buried, but failed to do so; the saddle was all that was left, no stirrup leather or girth—merely the saddle. We each took away a hoof of the horse as a *Memento mori*. Yes, here we are for certain at a camp of Burke's! I imagine they came down this creek on their way home; and if so, we shall fall in with many more, I dare say.

I wish they had marked the trees on their way, but perhaps they had no means of doing so; but they must have had a knife surely, and that would have been sufficient to mark the bark, even if not very deep.

We got to camp some time after the rest consequent on our stay in Burke's camp; cart not up, and won't be for a long time, so there will be nothing to eat; all of us very hungry till it did come, about 9 P.M. I took the bullock driver's watch as well as my own; I thought it would never end; six hours is a long spell; and I also had to keep a sharp eye on a native friend who had come with us a short way to prevent his bolting, as our long-tried companion, Mr. Nilmilly, vanished immediately on our arrival here, and has not been seen since; he got the funks on the march I fancy, as he was getting out of his latitude, and feared we should find no water ahead; he takes with him tomahawk, pannikin, clothes, and our good wishes for his safe journey to his people, for he has really been very useful indeed to the party, and I dare say we may hear something of him from parties who may be on the look-out for Burke coming from the north.

Ned had to leave one of his best bullocks behind; he was quite baked, and his mate was obliged to be left also to keep him company, as he would not leave him. The mate came into camp about 11 P.M., but the other, I fear, will be dead before morning. There is a large red sand hill close by, from which an extensive view of the country can be obtained—not a very cheering one, it must be owned; but there is a well-defined creek in the distance, well timbered. Close to this camp also we found camel-dung, showing that Burke had been here also, so that he could not have been making much progress.

15*th*. I did not have much sleep last night, having to keep such a long watch; consequently, feel rather done up this morning. Cut Mr. McKinlay's initials on a tree; party started first thing for the missing bullock; found him in the creek, and brought him into camp; he is better, but not quite right; he will be a great loss, for he is a splendid working beast. This delayed our starting till 12 o'clock, and we got into camp at 1·30, going only five or six miles; our journey is up a branch creek; there seems to be no good water-hole to bathe in at or near this camp, for which I am sorry, as I fear we shall stop here some days to make pack-saddles and packs for the bullocks, for at last the cart is to be abandoned, and quite time too, for this country is not fit for the passage of any wheeled arrangement, at any rate the roads we have travelled; it may be better on the plains, and very likely it is so, but it is so intersected by deep and steep watercourses and creeks, that it is almost impossible for a cart to travel at all, and had we not been fortunate enough to have a first-rate and experienced bullock-driver, we should never have brought it so far. Ned Palmer certainly deserves great credit for the way he has managed his team through this intricate and dangerous country. I wonder the cart has not been smashed long ere this.

Wind to-day disagreeable, blowing from north. The heat fearful in the extreme. Mr. McKinlay taken violently ill with dysentery. Our last native quite forlorn at being left all alone by himself, so Mr. McKinlay has taken pity on him and let him slip his cable and go; he seems delighted, and is off like a shot down the creek. It is a pity too, for they are very useful in pointing out the waters, and it does not seem likely that we shall see any more of them for some time, as we have not seen any lately; they must have gone up into the sand hills after their game, and left the creeks, as there are plenty of water-holes down the creek, and from the number of them they must be pretty numerous at all times.

Many fish to be seen in the water-holes, and plenty of mussels, judging from the number of empty shells round the fire-places at the native whirlies. The country on this side of the creek is better wooded than the other, but not a blade of grass, excepting in the bed of the creek and water-courses, and not much to boast of in them on the sandy side of the creek.

We found a small plant with a thick velvet leaf. We pulled a lot, and had it boiled; had we but salt and a little butter it might have been taken for asparagus, though not much like it in taste, only resembling it slightly; it is also very nice eaten raw, it has a slight acid flavour, and I should say first-rate for us, who have not had any greens for so long a time. It will improve the blood, a thing which we all require, as it is as pale and as thin as possible. The plant is best picked early in the morning, as, if the sun has been on it any time, it is tougher and not so acid. I hope we shall continue to find it, as it does us a world of good; besides being a great treat to us all, it helps out our small allowance of bread, as we can save half our bread at a meal having this stuff to eat with our meat.

Mr. McKinlay very ill this afternoon; he must have a very serious attack, as his face is very much pinched since this morning, and he walks really very ill indeed.

16*th*. Remained in camp. Mr. McKinlay in his tent all day, and looks worse than ever; he is taking some medicine; I think it is chlorodine—it quite warms you through after a dose of sixty or seventy drops. I hope it will soon restore our worthy leader to us in his usual health and spirits. We are all rather down in the mouth at this sudden illness of the governor, for he is certainly much worse to-day.

Ned and I had a nice walk up the creek after the camels some two miles; it was very hot up the creek, as we were obliged to follow their tracks. However, we managed a spell and a smoke or two; we found no beauties to flirt with, but spun yarns of the old country. We got the camels into camp all right, and found on our way some old horse and camel dung, so that Burke must have been here also. When we returned to camp we set to work to jerk mutton; the cart is to be left here, so we shall have a lot of traps to put on the camels—cooking utensils, rations, and God knows what else. There is no lack of mosquitoes here, but they don't seem to trouble me as much as they do the others, and a very good job too; what between the *swarms* of flies by day and the mosquitoes at night, we have a very lively time of it indeed. We retired to our blankets early, but, alas! not to sleep; at least several fellows were seen perambulating up and down, keeping the sentry company, for they could not sleep on account of these torments of the dark hours.

17*th*. Mr. McKinlay still very ill. Most of us hard at work, getting the baggage from the cart to separate the things that are to be taken with us from those that are to be left behind. Another long trudge up the creek after the camels and, *horribile dictu*, I forgot my pipe, and now I have only one left—a short clay. We have had no salt for some days past, and our meat, etc., is very insipid, but hunger is a good sauce, and we generally have it at meal-times. Very scanty food indeed for the horses, so they break up into different mobs and stray away. We take leave of the old .cart to-day, as to-night it is going to the top of a sand hill, to be there left to its fate; the goods are to be buried on the sand hill, also, in consequence of all this country being under water at some periods, from the flood-marks left on the trees. We bury no end of lucifers and candles, and, as the Yankees say, notions too numerous to mention.

Some of us weighed to-day, Mr. McKinlay one of the number. He weighed when he left Adelaide, in August, 15 st. 11 lb.; to-day exactly 12 st.! A slight shower with thunder this morning, and *promises* for some more. Mr. McKinlay a little better this evening.

Camels will miss the cart, as they now have a stiff load; the "old woman," as we call her, has over 433 lb. on her, which is a good weight for this difficult country. We did not get away till after 3 o'clock, and arrived in camp on a muddy water-hole about dark, long after all the others. Distance, sixteen miles. I fear Mr. McKinlay will feel the journey, as he is still very weak, though he says he is better.

18*th*. The country passed over to-day quite destitute of vegetation, the low, black flats looking as though they had been prepared for crops.

Passed a creek to east; no water. Crossing the plain one of our bullocks (the one that had been ill) was struck dead by the heat of the sun, though carrying nothing, only walking along by himself. Nothing could be done with him, as all the party save those with the camels were a long way in advance; so he was left to the tender mercies of the wild dogs. There was not a drop of water to be seen, and I feared for some time we should have been obliged to camp without any. We passed several magnificent creeks, and saw through the breaks in the sand hills others with timber. Passed over more flooded flats, on to a creek without water; then went on the same kind of country well wooded till we came to a rain-water hole, where we camped. Mr. McKinlay went further on in the hopes of finding water, but to no purpose, so came back to this water, and we found him and the horses camped when we arrived. There was sufficient water in this hole for all our purposes, first taking out enough in our water-bags and canteens to supply us to-night and to-morrow in case we see no more.

This must be a splendid country after the floods, for, though destitute of anything like grass, it is really very pretty, some parts of it undulating and well wooded; but it is desolate enough now. We find more similar traces of Burke and his unfortunate companions. Mr. McKinlay says he is very ill this evening, and hardly able to sit in the saddle, and he really looks so.

19*th*. Hodgkinson and Middleton are sent out up the creek to look out for water for next stage. Middleton returns about 11, having found plenty of water about eight miles up. Hodgkinson proceeded further, and is to return to the aforesaid water, where we shall camp to-night. So we all saddled up, and started for this water late in the afternoon, as the distance was so very short. Mr. McKinlay suffered a great deal, and we rigged up a kind of shade for him under the only tree near the camp with our blankets, for he did not wish the tents pitched, as they would keep us back at starting.

Mr. McKinlay and party found the water-hole from the direction given by Middleton, who was taken so ill by the way that we were unable to get him to camp that night; so he camped on a plain, under a large tree, without water or anything to eat. Poor fellow! he was awfully bad, and unfit to go further. He craved for water so much, and there was not a drop to give him, although I drained my canteen and bag for him. I lighted a large fire, and unpacked the camels, making him a bed under the tree. I thought he would have died. I fancied he had the cholera; he was doubled up, and rolling about so fearfully. I knew we could not be far from our camping place by what he told me, and I sent up a blue light and a Roman candle. I was very hungry and thirsty, and went to sleep after seeing Middleton a little better; strange to say, when I woke I was neither hungry nor thirsty.

20th. (Camp. iv.) Poor Middleton was hardly able to rise this morning, so I saddled up the camels and horses, and started. We shortly got to camp, Middleton very ill indeed. I was glad to get a drink of water and a scon. This creek where we are camped is some two hundred yards wide, and about eighty or ninety feet deep, with rather steep banks. We are on the east side; it is well wooded, which affords good shelter for the sick. The men in camp saw nothing of our blue light, though they had been looking out and keeping up roaring fires all night. Mr. McKinlay could not imagine what had become of us. We have, ever since we abandoned the cart, to carry the stock for the larder on the camels, so that the men at head-quarters had not much of a supper; we, as I said before, did not touch them either. Middleton was so bad on arriving at camp, that he had to be helped up the side of the creek to the place where we are to camp, just on the top of the bank, under some nice shady trees. The tent was soon up, and Middleton quickly between the blankets; I thought at one time I should never have brought him into camp.

After breakfast took the camels to water and

feed; I took a bath, and very much refreshed I was after; the water, nice and cool, but the bottom muddy. About 6 P.M. I went on horseback after the camels, the horsemen reporting that they were not to be seen on the creek for three miles. I overtook them about four miles down the creek on the tramp; God knows where they would have been in the morning had I not gone after them. There was plenty of feed on the creek, and they had a good drink on arriving, so that I cannot account for their getting on the spree; tied them up at camp to-night; Mr. McKinlay much better to-day, and looks quite a different man; Ned very bad; the day was hot in the extreme.

21*st*. This is not a very first-rate camp, but Middleton is too ill to move. Repairing camel saddle to-day, and doing odd jobs, others washing.

22*nd*. Up early; Hodgkinson and Bell start off with two days' rations to examine the stony ranges in the distance, and to ascertain if this creek receives any waters from the west or north-west, and to return by this creek and see how the water is in it. Parallel ruler not to be found; it must have been left behind or else dropped off the camel's back; unpacked everything, but *non est*. McKinlay quite well to-day, and Middleton improving, thank God!

There is only eight weeks' flour from to-day, but we still get a lot of that greenstuff, and relish it; it goes down well with a little sugar, when we can spare it from our tea. We must get to Finnis' Springs shortly, or we shall be in a pretty fix; we can't well starve, though, while we have plenty of sheep and horses to eat, to say nothing of a camel or so.

23rd. Up early to-day, to get mutton jerked. Wylde starts off to No. iii. camp, after parallel ruler, a stage of some fifty miles or more there and back, where we buried the things, and left the cart. I hope he may find it, as it is very useful to the leader. I did think we left it behind, but fear we must have dropped it. Middleton decidedly on the mend. McKinlay goes out on horseback, feeling all right, to the east, to examine the country; he went over flooded flats. Here is his account of the journey:—

"Over flooded flats, and a couple of sand hills. From top of the highest sand hill, changed course to 113° for two and a quarter miles to top of another larger sand hill, passing one other in my course then on bearing of 15° for six and three-quarter miles, over flooded flats, with a few smaller sand hills, but soon terminate on both sides of my course; the current over this tract of flat being to the south of east, then three-quarters of a mile on bearing of 15° over one sand hill to top of rocky hill, from which the flooded flat I have just passed gathers together in the distance to a creek, and goes off on course of 155°, and no doubt is the feeder of the waters now in the creek to south and east of our present camp, viz., Barrawarkanya, Marroboolyooroo, Cadrityrrie, Meinconnyannie, and Gnappa Muntra; then two and a quarter miles on bearing of 10° to top of sandy and stony hill, with four or five mallee trees and a few other shrubs; marked one of the mallee trees. From this hill the creek passed end of table-topped stone range, on bearing from six to nine miles distant north-west and round northward to east. Peaks and hills of stone with intervening flats, some of earth, others of stone, are visible as far as eye can reach; from this hill our present camp bears about 227½° and distant about eleven and a half miles."

This evening Bell and Hodgkinson returned; having examined the hilly country, but could find no tributary joining the creek, they saw a little water further up, and also a native and his lubra, but could not get any conversation with them, they were so shy.

24th. To-day a great event occurred; Hodgkinson tendered his resignation as second in command, so he will now join the ranks as horseman. He wished to return to the settled districts, but that Mr. McKinlay would not hear of. The bullocks all astray this morning, and could not be found in time to start.

Poole got a slight sunstroke going after the horses; he was brought in, and from the cold applications continually made, he soon rallied. Middleton all right again.

25th. (Camp v.) After a cool journey of eighteen miles, we camped on a small creek, with plenty of water. The country was flooded flats; passed a large creek, and numerous native "whirlies;" we crossed it, and then went over some high sand hills, the summits of which were almost perpendicular walls of drift sand, from two to five feet high, and very difficult for the animals to get over; the female camel gave us much trouble to get her to cross them; then over more flooded flats, then over small and stony hills, the stones of the same description as those of the Desert. We reached a creek we descried in the distance, and found plenty of water and abundance of good feed for the animals, which luxury they have not had for some time. Weather cloudy. We saw in the flats fields of very beautifully coloured lilies; the vegetation all this day's journey better than it had been some days previous. Mr. McKinlay has called the creek we left this morning "Burke's Creek."

26th. The weather cloudy, and threatening for rain. Maitland arrived this morning with the intelligence that the bullock that was ill before had dropped down, and would go no further; so they killed him, in order that the flesh might be made use of. He was too fat to travel. Another hurt itself to-day; although generally one of the quietest, it took to bucking, endeavouring to get rid of its saddle, when it fell, and must have hurt itself severely, for there it remains where it fell; the rest are all right, and off to feed. I expect we shall kill it also, but we must have more sun if we are to jerk them. Mr. McKinlay has gone up to the creek, and Maitland has written instructions for three men to bring on the meat and hide of the dead bullock. Wylde, Hodgkinson, and Poole went with three pack-horses to bring in the meat; the remainder of the bullocks arrived at 3·30. They brought in the meat shortly afterwards, but it was so awfully tough that we could hardly get our teeth into it.

Camels not found to-night; it came on so dark, I could not see their tracks; it would be a devil of a go if they were lost. I hope to find them in the morning, as they camp at night, and are, I dare say, now chewing the cud comfortably. The night is as black as Erebus, and if we don't get some rain it is a caution. It is spitting now, and if this continues we shall not be able to jerk the other bullock, so he will have to take his chance in the desert. There is plenty of grass and water here to last him for months; there was splendid green feed on the slopes of the stony hills and water-courses. There is an island in this creek formed by an arm of it; I should say it is 800 or 900 yards wide. Rained very heavily the whole night, and as black as pitch; those who have the middle watch will have a nice time of it to keep the sheep together, for there is no yard for them, for if they do get scared, it would be perfect madness to follow them; thank goodness it is my morning watch, when it will be light.

27*th*. Rained the whole of the night. Sheep bolted; it was no use trying to see them, much less to look after them; they were recovered in the morning, with the exception of fourteen, which were not to be seen anywhere. I started early in the morning after the camels; it was no use trying to find their tracks, as they had long since been obliterated, so I went on my travels, and came on the lost sheep, and brought them nearly into camp, when I met Ned in search of them, and made them over to him. I start again after the camels, up to my knees in water, but cannot see anything of them, and got a blowing-up from the governor for my pains; then I brought in a horse, and Middleton started after them, for I was awfully tired, having been walking in water up to my knees for the last two or three hours.

The creek that was almost dry yesterday is running a strong stream this morning, and rising rapidly. All the horses were brought to our side of the creek, and taken to the stone hill, where there was fine feed, as the rain still continued to pour down with a will. If the rain still continues in this style, we shall soon have to take to the sand hills for safety, for all this flat and where we are camped will be under water very shortly—a nice state of things. As it is, the camp is a perfect muck-yard, up to our ankles, and it sticks so to the boots that our progress is slow and tiresome. We are all as wet as drowned rats, and shall continue so, I suppose, till it holds up, for there is no use in changing, as we should be wet again directly. I talk of changing our clothes, we have only another suit to our back, and we all think it better to keep that dry till it holds up. Some of us I suspect will be having a touch of rheumatism—wet clothes all day, ditto blankets all night. We try and make ourselves as jolly as we can, and even Mark Tapley would allow that some credit is due to him who can make himself so here. The ground in the tent even is so soft that if we sit down we leave an impression. The flat is becoming quite a lake, and you can almost see the water rise, it flows over the ground so fast, and the trees are becoming shorter and shorter—of some only the tops are visible; the creek is now quite swimable, and running like a sluice. The camels arrived safe this afternoon, after a good hunt for them.

28*th*. It has been raining the whole night as hard as it could pour down. The water last night rose nearly three feet, and is rising fast now. We are making preparations to clear out of this, and high time too, or we shall have to swim for it. Our camp itself will shortly be under water; as it is the water is all round us, our camp being the only piece of high ground about. The rain held up about 12 o'clock, thank goodness, though everything is damp or wet. We shall get out of this in the morning, *i. e.*, if we don't have to flit before. We are all most miserable. Camels can't wander, that's a blessing, for the water won't allow them. It is as well we left the cart where we did, we could not have taken it further, and in all probability it would have been swept away by this flood now rapidly coming on. McKinlay says we are now in that position, and not far from the place where Captain Sturt dreaded being overtaken by rain. It will be awful work travelling through this sea, but we must make the best of a bad bargain and face the difficulty. There is one thing, the quantity of water will enable the governor to go where he pleases, as there will be abundance for months to come. He says, "I wish I had a couple of months' rations of flour, tea, and sugar, as then I could thoroughly examine the country in this quarter." It is very stormy, the creek is rising very fast still, and here we are quite isolated on about a quarter of an acre. Pleasant, isn't it? We shall have a swim for it to-morrow, and no mistake. Poor little sheep, it will be hard work for them. The weather looks very angry, and more rain coming.

Mr. McKinlay remarks in his journal of this date:—

"If this creek carries me much more to the north, instead of going to the east as it now does, I think it will take a run through to the Albert River; and if the steam sloop "Victoria," Captain Norman, has not sailed from there, I think I will be able to get flour or biscuits in sufficient quantity to carry me back, and enable me to do all, or nearly so, that was required of me by the South Australian Government; if not at the Albert, I will only be obliged to live the principal part of the return journey on animal food, and what vegetables we may find from time to time. It won't be a very hard case, but much more pleasant and agreeable if it can be obtained."

March 1*st*. And a very pretty first of March it was. Up early and had breakfast, so that we may be off about the animals. First of all the sheep are to be taken to some dry ground, half a mile off. They will have to swim, and there is a strong current too. Kirby and the horsemen go with them. They manage, with care and patience, to get them over in safety after a difficult job, they then go after the other horses some miles away on the hills. Sometimes I can see them swimming, and then a head suddenly disappears altogether, its proprietor having gone down a hole; they were never less than up to their waists. Middleton and self go after camels in the same sort of way, sometimes swimming, and sometimes just touching the ground with our toes. Thank goodness, they were all close by, two and two, on little bits of ground, just big enough for them to stand on. They came with us through the water quite quietly, and I fancy they must have felt some fear of danger, for the female camel in particular has generally a great antipathy to water. She followed me like a dog. We soon got to camp, down tents, load up, etc. Soon accomplished it, but it was frightful work, all our clothes dripping, for we did not take them off when we started, as they were wet already. To mend the matter the wind got up, and it went through us like a knife. We never felt it so cold as during this part of the performance. All ready to start, and off we go. We have to lead the camels to where the sheep are camped. We get on all right. The water sometimes up to our necks, and sometimes we have to swim a little way. Camels may well be called "the ships of the desert." They answered the purpose of boats to-day, at any rate, for us. The most of the provisions would have got soaked if the horses had carried them.

On our arrival on the spit of sand where the sheep were, Mr. McKinlay ordered two of the camels to be unloaded and to return for the ammunition, flour, tea, sugar, etc., which had hitherto been carried by the horses. So we had to take this most delightful journey again for the aforesaid traps, and very fortunate indeed it was that we had the camels, as otherwise all the flour, etc., would have been spoilt, as the water was over the horses' backs in many places, and their packs consequently more or less soaked. The creek this morning was rising some six inches, yesterday it was only three to four inches. It is none too soon for us to be on the move, I'm thinking. We are now in the midst of a vast sea, the shallowest part of which I should say could not be less than five feet. After getting all things to dry land we reloaded the camels with their proper burdens, giving the horses what belonged to them, and what we brought up on the second trip, and started for camp (we are all shivering and shaking, and teeth fairly chattering with the intense cold) on a sand-hill, where there is plenty of water and fine feed for the animals; but the road to it is our difficulty, the beasts all slipping and sliding about, and we expecting some of them to be down every minute. The poor little sheep were sometimes up to their bellies in mud, and had to be lifted out. It was horrid work for them. It still looks rainy. I suppose we shall remain here for some time, for I don't see how we are to get out of it. For the present we are in our new position, above all inundation, and in perfect safety for some time. From this camp the whole country is one immense sea as far as the eye can reach, nothing else visible but the large trees marking the courses of the different creeks and stone-hills in the distance.

Mr. McKinlay remarks again in his journal regarding this flood:—

"We were very fortunate to be caught in it where we were; had we been caught thus in making this creek, or a day's stage up it, to a certainty we should all have been washed away, or, what would have been just as bad, be perched on a small island of sand with all the animals round us, and nothing but starvation staring us in the face—as on most of the sand-rises down near the creek there was no vegetation of any consequence upon them."

We had a narrow escape from following in the footsteps of poor Leichhardt and party, who have never been heard of to this day, and it is now some sixteen years since they started. I should not be the least surprised if he and party were carried away in one of these floods, as not the slightest trace of him has ever been seen. This is mere supposition on my part, but I believe Mr. McKinlay agrees with me. After arriving and turning out the animals we got into some dry clothes, and not before they were wanted. Then we had some *hot* tea, and began to feel comfortable once more. Pitched tents, and we all looked more happy than we have done for some days. The sand here is awful, blowing into our eyes, etc., and everything we get to eat is covered with it.

Sunday, 2nd. It rained steadily for some time last night, and is showery to-day. The flats are considerably more covered this morning. Thunder and lightning from north-east. Some of us began to talk of our possible fate, others raking up stories of accidents that had befallen other explorers, and some painted the picture rather dismally; but it is of no use putting a sad face on, it will be time enough when the accidents do come. Threatening for a storm, but it went off in the evening and the stars shone brightly. No yard for the sheep, and we have to keep a special sharp look out for the wild dogs that are up here in numbers, out of the way of the flood. Mosquitoes very bad, no sleep hardly.

3rd. I hope, as the day promises, it may be fine and dry, that we may get our things out to air, they being all more or less damp.

There was a horrid row about 2 A.M. Mr. McKinlay caught the man *who should have been on watch*, not only asleep but absolutely coiled up in his blanket most comfortably. My stars! he caught it, and no mistake. I mention no names, but if he ever sees this he will remember the circumstance. After breakfast Mr. McKinlay called us all round him, and standing on a small eminence addressed us to the effect that if ever he found any one asleep on his watch, or even sitting down, which was as bad, he should erase that man's name from the list of those receiving pay; and that for the future he would have to work for nothing. It is very hard to keep on your feet two or three hours without resting, after a long march; however, the edict has gone forth, and becomes a law.

Began shoeing horses to-day, as their feet are rather soft, and we shall have to tackle plenty of stony ground on our course. Mr. McKinlay and Ned went out on horseback to look after the lost bullock which had been left behind on coming to last camp. They found him with the stifle joint broken, so that we shall jerk him as soon as the sun comes out hotter. Made a stunning currie to-day for all hands, which was duly appreciated, but the want of salt was a great drawback to arriving at perfection. Middleton unwell again.

4th. This morning four men started with as many horses to kill and bring in the lame bullock. The country is very boggy and travelling heavy. Mr. McKinlay went out yesterday, after he returned from finding the bullock, to see the state of the flood. He had to swim his horse some distance, the water was still so high, but he found that the creek had gone down nine inches. The last flood (whenever that was) was some seven feet higher than the present one, from the marks left on the stone hills and trees.

The high land up here is perfectly infested with wild dogs, but we have plenty of strychnine, and that soon settles them. They are so hungry, or voracious perhaps is the word, that when one of their gang gets poisoned he is quickly torn in pieces by his fellows, and some of them pay the penalty of their repast, and are in turn devoured themselves.

Mr. McKinlay and Poole rode out to some high

stone hills to the east to see from what quarter the creek flowed, but the haze was so great that the journey was of little use. From the stony hills to the west of north there was a perfect sea, nothing but the tops of trees to be seen here and there above the water. The ground was all but impassable in some places. Some days ago there was not a bird to be seen, but now thousands of cranes, gulls, ducks, etc., are here, and also a few black swans passed over our camp. We have seen very few of these birds up to the present time. The dews at night are very heavy, and you get quite damp on the watch, and those who sleep out in the open air have a wet blanket in the morning. Mosquitoes and sand still very troublesome, the latter blowing into the bread while it is being made, so you grind it up all the time you are eating, which is agreeable in the extreme.

5th. Every appearance of a magnificent day, the country beginning to look green, and pretty lilies in profusion in blossom for hundreds of yards. It is splendid, and the little birds chirping round and about give it quite the appearance of spring.

About dinner time the party returned with the bullock, in the shape of beef, in packages, and after dinner we all commenced the work of cutting up and jerking; while doing this an accident happened to Maitland, which might have been worse. One of the men while splitting down the head with an axe and cutting it up for soup, the head of the axe flew off and buried itself in his (Maitland's) knee. He is laid up for a time, so we shall have to cook by turns, he being our *chef de cuisine*. We got all the meat jerked to-night, and if the weather continues as it is it will be "first chop."

It is very hot indeed to-day, and I am cook; the sun blisters my back and the fire my belly, and I thought I should have been done before the soup. I must tell you there was no shelter from the sun at the cooking place, it was just on the open sand. There was not a tree on the sand hill that could be called a shade. Jolly, my cooking day is over! This evening we draw lots for to-morrow and consecutive days. Mr. McKinlay rather unwell to-day, and kept his tent.

6th. Every appearance of a fine day, and the weather appears to have broken. No signs of more rain. Still busy shoeing horses. A very painful touch of rheumatism in my ancle. Wylde takes charge of the pots and kettles and relieves me. (N.B. It is a relief.) We are looking forward to some roast beef to-day, which will be a treat after the jerked mutton.

7th. Wind very changeable, veering all round the compass. All the beef cooked yesterday gone bad, I regret to say, so that we must put up with the soup made of the bones, etc. What brutes those camels are for wandering; here they have left good food and are off over stone hills, where there is not a blade of green to be seen, so I had a nice walk after them, and found them going straight a-head, one after the other, and returned to a sorry supper of mildewed mutton and damper.

8th. (Camp vii.) In camp still. Mr. McKinlay calls this "Escape Camp." Finishing shoeing horses, and we shall make a start, if all be well, the day after to-morrow.

Extraordinary vegetation going on, grass springing up everywhere, in fact in places where you would think grass could not grow. This country will be beautiful in a short time, with flowers of all descriptions, and creepers, principally of the convolvulus family, are beginning to creep up all the trees along the creek. Innumerable black macaws flying about and discoursing anything but sweet music. Mr. McKinlay says, "in two or three months time from this date one could, with little difficulty (I am almost certain), start with any description of stock from the northern settled parts of South Australia, and go right across the continent to whatever point he might think fit."

The bullock has given us 116 lb. of dried meat besides what we have been using. 1 lb. of sugar to be served out to-day to each man, as this is the last, except a few pounds which will be preserved in case of sickness; so here goes the first of the stores; after all, what is it, we shall soon drink our tea (as long as that lasts,) without it, and think nothing about it! One of the fellows made all his into toffee, so that was soon done. Offers were made at 5*s*. per pound for sugar, and no sellers.

Had a nice job to-day to melt up all the extra fat to grease Mr. McKinlay's tent, but the sand was flying about so I was obliged to stop; it will make an additional weight of 50 lb. for the camels. There was a great game going on in the flat this afternoon, one of the nags could not be caught for two hours; having been without hobbles for some days she had got rather fresh, and at last we lassoed her.

Sunday, 9th. We are getting all ready for a start to-morrow; it will be a relief to get out of this disagreeable sandy camp. Middleton still unwell, he has not quite got over the shaking he had at No. v. camp.

10th. We start this morning, all being ready for it. The bullocks very refractory at being packed; they don't seem to like it at all. We did not get away till mid-day in consequence. Our journey was over stony hills and flats, crossing several small creeks; on the way we crossed the outskirts of a flat, about sixteen miles from Escape Camp, with plenty of water and fine feed. Mr. McKinlay arrived at camp some time before we did; he thought shortly after that the water was gaining on us, or rather that the wind being high it was driving it up the flat; but no such thing, we were again to be flooded out and had to move the horse-gear from where it was and bring it up to the most elevated spot, where all the other things were. The bullocks did not get in till after sunset, and one of them gave an infinity of trouble. Mr. McKinlay thinks of leaving him behind rather than be bothered with him. The camels came over the rough stones admirably. Mr. McKinlay remarks that they are "certainly the best animals for this kind of work. They will eat anything, from a gum tree to the smallest shrub, and then come and lie down by you;" whereas horses and bullocks, if a chance offers, will ramble all over the country: with sheep and camels, one could travel over any practicable part of the continent, and keep them in good condition.

I am suffering from rheumatism fearfully in one of my legs, from being so long in water and wet clothes.

11*th*. Where we removed the horse-packs from last night is now a perfect sea, and even up to the foot of some of our blankets; one of the men had to shift his quarters during the night, as he found himself getting very cold and wet. We start after breakfast for a gap in the hills, and have to wade through the water for a mile or more before we get to the foot of the sand hills. There are rather high table-topped ranges in the distance to the north and south of our course; then to the top of a high red sand hill and across a stony plain, with plenty of feed, thence to another sand hill, from whence there is a perfect sheet of water as far as you could see. Camped on a myall creek, after passing table-topped hills right and left; passed a native camp, with the fire still burning, and the tracks quite fresh, but we saw no human being. One of the bullocks did not come into camp to-night; knocked up, and charged the men who were with him, so they left him to his fate; he won't hurt, for there is plenty of good feed and water where he is. It is a great pity he should be left, for we want him for food. The cook not recovered yet, so we still do a little in the culinary line by turns. The men with the rest of the bullocks not in till late.

12*th*. Off early this morning; the bullock that was left never came into camp. We crossed several myall creeks on our course, over stony ground, the flood obliging us to diverge continually, over broken and stony hills and several creeks, to camp on a small creek with a frizzly barked tree growing about it, quite new, no one of us knowing the name; it is a beautiful, finely-grained wood, very heavy, and something like rosewood; would make very nice furniture. One of the bullocks dropped down within two hundred yards of the camp, apparently struck by the sun, though it was not very hot to-day. It looks for rain this afternoon; I hope we shall not get any, for we have had enough, at least for the present. Native smoke seen about five miles to west of north of the opening in the hills. Blew fresh to-night, and sent all the rain away. This bullock must be left also, as he cannot get up.

13*th.* (Camp x.) We start up the range about four miles, over some very stony country. The main range of hills Mr. McKinlay has named "Wills' Range," after the unfortunate gentleman who lost his life with Burke.

After passing this range we went over sand hills and rich pasture, with swamps full of water to east end of sand hills. Thousands of pigeons, ducks, and teal. They have commenced laying, and we found several pigeons' nests with eggs in, and also some ducks' nests; the latter had as many as eight or ten eggs each. Of course we gather up all the contents of the several nidifications for a glorious "*feed*" this evening. There are also quail, and numerous other smaller birds.

To the north-east of the camp is a very peculiar hill, with an immense stone on the top, which has been called by the leader "Elliott's Knob."* The country was very pretty to-day, the ground covered

* "A very strange round stone hill, capped with larger stone."—*McKinlay's Journal.*

with flowers of all colours and tints. One native was seen to-day on the top of one of the hills, but we could not get within speaking distance. We found to-day a quantity of the vegetable before alluded to: the native name is "adley."

Several ducks' and pigeons' eggs found to-day. Bell and Hodgkinson left camp directly after they came in for the purpose of shooting, and they brought home some ducks and pigeons. One or two new birds were seen to-day; flies very bad.

14th. Started early this morning on eastern course, to avoid the flood, and went some miles along stony ridges, then through swamp and water. On our left a small but pretty lake, and a long sandy range on our right; in the distance there is a well-watered creek, which seems to supply this small lake. We came to camp on a sand hill close to a claypan, with shallow water. The flood is seen some four miles off to the west of north. There seem to be interminable sand hills ahead. Country to-day was pretty, with much fine feed for the animals, and the "adley" in abundance, with its elegant little yellow blossom. The sand hills were covered with various flowers of all colours. The smell of the flowers is delicious, so no one must tell me any more that the flowers of this country have no smell.

15th. (Camp xii.) Off again, but detained a little, as one of the camels' saddles was wrong; it had become broken, and was galling the poor beast; it was soon righted, and we started afresh; passed through some fine country, also some stony and sandy rises, and came to camp in good time, on a fine creek, running nearly north and south. We shall again enjoy the luxury of a bathe here, as we shall stop some days, as we are going to kill a bullock, which will delay us. A splendid range of hills in the distance, east and north. This is a very pretty camp, but the mosquitoes are beginning to sing already. Lots of ducks killed to-day, and some eggs found. Old "Ranger" killed this evening, and will be cut up and jerked to-morrow, and some trouble they had with the old brute; he would not stand to be shot, but took to the water, and had a swim for it, but we got him at last.

16*th*. Oh, goodness! talk of mosquitoes, they were in swarms—if I may use the expression, in herds on this creek; every man of us was obliged to have his own fire to keep them away, but it was all of no use, they cared for nothing; they bit you through blankets, sheets, trousers, in fact, anything you had on; they could not have had such a chance before, I should think, and they made the most of it; very little sleep we got. I never saw them so bad except at a place called Maturne, up the Orinoco river, where we had gone to procure bullocks for the Government contractor for beef, and there we had to get into our mosquito-nets at 4 P.M., or we should have been eaten alive; here we had no such luxuries; what little we had was just enough to cover the face, and no more. No end of ducks' eggs found about the creek and swamps around. All hands jerking old "Ranger," except Poole, who is out with McKinlay on a scout to see the country towards the ranges to the east, some twenty miles from here.

Leaving Mr. Davis for a moment, we refer to Mr. McKinlay's journal, where he reports upon this excursion in a way rather perplexing, if we are to understand he is passing through the famous "Stony Desert." And yet the characteristic features of the desert ever recur in stone and sand, cropping out amidst all the verdure called up as by enchantment after the late rains. He says:—

"*Sunday, March 16th.* Went to have a view from the principal range eastward, the first and greater part of the road over magnificent pasture, nearer the hills very stony; found the hills distant twenty-one miles; from top of a large table-topped one I had a splendid view; the tier of ranges I am now on bear to east of north and west of south, but are very irregular, many spurs running off from main range, and forming a vast number of crown-shaped tops and peaked hills with innumerable creeks draining the country from east and south to west and north, and joining the main creek. Twenty-one miles travelled to-day, bearing 62¼°; from this hill another tier of similar hills is seen in the distance with a very large creek, draining the country between this and that, flowing northward, and then west round the north end of the tier I am now upon. The south-west end of distant range bears 125°, about twenty-five to thirty miles off, and the north-east end, dimly seen in the distance, bears 65°, which tier of ranges and creek I have called Browne Creek, after J. H. Browne, Esq., of Booboorowie, South Australia. The range I am on, and the tier northwards to where the Creek (Browne's) passes round the end of them, I have called Ellar's tier of Tabletops; the tier south of where I now am I have called Warren's tier of Tabletops, after my respected friend, Geo. Warren, Esq., of Gawler, for whose kindness I am much indebted; the plain or downs east and north of those ranges, I have called 'The Downs of Plenty,' as here there is everything one could wish in travelling over a new country. I would have gone over to the distant ranges, but unfortunately, my horse threw one of her shoes, and I was obliged to camp at a creek under the hills for the night. The creek I have now camped on I have named Ranger's Creek, after our bullock killed here."

We all took it out pretty well this morning, having had so little sleep last night, and the governor did not return last night, so "when the cat is away the mice always will play." All hands still at the beef; we have a fine sun, and it will be well jerked. Mr. McKinlay and Poole returned this afternoon, tired and hungry, having had very little to eat, and having travelled sixty miles. They brought some curiosities, found in a native whirlie, and saw plenty of emus; they saw also part of a European greatcoat, lined with red flannel, in the whirlie. To whom could that coat have once belonged? They also saw a head ornament, made of goats' hair, which must surely have been taken from one of the goats that Leichhardt had with him on his last trip; mosquitoes still very bad, and the sooner we are out of this the better. Mr. McKinlay has called this creek after the old bullock "Ranger," killed here. Mr. McKinlay saw three natives yesterday, but could not get near to them; they were busy gathering various seeds.

18*th*. Still at "Ranger" Creek; two of our fellows went out after eggs, and brought in seventy-six ducks', not a bad find; I should have gone, but I had something else to do; they were made into custards, without milk, boiled, roasted, just as it suited the fancy of the consumer—not that it much signified, as we *could eat in those days*. We were not in bed quite so late this morning, but were roused by Mr. McKinlay just before daylight, and we pack everything for an early start to-morrow. The beast gave us 162 lb. dried meat, and well jerked it is too, and glad I am that we are off first thing.

19*th*. Up early as usual, just before daylight, and breakfast by the first dawn, and off after the animals saddled up, after about two hours' detention, and started on north of east course, about 14 miles through a magnificent country, the plain alone extending for miles and miles, level as a billiard table, and beautifully grassed. High ranges in the distance, the scent of the flowers as we passed over them was delightful. Sure it is that

> "Many a flower is born to blush unseen,
> And waste its sweetness on the *desert* air."

20th. Started this morning at 10 A.M., our course a little north of east, and travelled till we struck a large creek, and then over sand hills and flats, covered with magnificent grasses of every description, many creepers, and the blue convolvulus, also another beautiful small blue flower, with a dark purple eye. It seems quite tropical, and everything has changed these last few days, flowers, shrubs, and weather too. Only about six pods of the blue flowers could be obtained. Plenty of pigeons to-day, and a few nests were found also with eggs in. A native brought into camp, and decorated with necklaces; he also got a good feed to console him. Mosquitoes worse than at "Ranger" Creek I really believe.

21st. Our journey to-day was over red sand hills nearly all the way, our course north-north-east. We had to cross an immense sheet of water. We found eighty ducks' eggs. The grass nearly up to the horses' knees. Bullocks and sheep not in to-night. Not one of us could sleep to-night; the air was perfectly alive with mosquitoes. Every day we meet with fresh flowers. Distance to-day sixteen miles, and camped on a plain by the side of a claypan with a little water, and not very good.

22nd. Bullocks not up, so had to spell here, and a fine place too certainly. Two or three of us went out to look after them. The sheep arrived about 8 A.M. Thunder, with a little rain; then the bullocks came up; they had strayed a long way from where they camped the night before; the men were hungry, as they had nothing to eat since yesterday morning. Mr. McKinlay took a ride to-day, to see what sort of country was ahead of us, leaving orders that if the bullocks came in before 12 o'clock, we were to follow his tracks, but as they did not arrive in time, we shall have to stay here another night. Kirby was much knocked up on his arrival; he had been up all night with the sheep, so I relieved him, and he took his sleep out. Looking much for rain, so preparing for it; covering things up with tarpaulin. Mr. McKinlay returned in the afternoon. Ned, the bullock-driver, reports that when he was after the bullocks this morning, he was stuck up by a lot of niggers; he fired over their heads, and they soon scampered off, leaving him to go his way in peace. Perhaps they thought to have a good breakfast of him, but they were scared by the fire-arms.

23*rd*. (Claypan Camp.) No tree marked here, as there was not one large enough. We travelled seventeen miles to-day, the first part over sand hills and flooded stony and sandy flats, then crossed a myall creek, afterwards a box and myall one, some ten miles from our starting place, with plenty of water on both sides of the creek; stony flats and undulating ground, well grassed. We camped on a myall creek, after following it down for two miles to where there was plenty of water and good feed; the flood was close on our left for some time after starting. Mr. McKinlay callèd me into his tent at 3 A.M.; he could not sleep, and was very anxious to be on the move.

After a sorry breakfast of jerked beef soup we started, and glad enough to get out of this. We are allowed only 12 lb. of this meat per diem for the party of ten, with 4½ lb. flour per week. What shall we do when the flour is all gone, and nothing but this jerked stuff? it is very like thick mahogany shavings. We feel almost as hungry after having had our allowances as before, and it is no use "asking for more;" for, like Oliver Twist, we should not get it. The feed all along our route to-day was magnificent. We found a wild cucumber, but it was so bitter that it could not be eaten.

CHAPTER VIII.

CENTRAL DISTRICT.

Editor's remarks on the Central District—March 24th, Scott's Ranges; Emu Plains—26th, Petrified Wood—29th, Brown's Creek—30th, Hamilton Range—31st, Hunter Gorge—April 2nd, Prospects as to Food; flour finished—4th, Daly River—6th, The Euro, a small Kangaroo—8th, Mueller Creek—9th, Manserg Creek—10th, Cadell Creek—20th, Blackeye Creek—21st, Hamilton and Kirby Ranges; Warburton Creek.

THIS chapter comprises the journey and its incidents between the dates of 24th March and 21st April. The part traversed we have named the Central District, and we have marked out the somewhat distinctive features of its southern limits where it meets the region of desert. There is more difficulty in finding any distinctive boundary to the north—any features separating the central from the tropical region. In this paucity of such signs we are glad to seize upon Mr. Davis's account of large trees of a new description growing on the banks of a fine creek; and, as the party came upon this scene on the 22nd April, so we close the central region on the 21st, and open the tropical in the succeeding chapter on the 22nd April. The position is in south latitude about 21° 45′, and it is where the party have just crossed the dividing range and are descending its northern slopes to find the waters henceforward taking a northerly course like their own.

We are now in the autumn of the antipodes and in latitudes bordering on either side of the tropical line, so that, but for the moisture with which the late rains have covered the country all around them, the travellers would have found the weather much hotter and less comfortable than it actually was. The cold at night was sometimes intense, although the days were hot under a bright sun. For example, McKinlay says, on 6th April, "Beautiful cold morning," and on 7th, "Exceedingly cold during the night," and again on the 13th, "Evenings, nights, and mornings beautifully cool; the days hot enough."

The country was often exceedingly beautiful in its luxuriance of vegetation; for instance, on 3rd April we find the party "camped on a magnificent lagoon, about one mile long and about two hundred yards wide—a perfect flower-garden." But the cause of all these beauties—the late abundant rains, had brought also its disagreeables to the travellers in the generally wet and boggy state of the country; there were many running creeks—a rare and pleasant spectacle of Australian scenery. The country passed through may be described as consisting of valleys and great plains bounded by hill ranges. "On some of these vast plains," remarks McKinlay, "the traveller, if overtaken by such heavy rains as his party experienced, would be certainly washed helplessly away, for there is not a knoll six feet in height within range of the eye." Notwithstanding this luxuriance of the hour throughout this country caused by the fitful rains, the prevailing spinifex grass guides us to the poverty generally of the country. It is a country similar to that described in much less glowing language by Waterhouse while passing in the same latitudes at some distance further to the westward. The spinifex is the only permanent vegetation of the smaller kind that can face the sun and climate upon the open country; a month or two of the winds and droughts of summer and autumn sweep off everything else, and the country returns to its customary bareness and aridity, as if awaking from a casual dream.

Bright and pleasant, however, are these its dreaming intervals; as the party traverse the grass and inhale the fresh perfume of the flowers, the whole scene teems with life, animal as well as vegetable. The Emu Plains are so named from a troop of these remarkable wingless birds, the ostriches of Australia, having been seen there, and many more were afterwards visible over the other plains. The "native turkey," a kind of bustard, is also plentiful. Fish, too, are abundant in the creeks and water-holes, and were seen jumping and snapping at the flies. We commonly think that all such pleasant scenes were made for man, but man hardly ever appears in all this magnificence and busy life; there were only signs of his existence in the smoke occasionally rising from the distant ranges. Let us return to our journal.

March 24th. We travelled to-day some eighteen miles on a course a little west of north, over nothing but one grand plain with plenty of small creeks crossing our line of march, with a high range of hills running to north-west and south-east, the tops of which are well-wooded. These Mr. McKinlay has called "Scott's Ranges," after John Scott, Esq., of Adelaide, who kindly lent Mr. McKinlay two horses from his run, and also gave him leave to take anything from his station that he thought might be of use to him. This plain is undulating in some parts. Here we saw some fifteen emus, and have called it Emu Plains. Camped on a small box creek with plenty of water; there was no timber anywhere except on the banks of the creeks and the tops of the ranges.

We are getting on well now, and hope to continue making good days' work, every one being in excellent health. A sheep to be killed to-day to keep us up a bit, as the jerked meat does not satisfy us. We shall have to eat horses yet, I expect, and then—but don't let me think of it at present, quite time enough when the sheep and bullocks are all eaten. We had a jolly supper to-night—curry and mulligatawny soup. Beautiful weather now, and we all enjoy it much; we only want a little more to eat.

25*th*. A long walk after the camels this morning; they had gone beyond the horses; country same kind as yesterday, beautifully grassed all the way, but a little more undulating. Crossed a box creek with plenty of water, at about fourteen miles, to another box creek that was dry. Two miles further a creek with plenty of water, where we camped. Some rising ground in the distance to the west.

26*th*. (Camp xx.) The climate up here must be very healthy; the air is quite invigorating, and different to what we have had heretofore. Same kind of country as the last two, and finer could not be found for pastoral purposes. Weather beautiful; dews very heavy at night. We struck and crossed a box creek, where it loses itself in a flat. The latter part of the journey was through a large boggy swamp full of water, then over a fine plain for two or three miles, magnificent, to a large swamp running a long way to the east; so we made a long *detour* in that direction, and round it. Country here very flat, not a rise within sight, a nice place to be caught in a similar flood to the one we had to clear out from the 1st of the month. I don't suppose we could by any chance save ourselves, much less the animals and stores.

The plains we have been travelling over the last few days are covered with pieces of petrifaction. We saw one or two large logs quite petrified, and we got some specimens, which if we can get them to Adelaide will be considered curiosities. Camp xx., or Carbine Creek Camp—having left a carbine here that had lost its hammer and was unfit for service.

27th. Still journeying over an immense plain, and the low part of it awfully boggy, with hills on the right of the way. Crossed a creek with water, plenty of seed, and new flowers; one a kind of hollyhock, another on a large stem so like wax that we named it the wax plant; it was nearly white, with a very pretty puce eye.

Very hungry when we got to camp; found a sheep had been killed, and to which we paid great attention as soon as the supper was ready. I got some seed of the blue flower on the small creek near our camp, not quite ripe, but I shall take care of it in case I see no more. Mr. McKinlay also got bogged to-day, and got out with some difficulty; found that it was impracticable to go that way, so changed his course, found the ground for some distance better for travelling, and camped. He climbed a tree, and could distinguish hills in the distance to the north and south of east, and some high ground near. We are a long way from the main creek; the ground is sadly boggy.

28*th*. (Camp xxi.) Morning splendid, and most of us hearty and in good spirits; kept changing our course to avoid water until we camped on a small stony rise, beyond this there is a net-work of creeks a mile in width; we crossed a great many to-day. These creeks must drain an immense area of country. Northward also appears to be a regular nest of creeks. This is a first-rate pastoral country.

29*th*. A new fruit to-day; the ripe ones have rather a nice taste, the seeds of it are quite hot and fiery. The fruit is about 1½ in. long, and ¾ in. in diameter, and ribbed quite sharply outside. We found here also the "bean tree," and the fruit tree of Cooper's Creek. Distance done to-day about seventeen miles. Camped on a small creek. The day was very fine; the first part of our journey was over rather swampy ground, but good travelling on the whole. For the last two miles the ground has been more swampy and full of watercourses, with plenty of water in them, caused by a large creek from the east emptying itself out in this direction. This creek Mr. KcKinlay has called

"Brown's Creek," after a gentleman, a friend of his in Melbourne.

30*th*. (Camp xxiii.) Our road to-day was rather level, till we came to a sand hill about eight and a half miles from last camp; the country well-grazed, passing on the left two more sand hills also well-grassed, but higher. From the top of one of these there was an extensive view of the surrounding country. To the west of creek a high range running all along it; hills in all directions, some of them well-wooded; these Mr. McKinlay has called the "Hamilton Range." In the distance apparently a mass of heavy ranges running north, or perhaps a little west of north. This country has been terribly torn and cut up in all directions by recent floods, regularly *furrowed*, you may say, in many places, but quite firm and good travelling; not so much feed quite the latter part of to-day's journey, the ground being so torn up.

We camped on one of the main channels of the creek, with plenty of feed and water. Each man received to-day three-quarters of a pound of sugar from the fourteen pounds kept for the sick; so that he can eat it with his "adley" as we have come upon lots of it, and it will do us (as it did before) a vast deal of good, and I don't see why we should get sick with a fine climate, plenty of exercise, early to bed and early to rise, and no spirits, so that you cannot undermine your constition with the "ardent" if you wished. Plain food, God knows it is plain, no "provocatives," nothing to hurt us, so how are we likely to get ill? We killed a sheep to-day, and we are to have two a week to vary the food. Verily, in this instance variety is charming, when you can get it.

31*st*. Came over some nasty swampy ground to-day for eight miles, when we rounded a large table-topped hill, crossed a flat-topped one, and descended again into the swampy country; the main creek passes through a gorge in the hills, and then branches off into innumerable smaller ones. I wish we were out of this low swampy country—looks like fever and ague—a pleasant thing to have clinging to you on the march. The floods must be severe here, I should think, judging from the drift-wood and scrub left in the trunks of the trees, some twelve to twenty feet from the ground. The hills Mr. McKinlay has called "Hamilton," after G. Hamilton, Esq., inspector of police in Adelaide, and the gorge through which the river passes, "Hunter."

We are to-day some 360 to 370 miles from Peak Downs, due east of us, and about the same distance from the head of the Gulf of Carpentaria. We were all wishing we could make off for the "Downs" to get some flour and tea, and especially tobacco, as we have none, and we all feel the want thereof.

April 1st. All fool's day, and 200 and odd days out. Started early to-day, and our journey was entirely through swamps and water holes, with mud up to your neck—a frightful country. The day was fine, however, and we went to all points of the compass—Mr. McKinlay calls it a "zigzag" course—till we camped on a large creek well timbered. The country round and about it is a perfect bog; a man can hardly get out of some places. We shall have a job to cross this creek. I expect Mr. McKinlay is going out to find a crossing place if he can, and there is not much doubt but he will. Our camp is in a "Dismal Swamp." We passed to the right of us some very peculiar hills on our way to-day, one was exactly like a tent. Mr. McKinlay has just now returned with the news that he has found a crossing place, and describes the country on the other side of the creek as being one network of creeks, with magnificently grassed flats, very different to this.

There is a native weir here, and the fish are very numerous, jumping up at flies and other insects on the water. Had we the proper tackle we could have good sport. The creeks to the east are drying fast.

2nd. We went only about one mile to-day. The crossing of the creek was a long and nasty job; it was as soft as mud could be. One of the camels got into it pretty deep, and it was the devil's own work to extricate him. We saw the same range of hills. They certainly are very curious, and appear as if they had been thrown up by some volcanic irruption. I regret I did not take a sketch of them, but I forgot it. We got to blind hookey, and that was the cause. Mr. McKinlay found us at cards, and we *caught it*. Why, I don't know, for he likes a game as well as most men I expect. We had to give in till he had *turned in*, and then we went at it again till 12 o'clock, playing by fire light.

To-day is a memorable day, the last we shall have any bread. The flour is all gone except two bags, which are to be kept for the sick, and to have a jolly big feed when we reach the salt water. It will seem odd to have *nothing* but meat and water to live on for the next three months perhaps. I suppose we shall get used to it, and not miss the staff of life in a few days. We are drawing so far to the east to avoid a creek that I should not be surprised if, after all, we went for stores before proceeding to the Gulf.

3rd. Started along the creek a mile and a half, then altered course, and passed many boggy creeks. The travelling infamous. The poor little sheep were in such a state of mud they could hardly walk. We had several times to halt while the governor went ahead to reconnoitre, and after several vain attempts to cross one of the boggy creeks, we had to "hark back." We lost a lot of time, but after going back a short distance on a different course we came on a fine lagoon, about one and a half miles long, and three hundred yards wide, with the camel food growing in profusion six feet above the water, and in full bloom it looked very pretty. Here was a native whirlie, and some utensils, stones for pounding the "adoo." From the appearance of the place it had not been visited for some time; very boggy round lagoon, and had to take off our boots to dip water for use. Fine bathing, about twelve feet deep in the centre. Plenty of mussels. Some liked them, I can't say I did, they were so muddy in flavour; and if you, gentle reader, have been "spilt" into a mudhole or dirty ditch out hunting as I have been, you will recollect the peculiar taste I mean.

Here I got a true piece of petrifaction from the bottom of the lake whilst diving for mussels, which with other curiosities I gave to Mr. Harris, the mayor of Port Adelaide, who was very kind to me on my first arriving in the colony, and who, in fact, first introduced me to our worthy leader.

No bread, and don't we growl, that's all. The meat alone is not enough for us, and we are all as hungry as hunters. Perhaps it will do us good to feel a little *hollow*, at all events it won't do for explorers to be particular in their habits.

4th. (Camp xxvii.) Camped in this beautiful flower-garden, for it is nothing else. The governor, Wylde, and Middleton are gone to the hills to the right, to look out for the course of the creek, and see if we could get round it, for we are going much to the east. I hope it will drive us into some place where we can get some grub, and I shall certainly call it "Salvation Creek," and a very fine one it is. Called the "Daly" after our present governor. It is a great pity the native names cannot be obtained.

5th. (Camp xxviii.) Started on a north-east course early, the weather looking rainy, with a strong wind blowing. The flies here lately very troublesome. We crossed a large swamp and to our right appeared another, or else a lagoon. Crossed between two sand hills, with a splendid feed all the way. Altered our course on account of some high sand hills ahead, saw two natives going over a swamp, they did not see us. There is a large creek on our left. We passed also on the same side some myall and sandy country but feed excellent, and the foliage on some of the trees grand. More sand hills and creeks on the left, and camped on a branch of the large creek very hungry, and only jerked meat and water for grub.

6th. (Camp xxix.) Very cold this morning and not a fly to be seen, which is a great relief. The chaps are growling about the jerked meat, which is magotty; it may be an addition, but certainly not an improvement. Had we any bread we should not feel it so much, but when I tell you that there was only twelve pounds of this horrid stuff served out daily to make SOUP, water bewitched, between ten hungry men, you will say that it was hardly sumptuous or plentiful fare. We used to find some "adley" and other greens occasionally. We came to camp after fifteen miles in some "mallee" scrub, with some fine water-holes. Our way to-day was through scrub and heavy timber. Sheep to be killed to-night thank goodness, for that soup with maggots floating on the top is horrible.

The governor has just returned from some high hills, where he went for a view. He brought a young euro. Pity we killed the sheep to-day. The country to-day was hill and dale; tiers of hills on the right, all along; from six to seven miles distant well-timbered detached pyramidical hills; one seen between us and the main range, Euro (called so because Mr. McKinlay shot the euro there), is about four miles off, composed of sandstone and quartz. Euro meat very good. Hope to see many more soon, to save our sheep for harder times; as it appears not improbable that we may have some such.

7th. The country to-day very much resembles what we passed through yesterday; the ground was covered with small bronzed stones. Distance travelled about seventeen miles, when we struck a very magnificent creek, 250 yards wide; in fact, it might be called a river—the water running about half a mile an hour; very steep sides, and the water so deep that none of us could get to the bottom. Feed and flowers in profusion; here magnificent gum, box, and bean trees lining the banks. Cockatoos in thousands, very wild ducks, cormorants, magpies, pigeons of various kinds, and various other kinds of birds very numerous. There is a small hill visible from our camp, with a large plain between us.

8th. (Camp xxxi.) Started at 8·30 A.M. Very fine; hardly any wind; dew heavy this morning. Crossed a small boggy tributary not far from the creek, then through stony rising ground well timbered, good feed, and plenty of it. Plenty of bronzed pigeons about. Passed through myall and stony country, showing unmistakable signs of having been flooded. To the right some fine plains, with low myall ridges behind them. Crossed a boggy creek, but the old female camel "Krishna" got fast. She was soon right again. The old beast hates water and boggy places. The others are not so bad. Then over ground covered with stones, limestone, and flint. I wish the large creek did not keep so much to the east, so that we could lay our course nearer for the gulf. Vile travelling, plenty of water in creek, and running fast. Our leader has called this after F. Mueller, Esq., of Melbourne.

We had travelled fifteen miles to camp. On our arrival, Mr. McKinlay took a fresh horse and went to the north-west. On his return he told us that he had seen a creek to the west that he thought would do to travel down. There is also, he says, a large creek from north and east going south, not flowing now, with broad stony bottom, with splendid reservoir of water. A long way to the east is a fine high range running north and south, named also after F. Mueller, Esq. It was rather amusing to hear some of our fellows wishing for something they should like to eat. One, a loaf and one pound of Cheshire cheese; another, loaf and some cheese; another did not care what it was, so long as there was enough of it. We certainly did have something, but it was the "*enough*" that was wanted.

9th. (Camp xxxii.) A very heavy dew this morning, everything quite wet, fine, though with no wind, and a few fleecy clouds floating about. Started rather early this morning after breakfast on a course 15° west of north. After crossing the creek mentioned yesterday, went over a splendid plain, and crossed another nice creek, which Mr. McKinlay has called the "Manserg." Some spinifex ranges on the right, with good open country and fine soil. A creek to the left about two miles. Went into a low range, with bronze stone to the left, but plenty of food growing between. Saw innumerable traces of kangaroo, but none of the animals. Plenty of emu in the plains, but so wild that one cannot get within 500 yards of them. We shall never cease crossing small creeks to-day. The country is pretty; at least it is diversified with plain, river, and wood, and now and then a nice view—pastoral, decidedly, as I should say. There is plenty of permanent water; pigeons by thousands. Hodgkinson went and shot *at* some, and that's all, they are so wild. This country differs in that respect from Alexander Selkirk's, for there their tameness "was quite shocking to him;" and here the reverse is the case in every respect, their wildness being excessively disgusting to us. One wild turkey also made his appearance, and he had a shot from a revolver, but also with no effect: he flew away quite coolly. Had we only bagged him, just imagine the breakfast!

We came to a halt while Mr. McKinlay went to the top of a high hill to see the country on the other side. We soon got the "coocy," and off we were again, and soon camped on the creek down which we went a quarter of a mile. The last two miles rather miserable country, spinifex and porcupine grass, with detached conical white clay-slaty hills, timbered however with small white gum.

Helped Mr. McKinlay to lay down his course and distance to-day, when we found we were somewhere about 21° 37′ south, 142° 17′ east.

10th. Started rather late this morning, as the animals had wandered some distance, so went only about twelve miles to-day for the above reason. We made a great deal of westing to-day, for we are nearly or quite 2° east of the Albert River, and the more we make the sooner we shall get to the Gulf. We had a horrid day's journey through a miserable country covered with rough stones, spinifex, myall scrub, and white gum. Obliged to change our course on account of the heavy creek to the left crossing our path, and went a little to the west. Innumerable creeks with plenty of water intersect the country. We camped. The hills run a good way back, and are not such rough ones to look on as yesterday. The large creek Mr. McKinlay has called Cadell Creek, after F. Cadell, Esq., the enterprising navigator of the Murray and Darling.

11th. (Camp xxxiv.) Fine morning again, and we all came along well; caught in a squall from Mr. McKinlay for losing tracks; governor not very amiable lately, and no wonder, he having to go so much out of his course, and devilish little in the grub locker; however, we went a good westing stage of nineteen miles; we had a very light and delicate breakfast, this only consisting of two table-spoonfuls of flour, with water, made into a sort of pap; I took a little laudanum, as I had a slight touch of diarrhœa, which soon put me all right. Maitland left the handsaw at the last camp, and the skipper rather astonished him; Hodgkinson has to go to-morrow and get it, then catch us at the next camp, and a very nice ride he will have all alone—solitude may be very agreeable sometimes, if you are not hungry, but when combined with short and bad grub it is not exactly the thing. Our course lay through upland plains after crossing the different branches of the large creek, passing a small line of detached hills. Distance to-day eighteen miles, through generally a good country. Numbers of very curiously topped hills, one in particular seems as if it had a coronet on its brow, bearing north by east from camp.

12th. (Camp xxxv.) Started rather early this morning; the country passed through to-day was peculiar, many small hillocks scattered about the large plains, which were all well grassed; we made a short stage on account of the man sent back for the saw; about fourteen miles was the stage, and we camped on another little creek; we shall not be short of water at all events, if the country continues like this; man and saw arrived safely.

Sunday, *13th*. (Camp xxxvi.) We went through some pretty country to-day, with hills on either side for some distance, and then up a beautiful valley, with fine creek on our right. Valley well wooded with white gums; there is also a small tree, name unknown, from which we obtained large lumps of amber-coloured gum, very pleasant to the taste, and consequently devoured as soon as it was found to be palatable. After we came to camp we found abundance of the native oranges. Why it should be called "orange" I don't know, as it is as much like that fruit as a gooseberry is like a pine-apple. They are not first-rate eating, but still they served to fill up vacant places. We also found a new fruit here, something like the last, it splits open when green, and ripens in that way. It is somewhat larger than the orange, growing on a prickly shrub, which sticks close to any tree in its reach.

Kirby with the sheep is not up to-night, he has lost the tracks and gone up the other side of the western range. We shall stop here if he does not come in early to-morrow. A good fire is being lighted on the highest point of the range, and blue lights are being burnt in case he is in the neighbourhood. Mr. McKinlay is rather uneasy about him, and some of us will have to go and look for him in the morning.

14*th*. Slept like a top, but up early, as some of the men must go and look after the lost sheep and shepherd. They all came back about 1 P.M.

He says he got bothered among the creeks and lost the tracks. He is all right and so are the sheep. Lots of kangaroo and emu, but very shy. Looking like rain and rather hot. Worked up course and distance with governor, for be it known we have never taken an observation all the way, he having done it all by dead reckoning; he makes it about lat. 21° 5' south, lon. 141° east.

15*th*. (Camp xxxvii.) We made a very short stage to-day *on our course*, on account of not finding water; we went about six miles north, and then four miles east, as the appearance of the country did not promise water, and rather late at starting this morning, as some of the nags were absent without leave. We followed right bank of creek, and passed tributaries coming in on both sides; passed a remarkable table-topped hill on the right; the hills on either side. After coming to camp Mr. McKinlay went out to examine. His journal at this date says:—

"After camping, got a horse and went out over the ranges in a west and north direction, and saw what I suppose will be a course to suit me to-morrow; otherwise it was my intention to have taken one man and a pack-horse, and pushing over the range northward, to see if we are near the north watershed, or to have found a practicable route. Ranges are covered with spinifex and rough stones. Hodgkinson shot an euro, which will help us on, and save a sheep."

16*th*. Started over ranges, and at about seven miles came to a splendid flat, covered with myall for two miles, with reddish table-topped ranges close on our right; passed through them and made for a gum creek that appeared to come from the ranges; no water in it or on the flat, but found some in a side creek where we camped. Saw a native signalizing some distance off. Jolly feed of "euro," small species of kangaroo. Currie, my boy, for supper!

17*th*. Up by starlight this morning, which was delightfully cool, in fact cold. After breakfast started over a fine flat, well wooded with box, myall, gum, with numbers of small creeks running into it; water in many of them. We went on our course 305° for eleven miles, and crossed a fine creek going to the north; then changed our course five points, and crossed one spinifex ridge on to a splendid open flat with beautiful grass, high ranges to the east, and camped on the first creek, with abundance of water in it. The scenery here is very pretty from the spot where we first struck—the plain from the range, the high hills, the high but undulating country, the timber intersecting the plain, marking the course of the creeks, was really a sight not to be forgotten. What a park it would make should this part of the country be ever inhabited with the Anglo-Saxon!

To-day Kirby and sheep got astray, and Hodgkinson was sent to find him and bring him on our course; but they having to travel through so much spinifex he could not get their tracks at all, and returned to Mr. McKinlay on the march, who started him back again *instanter* with a flea in his ear. He arrived about 10 P.M., without having ever seen the sheep tracks. He went back to our last camp to try and pick them up; was unsuccessful. Old Kirby and sheep won't be here to-night, it is too late; poor fellow, he will be very hungry. Mr. McKinlay says here:—

"After getting into camp I rode out south, towards the water-shed, but found it further off than I anticipated from this camp. It must be from ten to fifteen miles, and most excellent country. The main range, west, from what I could see of it, is very stony; few trees, and a great abundance of kangaroo and other grasses. Emu and kangaroo in abundance. Range runs to east of north a little, and to south of west a little, and is formidable. Distance travelled seventeen and a half miles."

18*th*. (Camp xxxix.) Up early, and got breakfast over as soon as possible, so that the men could be off after the sheep. Middleton and Palmer started immediately after the meal. It was bitter cold last night, and Kirby must have felt it without his blankets, though I dare say he lighted a good fire, as he would have to watch the sheep all night, there being no fold for them. Mr. McKinlay and Poole started to try and cut his tracks. The horse Jemmie that Ned had to ride gave great trouble, neither whip, nor spur, nor a touch-up with a long pliable stick, administered with no light hand by the governor, had the slightest effect. Middleton then tried him, and after horse and man coming to the ground three times, he "gub" it up, and away they went across the plain, Middleton riding him as if there was a bush fire or a tornado behind him; he stuck to him like a brick, and fairly, by putting plenty of it in, took all the steel out of him. I hope they will be successful, it would throw a gloom over the party should he be lost, to say nothing of the sheep, and that would put us all in a queer state. We have nothing for dinner, and till Mr. McKinlay comes back we cannot get even a little flour. Should they not find him we shall have to kill a bullock, and then "two birds with one stone," viz., jerk him, and keep on looking out for Kirby. Mr. McKinlay adds in his journal:—

"Middleton and Palmer got on his tracks, and followed them to about dark, when within a very short distance of our tracks here, and more than half the distance to this camp, and thought it not improbable, from the course he was then pursuing, that he had got to our camp, and came home, but the unfortunate had not. Had he been followed the day before by Hodgkinson with the same perseverance, all would have been well, and much anxiety spared to all. If the poor man has kept to the ranges, I'm afraid there is little hope of him —it will be a sad end for the poor fellow; a better man for his occupation could not be found. Just fancy an unfortunate man lost between two and three hundred miles from the coast, in a perfect wild, with twenty-three sheep (and I question if

he has any matches), left to sink or swim beyond reach of any Christian soul. If he is recovered he may thank God. Will still keep up the search for some days to come, in hopes of recovering him."

Some of our fellows who have been successful in the diggings, say that there is every indication of gold being here. I know nothing of the matter myself so cannot venture an opinion. Mr. McKinlay and Poole came in about sundown, and we dined on flour and water (paste). Poole says that there is gold in the ranges. Not a bird to be seen all day, or we might have had something, if only a hawk, to fry, but there is nothing alive at all about here.

19th. Up before daylight. Mr. McKinlay called out to me to give the unwelcome cry, "Turn out, boys." I sleep near him, with the camels' packs, etc., the horses being a little distance off; bitterly cold all night, and this morning worse; but Mr. McKinlay, after he turned in, determined to kill a bullock, so we had to fetch them up and all the other animals, for you see we had nothing to eat but that horrid "paste" ever since Kirby was lost, so up we soon had the said animals, and before the first blush of morn had tinged the sky "Mr. Blackeye" lay a helpless mass of beef, with a revolver bullet through his brain; didn't we all work with a will, McKinlay with one knife, and every one doing something towards getting an early breakfast, which was soon made of some of the late Mr. Bullock's liver, to which we did ample justice; then immediately off went Ned and Middleton, with plenty of it, in search of Kirby; there are only three bullocks remaining. Mr. McKinlay remarks on this:—

"In the event of Kirby not being found, with the sheep all correct, not very bright prospects for the party to travel to the Gulf and round to Port Denison upon; certainly we have the horses, but I would be loath to kill them, except in extreme need, but I will still hope for the best, but cannot stay beyond a week, whether found or not, as our provisions, beef, will be lessening daily; the flour we still have in a small quantity, reserved in case of sickness, and for the purpose of putting a small quantity daily in our soup, to make it appear more substantial; at present the vegetable the party were all so fond of has disappeared, except some old dry remnants, which all feel the want of much. I hope it may reappear. By noon of same day, on our not coming across his tracks, I started out and skirted the foot of the range where he ought to come out on his course, but was unsuccessful in finding the slightest trace of the unfortunate man. What thoughts must pass in his mind. Not a probability of ever again seeing any one of his own colour. Possibly destroyed by the natives, whose fires are to be seen daily, although they don't make their appearance. Never again to see his home nor his friends; it must be awful for the poor man! Dusk now setting in; I have better hopes of his recovery, as neither of the three horsemen have made their appearance. Just at dark up rides Middleton with the joyous intelligence that man and sheep are found, Palmer staying behind to push on and overtake Bell and Kirby with the sheep on our track here, and Middleton took a more direct route here to give information of the good news, at which all of us were glad and thankful. About 11 P.M., horsemen,

Kirby, and sheep arrived safe, and I was truly grateful for the deliverance. The poor man says he never expected to see us again. Bell fortunately picked him up within three miles of our last camp; he was then, after having been considerably south, and now completely bewildered and thinking he had missed the camp while travelling in the dark, steering a north-west course, and in ten minutes longer would have been on our track for this place. Middleton and Palmer had traced him throughout; and as they found they were drawing near our track, Palmer went to the track to see if anything was to be seen of him there, and called out to Middleton that they were found, and gone towards home on the tracks, when Middleton immediately started with the information, leaving Palmer to follow and overtake and assist them to camp with the sheep. The man Kirby, on arrival, was completely worn out, not for want of food, but with a troubled mind and want of sleep. He had killed a sheep the second night after leaving last camp, and had with him a small portion for his use. How thankful he must have been to see Bell!"

Were we not all glad to welcome back a comrade that we had all but given up for lost; after the second day we certainly did not expect to see him again; it would have been bad enough to return with a death to report, but such an awful thing as this would have been, indeed, a thousand times worse; thank God he is right, and many a hearty shake of the hand he has had this night of our Lord.

20th. Kirby rather done up this morning; he looks rather pinched up in the face, but otherwise well; he had hardly any sleep since he left us, having stuck to his charge like a Trojan; finished cutting up and jerking to-day. A pity this delay has occurred, as we were going on swimmingly for the gulf; as we are only about 250 miles from the mouth of the "Albert," we ought to do that, say, in thirty days, if we have no more stoppages, as we shall have a good store of jerked beef to take us along, and help out the mutton. "Forward" is Mr. McKinlay's motto; ours *semper parati.* The creek we are on is to be called "Black-eye," after the bullock, and first-rate beef he made. Doing odd jobs, mending and repairing, etc. etc.

21st. We shall be obliged to remain here another day, as the meat is not quite fit for packing. The ranges Mr. McKinlay has named after different officials and friends, among whom he certainly has not forgotten G. Hamilton, Esq., for here he is again represented by a fine creek running west of south, containing plenty of water. More power to him, for he worked hard enough to my knowledge, before we started, to get everything ready for the trip complete, and took great interest in the expedition. The one flowing south from No. 39 camp he has called Warburton's, after P. E. Warburton, Esq., Commissioner of Police of Adelaide, so the police is well represented in the far north, and I hope it will not be long before the gallant troopers of the mounted police will be pushed forward here to look after the duties that may fall to their lot from the quick occupation of the country in these latitudes. The corps of cavalry police of South Australia are second to none in the Colonies, and are as fine a body of men, both as regards education and *esprit de corps*, as one would wish to see, and Mr. Hamilton may well be proud of his command. They are few in number, more's the pity; but they are the right sort.

The ranges on the east side of the creek Mr. McKinlay has named after Kirby, to commemorate his providential escape, not but what I fancy it will never require the chart to remind my friend Kirby of *those here ranges*. Plenty of mussels in a little water here. Strange it is that now we have killed a bullock, we could shoot any quantity of curillas, hawks, etc.

Fine pastoral country, the Government ought to make each of us a present of a bit of it somewhere out here toward the Gulf. We would soon get it stocked, I warrant you, if we go to the Gulf and back to Adelaide all well, under the guidance of John McKinlay, Esq., our worthy old leader. I hope he won't punch my head for calling him "old," for since I wrote this in the "far countree." he has taken unto himself a superior moiety, so I do not mean the word to be taken in its literal sense. Some government or other, I don't care which, ought at all events to give him a tidy slice of all the plum-pudding—*stone*, etc. etc.—that he has gone over, or, what would perhaps be a more graceful way of doing it, let him select a tract of land for himself, not forgetting the "heirs for ever," and if they like to give us each a slip we won't say nay. Kirby is as sound as a trout. Off to-morrow.

CHAPTER IX.

AUSTRALIA TRAVERSED: TROPICAL DISTRICT.

Editor's Introductory Remarks; the Approach to the Sea; Tropical features; the Leichhardt; Aborigines, etc.—April 22nd, etc., Still Cold Weather—23rd, Sarah's Range—25th, Marchant's Creek—26th, William's Creek—27th Elder's Creek—28th, Poole's Creek; Elephant, M'Pherson, and Margaret Mounts—30th, Jessie and Jeannie Creeks—May 2nd, William Creek—4th, Davis Creek—6th, The Leichhardt River—8th, Sturt's Pigeons—12th, Baggage on Fire in Grass-burning; Description of the Leichhardt—18th, Indications of nearing the Sea—19th, 20th, Unable to reach it—21st, Start for return Journey.

We might expect some enthusiasm in the contents of this chapter, as the party approached the goal of all their exertions, and had the hope of presently emerging upon the northern sea. Our travellers, however, plod on without much troubling the poetry of the occasion. As they descend the Leichhardt, the first of the known gulf streams they have made, they find a gradually increasing rise of the tidal wave, until, on the 18th May, the salt water comes in upon them like a sluice, running through the mangrove creeks.

The network of these creeks, and the bog and swamp that appear to fringe the southern shore of Carpentaria, are a sad check to the enthusiasm that might naturally be otherwise called forth upon the successful accomplishment of so great a journey. On the 20th they can reach only within from four to five miles of the sea, and on the 21st they joyfully commence the return to home and the civilized world.

Geographically speaking, we are now within the tropical boundary, but the extra-tropical features still follow us. The weather is fitfully hot and cold, and the nights sometimes bitterly cold, and still there is the ominous spinifex, the sign of a poor soil, such as has not the advantage of regular tropical rains. There are still the marks of great and sudden flooding—the symptoms of a precarious rain supply. At Elder's Creek, for instance, reached on 28th April, there were the marks of a recent great flood, which had left its traces in logs, grass, and rubbish, at a height of thirty or forty feet above the travellers as they lay down to sleep, peaceably enough now, on the sand in the bed of the creek. Tropical indications, however, gradually increase as the party proceed northward. Here they pluck an edible fruit growing on a palm tree, there the dense and substantial vegetation shows it is no longer the creature of a casual shower, and everywhere the range of the spinifex is gradually narrowed.

The considerable river Leichhardt was struck on 6th May, at a point about one hundred miles from its mouth, where it was a hundred and fifty yards wide between its banks, with a stream about twenty yards in width. Some fifty miles lower down, it presented a more imposing appearance, "its bed," says McKinlay, "vast sheets of stones, and the water in it one hundred and fifty yards wide." Two miles lower down the river goes over a fall fifty or sixty feet in height, and some miles below the fall occurs a sand pit, indicating a tidal influence. Diverging to the westward, on the 13th, a branch of the Albert was met, but its waters proved to be salt, and the party returned to the Leichhardt. The Albert had, at an earlier time, been an object of attention to McKinlay, because the steamer sent round from Melbourne by the Victoria Government the year before had been instructed to lie off that river in readiness with provisions and other assistance for the use of any of the several exploring parties then traversing the country. Latterly, however, this contingent prospect is not alluded to, no doubt from the impression that the long delay in the lake district had brought the party to the Gulf at a date long subsequent to the return of the steamer, as was indeed the case.

The aboriginal population are evidently getting more numerous—another indication of the comparative plenty, and of the permanent supply of water and food of tropical regions. They still keep to the ranges, where they seem busy burning the grass. On the 1st May the party came suddenly upon one of them, who ran off in great fright. It seemed strange that more should not be met with in so fine a country. On the 8th, while in the neighbourhood of the line of trees that marked the course of the Leichhardt, the natives were actively burning the vegetation in all directions. A fuller share of tropical life now clusters around the travellers. Pelicans are abundant; like the kangaroo and other Australian denizens they pervade the entire country. Sturt's pigeons are in such numbers that they are described as vast clouds darkening the ground beneath them. The multitudes of ants and their habitations are alluded to by most Australian travellers. In their migrations these industrious communities leave behind them memorials that may well bear a comparison, after its kind, with a Nineveh or Babylon. Writing on 24th April, McKinlay remarks upon the numerous red-ant hills which the expedition, for the previous hundred and fifty miles of its course, saw upon the slopes and tops of the ranges. Untenanted and going to decay, many were like sharp spires, and all were washed or worn by the rain and weather into some diversity of shape. Again we are with Mr. Davis.

April 22nd. (Camp xl.) Started early this morning. Very cold. Wind from the south. The journey was through a varied country, after crossing a good-sized creek and several smaller ones. The larger one had a fine sand and gravelly bed, with large trees on its banks of quite a new description. Mr. McKinlay, who has been in the colony thirty years or more, has never seen them. They had a short, broad, dark leaf, and saplings growing all round the bottom. We passed a creek to the right. The country here is splendidly grassed up to the ranges, which are some distance off, though we are approaching them fast. Several more well-wooded creeks, sandy bottoms, the last we came to we went down some short distance, and camped at the junction of two creeks, in one of which Palmer found a piece of copper ore. No end of quartz and mica to be seen. Gathered some seeds. Cold roast beef for dinner, *hot sirloin*, if you please, for supper.

23rd. This morning the horses were not to be found, and when they were, only a part were brought in, the others had gone back on the old tracks, the sheep and bullocks sent ahead, and two men after the horses. The fellows who brought in part of the horses got McKinlay's blessings. It is very vexing, here we are all ready for a start, camels laden, etc., but Mr. McKinlay says we must wait for the horses, and so we did till 12 o'clock, when we unpacked, unsaddled, and turned them out to feed. I don't suppose we shall get away to-day. Dinner over and no horses, one man sent after sheep and bullocks to bring them into camp again; it was a fine day for travelling, but, alas! here is another delay of a day or more. They all came in about sunset. Mr. McKinlay went out on a voyage of discovery, and thus reports the results:—

"I took a horse and went to the nearest hill, about seven miles distant, to observe the course of the main creek, but the day proving warm and misty I did not get so distinct a view as I anticipated; it was extensive enough but indistinct, although the elevation I was on must have been more than three thousand feet from level of the creek, and much higher ranges on to west of it; from top of it portions of the main range appear in the far distance at 347½°; no other eminence round the horizon to 95°; the whole intervening space filled with creeks running in all directions towards the main creek that must be distant from the hill I was on easterly, nearly twenty miles, with an apparent northerly course; this hill is detached from the main mass of range and distant from four to five miles. It and the most of the intervening space between the camp and it is literally one mass of quartz and quartz reefs, mica, etc., and on top of range is a sort of flaggy slate, all apparently having undergone the action of fire—this range I have called Sarah's Range; it bears from camp 320° seven miles; a great deal of spinifex and abrupt creeks between camp and it, not a speck of gold visible, but it appears to have undergone the action of fire; this is another day lost. Such detention makes me quite irritable and fidgetty."

24*th*. (Camp xli.) We made but a short stage to-day, the bullocks having taken it into their heads to have a ramble; we did not wait for them though, but left Palmer to bring them in. Distance travelled about ten miles, and Mr. McKinlay being doubtful of finding water farther on, and there being some very good here, we camped.

Country passed through to-day very auriferous, plenty of large quartz reefs, and Mr. McKinlay says there is any amount of pipe-clay under the quartz on the hills where he was yesterday; all these are also found in the creeks.

The natives are busy burning away on the ranges some distance west of this, and have been doing so daily ever since we came on the creek. I suppose they are still unaware of our presence, or they would have paid us a visit.

For the last 150 miles at least there have been on the slopes, and on the tops of all the ranges, decaying red-ant hills, not tenanted, but gradually decaying; many of them appearing like sharp spires, and washed in all kinds of shapes by the rain and weather. Perhaps the inhabitants were nomad tribes, and wander about like the other natives. Some of the ant-hills formed quite townships, and were rather curious.

25*th*. (Camp xlii.) The country passed through to-day was undulating and stony, the quartz-reefs extending all the way on our left, or west of us, as far as the eye could reach. Distance to-day, twenty-one miles, and camped, without water, at the foot of a small stony hill some twenty feet high. Mr. McKinlay went on by himself to look for some, which, on his return, he told us he had found in a fine large creek three miles ahead. We had unpacked and pitched camp, so we had dinner, and then re-packed off for the creek, called "Marchant" by Mr. McKinlay, after W. Marchant, Esq., a friend of his, who has a run called "Mananarie," north of Adelaide. This fine creek, on which we are now camped, is still running, and comes in through the ranges from the west and south. It is heavily timbered with white gum. We lost the marking-chisel to-day from off the camel, by some means, so there will be no more tree-marking. Passed several small creeks on our way, and we also found a good deal of spinifex.

26*th*. The fine ranges still on our left. Crossed Marchant's Creek, and in ten miles came to a very fine one about 400 yards broad, and water as far as you can see south and west. This creek is called "Williams," after Edward Williams, Esq., North Adelaide. A quantity of small fish in the water-holes, and some very pretty, with fine black stripes, something like a tiger's.

Sunday, 27*th*. Passed through good and bad country to-day; some magnificent pastoral land. Crossed this creek only three times, and then followed it for some distance till it went off to the east. At thirteen miles we came to a splendid creek. Lots of water coming from the hills to the west, and running east. This creek is named after Thomas Elder, Esq., of Adelaide, who joined us at Lake Hope.

28th. We had a fine bed of sand last night, which is rather more comfortable, as you can make your nest *à la turtle*, and curl yourself up snug. There must have been some fearful floods here at times, as, forty feet above us, in the fine gum-trees that edge the creek, is to be seen bush and *débris* lodged up in the boughs; some trees broken off short thirty feet above their roots. I dare say, from the quantity of stuff lodged in the branches, and the force of the current, some of the large trees are even torn up by the roots. Rather milder than it was yesterday as regards heat. There is another creek joins this just about where we struck it, with plenty of water coming apparently from south-west. Fine pastoral country to-day on the whole, lightly timbered, and some of it flooded. Crossed several small creeks, and one large one, which Mr. McKinlay called after Mr. Poole, of Willaston, the father of one of my comrades. The governor took horse after getting his dinner (no fear of his going before) to a detached hill two miles away. Mr. McKinlay shall speak for himself:—

"After getting into camp, myself and Middleton went on to the hill in front, and at two and a-quarter miles arrived at it. It is perfectly detached, and stands in the open plain—is very stony, or rather rocky. Open plains to the north and west, as far as you can discern; to the north-north-east appears dark timber, which I hope to be the main creek, and appears to be bearing to north and west. A couple of isolated hills from fifteen to twenty miles off, bearing respectively, the southern one 251½°, the northern one 254°. The southern one I have called Mount Elephant; the one to the north, Mount McPherson; and the one I am on, Margaret. Another in the distance, bearing 258°."

Sheep and bullocks not in till very late. Had the satisfaction of some emu soup for supper, Mr. McKinlay having shot a very fine one. Distance twenty-five miles.

29th. Left Poole's Creek about 8 A.M. Over some fine undulating and well grassed plains, with small belts of bushes here and there. Some emus were shot to-day, and were left on the plains with a stick stuck up, and a piece of paper with the order in pencil from the governor, "Davis, bring on the emus on the camel."

We do not much like the flesh of the emu; it is so rich, it made some of the crew sick. We camped at a watercourse, to let the sheep and bullocks have something to eat, as they were so late in last night.

30th. More fine country to travel over to-day; nothing but one immense plain. The natives are burning grass to the east-south-east. This is the first real bush-fire we have seen. The emus made us sick; the meat is so oily. They weighed, when ready for the pot, 48 lb., 31 lb., and 33 lb. The smaller ones were better, and they have saved us some sheep, which is a consideration.

We quote from Mr. McKinlay a description of this country:—

"The grass passed over yesterday, although abundant is rank, and not of that sweet description we have before seen, but no doubt excellent for cattle and horses. Just as the animals were being brought in for packing, Davis found, in a small shallow pool, nearly dry, numbers of small nice looking fish of two sorts—longest not more than three and a-half inches; one sort like the cat-fish of the Murray, the other spotted like a salmon. For five miles over timbered plains on a bearing 345°; at three and a half miles, struck a small creek coming from west and south, with plenty of water; and, at five and a quarter miles further, an immense deep creek with water (gum), crossed at right angles from the western banks, which are very precipitous. I have called it the Jessie. At six miles came to and crossed a noble river, now a creek as it is not running, but plenty of water; from 300 to 400 yards broad. At crossing the first, cabbage palm seen on its western bank between this and the last creek; on left of course is a splendid belt of white gums on the dry sound flat. This river, like the other creek, flows from south of west after crossing a northerly and easterly course; I have called it the Joannie, after a young lady friend of mine. At fourteen and a half miles came to a fine lagoon running easterly and westerly; good water in abundance; went round it and camped north-west side, as the natives are firing close by on the south-east side; distance nineteen and a half miles. For some considerable distance back, it has been an open timbered country; plenty of myall and useful white butt gum; drainage, as yet, all to the east and slightly north. I thought the

Jeannie bore more north, but it bore off again to the eastward; no game of any kind seen to-day, except a turkey; a great quantity of vines on which grows four or five black fruit, like peas and extremely hard, from every flower, and on which the emu appears to feed much. There were also two other vines or runners, on which grow an oblong fruit about one to one and a half inches long, green like cucumber, but bitter; the other is a round fruit about the size of a walnut, darker in colour than the other, not so abundant, and which the emu seems to exist much on at present. Some seeds of each, and many shrubs, flowers, and fruits before new to me, I have obtained. A number of partially dried lagoons all round this, about three-quarters of a mile long. One is about six feet deep; a very fine sheet of water."

May 1*st*. (Camp xlviii.) Beautiful May morning, with a fine breeze. Palmer saw a solitary native on the horses' tracks as he was coming up with the bullocks; he "cooeyed" to him, and as soon as blacky descried him he was off like a shot. We have seen but few natives. The country fine, with lots of grass seeds. We crossed a fine dry lagoon, well grassed, in the open timbered land; then struck a creek flowing nearly north, with a fine white sandy bed, but no water. We followed it down some way, and crossed. The bank, where we struck it, was too precipitous to get up on the other side. Here we saw some dead palm-tree leaves. Crossed again in the opposite direction, three miles from where we struck it. Distance to-day, eighteen miles.

2*nd*. Started early over a beautiful plain, and at three miles from camp crossed a water-course, and at about 6 A.M. crossed another; plenty of water, and then further on a deep narrow creek flowing about north-north-east. Saw small ranges when crossing the creek, on the other side of plains, about south-west. [Here my Journal is so rubbed that I cannot make it out exactly, so I must crib from the governor's a bit, with what parts I can make out in mine here and there, and it continues as bad till the 11th.—J. D.]

Mr. McKinlay says at this date :—

"The large creek when last seen was bearing to west of north, a long distance off; beyond, an open plain. The creek I am now upon divides into several branches just here, which makes this one so small. Shot a new bird—dark grey, large tail, something like a pheasant in its flight; it always starts from the ground, and settles awkwardly on the trees, its tail appearing a nuisance to it; the specimen shot is too much torn for preservation. The days now are very warm, and the nights very agreeable. Short as the time is since they must have had the rain here, it is astonishing how it has dried up in many places. The large creek crossed yesterday I have called the William, after a young friend of mine."

3rd. (Camp l.) Blew pretty fresh this morning. Off early over a large plain, where at the end was some heavy timber, over a stony spinifex range. At about fourteen miles came to a water-course with abundance of water. Numerous courses on either side of us. The principal creek here is dry nearly, the grass quite dry and not so good quality as it has been lately. Any quantity of those beautiful broad leaved shady trees we saw before. Very hot indeed. Distance sixteen miles.

4th. (Camp li.) Very mild this morning. The sheep escaped last night, and half of them are missing. I hope we shall find them. This creek I was going to say is mine; at all events, Mr. McKinlay says it is "DAVIS." Found the sheep not far off. Went across plains of myall with gums. Crossed a small creek, then two more flowing north, then over good country with a little thick myall forest, then over pretty thickly timbered, well-grassed table-lands and spinifex ridge, ending our journey over fine plains to a creek, the only water seen to-day. Distance, twenty-seven and three-quarter miles! Poor sheep!

5th. (Camp lii.) Nice calm morning with dew, but looks like rain. We heard a native last night making an awful row, but as yet have seen none, though they were pretty near to us yesterday with their fires. This creek has plenty of box on it. We crossed it first thing, then over a plain country, next to a swamp, and afterwards plains with shrubs on them, and belts of timber. We camped at a water-course, rather muddy; but the leader is making a short stage of it to-day to make up for yesterday. The sheep, though well, are not in such condition as they have been. Distance to-day, thirteen and a half miles.

6th. (Camp liii.) Cloudy this morning. Started

early, over plains and small belts of timber. Saw a native at a swamp for water, and two more in the distance, but they made off instanter. Birds of all kinds—cockatoos, parrots, hawks, macaws, curillas, grelas, crows, etc.

At twenty-two and a half miles struck the Leichhardt. Banks too steep to get any water for the animals, but, on following it down, came to a capital place; nice beach for about one mile. The width from bank to bank may be 170 yards. Hodgkinson caught a small fish, and we saw a large one, but he was too knowing. Camped; distance twenty-five miles.

7th. Very sultry, with every appearance of rain. Made an early start down the bed of the river, the water here being only fifteen or twenty yards wide. Crossed it, and followed along the western bank, where it is full of sand and timber, and full 500 yards wide; through some pretty forest-looking lands to a fine lagoon, with plenty of water and good green grass. Crossed two creeks, and came to another lagoon; plenty of water and feed. Then through open forests and plains. Mr. McKinlay, seeing we were not likely to meet with any water, changed his course for the Leichhardt, which we had left some distance away on our right. We arrived at it in about three miles. Crossed it, and camped on some sand. Lots of stones for the last two miles, and plenty on the river bank.

8th. Strong breeze, and all our previous prognostications of rain vanished in that air. We started in good time. First part of the way over stones with spinifex, then over plains with belts and clumps of trees. At about ten miles we halted. As for the Sturt pigeons, I never witnessed such a sight; the enormous flights of them completely darkening the ground as they flew over in flocks from south-east to north-west, though thousands of them remain here. The blacks are burning on the river in all directions, and there are fires also in the direction of the "Albert."

The leader with Middleton rode out to ascertain what sort of country it was between the camp and the coast.

Mr. McKinlay here says:—

"Took Middleton with me to ascertain what kind of country there is between camp and coast. On bearing of 355°, at six miles, came to and crossed a creek, plenty of water, flowing to north-north-east; at sixteen and a half miles struck a creek with heavy box and gum timber, and water where we struck it in small lagoons and side creeks. Camped; natives burning ahead of us, and a little east. A great portion of the country we have come over from camp is inundated, and has now coarse grass and reeds. This creek flows here about north; south of this, it comes more to the north-north-east.

"*9th.* Middleton and I still out; party in camp. Started on bearing of 40°; wind strong, south; at three and a half miles struck the creek, now a very considerable size, and flowing to the eastward and a little south; followed it for a quarter of a mile, keeping it on the left, on bearing of about 110°, and crossed it at a long grassy flat. In its bed native whirlies between where we first struck it and crossed it; bearing of 40°, long deep reach of water, banks well defined; bearing of 40°, at three quarters of a mile creek, recrossed same on a bed of lava, all rent, abundance of water. At five and a half miles further struck the Leichhardt, its bed vast sheets of stones—rocks and small stones opposite side, lower down; the water in its bed is about or upwards of 150 yards wide. At two miles, bearing of about 210°, struck the river at a stony and rocky fall, and went westward half a mile to avoid the bend. Struck river again at three miles on same course as above; then, at four miles, struck a lagoon to south; then, at four and a half miles, struck the river, water in its full width, now upwards of 250 yards, a splendid-looking place, and lined on its banks with splendid timber of various kinds, with a variety of palms, etc.; then to the southward of south-west for between six and eight miles. But the rugged banks were so intricate that it was impossible to calculate the distance correctly; in a great many places, half a mile from the river banks, the plains drop off precipitously from three to ten feet, and slope off in undermined deep earthy creeks, finishing at last in deep reedy creeks close to the river. Water in nearly all the side creeks, and compelled us to keep out, but sometimes we were caught in them, thinking the timber we were advancing to was a lagoon or belt of timber, and then we were compelled to go round it; then cross a very fine creek running into the river, the same, I believe, we crossed yesterday about six miles from camp on our outward course. From this to our camp I make out about thirteen miles, on a bearing of about 200°. Got to camp about 8 P.M., for the last seven miles guided by a roman candle shot off at the camp. Fireworks are most useful in expeditions of this kind, as in many cases, some of our party have been guided up to camp near midnight."

9th. All of us save the governor and Middleton in camp awaiting their return, and resting and amusing ourselves as best we may.

10*th*. (Camp lvi.) Beautiful weather, but very cold in the night. Started in good time and order over land subject to frequent inundations, judging from the reeds, etc. Crossed a creek about six miles from camp. Six miles further on, three fine lagoons in succession, all of them containing plenty of water, and at the last we camped where there was excellent feed.

Here Mr. McKinlay says:—

"I forgot to mention that yesterday, on return to camp from first striking in Leichhardt's river, I observed apparently a native firing the grass a short distance on my right. I made towards it and saw one coming steadily towards us, till spying us, retreated at full speed; as I had some fish-hooks and line, I was determined to pull him or her up. Started off and overtook what turned out to be a gin and her piccaninie, and had a load of something which in her retreat she dropped. She screamed and cooed, and set fire to the grass all around us to endeavour to get rid of us, but all to no purpose. I held out to her a fish-hook, but she would not take them to look at even, but busied herself screaming and firing the grass; upon which I got off the horse and approached her. She immediately lifted up her yam-stick in the position the men throw their spears, and prepared to defend herself, until at last she quieted down on observing the fish-hook, and advanced a step or two and took it from me, evidently knowing the use of it. I then gave her a line and another hook, and by signs explained to her that I would return in the direction the day following. She wished me to understand something, holding up four of her fingers, but what she meant I could not guess. I tried to make out from her how far the coast was, making motions as if paddling a canoe, but could not get any information; as soon as we were clear off, she set to work to make an immense smoke to attract the notice of her people to give them the news. This afternoon three of the party went over east-south-east about three-quarters of a mile to the river and caught about a dozen of fish of small size and three different sorts, and a turtle about a foot long. The river during the day has almost always been in sight from three to six miles off, till crossing the creek when it was not more than one mile off."

11*th.* (Camp lvii.) Started over some broken slopes in the direction of the river, then over some plains, and crossed a creek running into the river, then into open country, sloping to north-east, with plenty of water on either side. Struck the river again at the falls. Camped on a small creek with running water and beautiful green feed. A bullock was killed, as he objected to go any further. The fish under the falls are numerous, and consist of guard-fish, sword-fish, and sharks. The falls are some fifty or sixty feet high; no current, deep water above and below. Found a tree of the palm species, with good fruit on it.

12*th.* This is a vile camp, high grass and no shade. The scenery, however, is very pretty, undulating fine grassed country, intersected by small creeks, their courses defined by trees on their banks. The grass is nearly up to one's neck, and it is very hard work to get through it. The men are busy jerking the beast; there won't be much trouble in that, as he has not one ounce of fat on him, and his meat smells rather like musk.

Two of our fellows went to the falls to fish, and succeeded in bringing home some very good ones, black bream, and an excellent firm fish, and some flat-heads, not quite so good, but still very acceptable for a change.

A nice accident happened soon after Mr. McKinlay had left. He had told me to get the grass burned round the camp, so that it might be a little clear; so before he left I had commenced and burnt a good piece, and had finished, as I thought, and the fire all out and secure, the wind at the same time being very still, hardly a breath, when all of a sudden there was such an awful row in the camp, and all of us being a short distance away, we were perfectly astounded. Bang! bang!—fiz! fiz! We ran down as fast as our legs could carry us, and found to our dismay that some fire that had been smouldering had been fanned into a flame, and communicated with the pack saddles (some distance from the clearing), in which was our ammunition, to say nothing of fireworks; so rockets and blue lights were vieing with each other in their praiseworthy endeavours to celebrate our arrival at "The Falls." It might have been worse had we been farther afield, as the packs would inevitably have been destroyed. As it is, every rocket is absent "without leave," which is a great pity in case we should want to signalize the "Victoria," should she be in the Gulf. I hear from the two who went to the Falls (Mr. McKinlay only allows two to go away at a time) that they are very pretty. The fruit tree that grows there is very like a medlar when ripe. Many native tracks about the tree, showing that they are partial to the good things of this land when they are to be found. The pigeons came over the camp by hundreds of thousands to the Leichhardt for water. We knocked over a few, for the beef is positively *soft*, not tender. What shall we do when we have nothing else?

13*th*. In camp. Finished the beef. McKinlay and party not returned yet; the camels a long way off this morning—four miles, I should say. They don't seem to like this feed; I wish they would not ramble so. It is not good travelling, in fact very fatiguing; tramping through this high, rough grass is anything but pleasant. This appears to me a very long day, and the breakfast burnt to rags, for which the cook got a blessing or two. After returning with the camels sat down to repair our small stock of clothes and play cards; some went off to fish. I wish I could, but orders from head-quarters prevent me.

14*th*. Two as usual off early to fish; I wish them luck; the two yesterday only caught a few, and those small. Took a nag and went after the camels, but could not find them anywhere; returned, after some hours' fruitless search, to my dinner, and afterwards Bell and I started again, found yesterday's tracks, but no new ones. We shall be in a nice mess if they are lost; we looked for them till dark, and went on to last camp, but could see no sign of them. We stayed at the old camp all night without supper or blankets; mosquitoes very bad, but when we did get to sleep we forgot all about them.

15*th*. Up by starlight, and started across country to try and cut their tracks and make a circuit home again. The country covered with small trees, which is much against our seeing the brutes; had it been open plains, we might have seen them a long way off; I am afraid we shall not find them. Saw plenty of turkey, but could not waste time to go after them. After a long round we sighted camp about two o'clock, having had nothing to eat since one o'clock the day before. Just as we came in view of the camp I saw McKinlay on horseback coming up the creek. I reported our loss; he did not say much, as it was no fault of ours, but I dare say that he thought the more. Bell and I rode forty or fifty miles to-day, and crossed any quantity of small creeks and water-courses. Immense tracks of country burned by the natives. We came on a deserted native encampment, where we found the bones of birds and a snake by the ashes of an old fire; there was a "whirlie" there too. I had to set to work after coming in to repair some things for the governor, and did not finish till after 11 P.M.; pleasant that, and I as sleepy as an owl. Mr. McKinlay, Bell, and I have to start in the morning, but before we start let Mr. McKinlay tell in his own words where he has been since he started from us on 12th instant, and what he saw and did down the Leichhardt.

"*12th.* I started out to-day to examine the country ahead, taking with me Middleton and Poole. At one mile, over plain 5°; changed course to 355°; at five and a half miles struck the river and changed course to 285°; at five-sixths of a mile struck and crossed creek from south to river; at two and five-sixths miles crossed smaller one from same direction; at a quarter of a mile further changed course to 340°; at eleven and three-quarter miles over very bad travelling country, plains subject to much inundation, to a creek running into the river, with splendid water and feed; at twelve and a half miles came to the river, with an immense sand pit opposite; appears to be within the influence of the sea, and is about 600 yards wide, and dry half across. A number of pelicans up some distance; water either brackish a little, or with some other peculiarity about it. Started, for apparently another bend of the river, on bearing of 329°. One and three-quarters miles saw a lagoon, on the left, ahead; and, as the horses are tired, will bear for it and turn them out. Course 282°, three-quarters of a mile; abundance of water and feed; lots of geese, ibis, ducks, and spoonbills. North three-quarters of a mile from this is the river, about 500 yards wide, treeless on the west bank, and cliffs about twenty to thirty feet high, all round an immense sweep; sandy beach opposite, within the influence of the sea; a rise and fall of four feet observed—and, at high water, a little brackish. Caught a few fish; the only thing we had for supper; would have done well had there been sufficient of them.

"13*th*. Started, on bearing of 330°, for a distant point like river timber, which turned out to be a small hill or ridge with spinifex; a lagoon on the left at its base; struck it at five miles. At five and a half miles changed course to 355°; at ten miles, first part over firm small stony plains, good country; then, at four miles, crossed a salty timberless creek; and then over a succession of salt swampy flats, with grassy plots intervening. Middleton's mare, "Counterfeit," knocked up, and he had to stay with her. I and Poole went on, on a bearing of 355° still; at two miles came to a mangrove creek; at two and a quarter miles the banks of the Albert River; salt arm, from half to three-quarters of a mile broad. Returned to Middleton, and started back for the Leichhardt River, on bearing of 110°, to camp as soon as we could get water and feed, to endeavour to get the mare back to camp or part of the way. On bearing of 110° for about four miles, first part over salt swamps; passed a long rocky lagoon full of water, and half a mile long from north to south—and several other smaller ones between that and the river; mangrove banks in all the flat parts. Banks on this side treeless; country much burnt up. Top tide at least five hours earlier than when we camped last night; caught a few fish—in all about enough for one, but had to do for the three of us. Rise and fall of river somewhere about five feet.

"14*th*. Wind south; was very cloudy during the night and this morning; mosquitoes very troublesome during the night. Bearing homewards, 170° to 215° for the first eight or ten miles, leaving Poole and Middleton to get on to our first camp, till I bring on the party on the morrow. Got to camp myself a little after sundown, and to my disgust found all the camels astray, and Bell and Davis in search of them.

"15*th*. Start Hodgkinson and Maitland on to Middleton and Poole's camp, with four horses, bedding, and provisions, on such a course, 25½° west of north, as will cut their camp. No tidings of the camels. I went out and hunted about for them till noon, and just as I got to camp Bell and Davis returned, having camped out all night after them, but saw nothing of them—the ground is so hard they leave so little impression on the ground that it is a difficult thing to trace them; however, they have got bells and hobbles on, and will at once be again sent after, with I hope more success. I am exceedingly annoyed at the detention here, more so as the animals don't do so well here as they have done. Hunted still during the afternoon for them, but without success. All spare hands will start out in search in the morning; it will be the sound of the bells or the sight of them only that will recover them, as track them we cannot in this dry country. Promised the party a treat on arriving within the influence of the sea on the north coast, so had baked some flour kept in reserve and each had a liberal allowance served out to him—that with fresh and excellent mutton, and some salt I brought back from the flats, gave all quite a treat. Sent Poole and Middleton theirs on by Hodgkinson and Maitland, which in their present half-starved condition would be a still greater treat. We would all have been in better spirits had the camels not been absent, but will hunt well for them to-morrow, and trust we may recover them."

When Bell and I arrived in camp we found Hodgkinson and Maitland away down the river with provisions to where Mr. McKinlay had left Middleton and Poole, and started Hodgkinson and Maitland to them with provisions. Fancy our delight on arrival to have three immense junks of bread put into our hands! Mr. McKinlay promised us a treat when we came within the influence of the sea on the north coast, and he kept his word, and we certainly did like to see the bread; but, strange to say, that I sat down, and so did Bell, and quite forgot the bread till we had nearly finished our roast mutton and soup. The governor had brought us some salt from the salt lagoons, and we should have been as jolly as sand-boys had we only got the camels here with us, as it is a sad damper to us now not having found them.

16*th*. Mr. McKinlay, Bell, and self off early after the camels, but could see nothing of them. A few bushes were bitten, so we still kept on till we arrived at the old camp, where Bell and self had the *al fresco* turn in, where we had a little lunch, and turned the horses out, and rested a bit for an hour; then off we started across a large plain, when we saw at the distance of half a mile the old female camel walking very quietly towards the south. We then shaped our course, and stopped her, and then we saw the others marching straight ahead. We soon collared them, and turned them on the way to camp, the governor leading. It was a mere chance we found them, for we could not track them; it was just luck, and nothing else.

17*th*. Started early for the lagoon, some twenty miles distant, where Middleton and Poole had been left, and where Hodgkinson and Maitland had gone with their grub on the 15th.

All the grass around us is one mass of flame, and what was beautiful grass is now nothing—a black desert. Why the natives set it on fire we don't know. It was very warm travelling through this conflagration. The hawks soaring above in hundreds, ready to pounce down on the poor frightened lizards, mice, or any other little animal that escaped from this fearful monster fire. Plenty of water on our road to-day, keeping the Leichhardt on our right all the way, the fine timber on its banks marking well its course.

18*th*. (Camp lix.) Everything at camp all right. We were all off together this morning. We shall soon strike the Gulf; at any rate we cannot be far off from the sea, as the tide rises some four or five feet here, and perhaps more. We had rather nasty travelling over plains, not a hill to be seen; look where you will, the grass nearly all burnt off the ground; in places the stumps were rather trying to the camels, they being as sharp as spikes. Passed several lagoons on our way, and any number of cockatoos in the trees on the banks, and very pretty they look. There is a great sameness in the country, down this river at least, as far as we have come (over 100 miles). We passed a fine creek, with plenty of water, with game, ducks, etc. A few miles further on we struck a pretty mangrove creek, and further on crossed lots of little rivulets of salt water, running inland with the tide, which was just making, and we saw it coming up quite fast. There seems to be a heavy mangrove swamp ahead of us. We camped on a small lagoon of fresh water, the water all round us being quite salt. The river too is salt. The tide here where we are, for we are within a stone's throw of the river, rises ten or twelve feet, and a ship of 800 tons could be alongside the bank, and take in or unload her cargo with ease. The river has a very pretty and picturesque reach here, and it is some 400 yards wide. Natives burning in every direction, but they are not to be seen. The water lilies are in bloom. There is also a *tree* with dark green foliage and beautiful yellow blossoms. We caught a small shark and several flat-heads to-day.

19*th*. This is our sixtieth camp, and I cut MK. on a small tree. Mr. McKinlay, Middleton, Poole, Wylde, and Kirby started very early to get to the seashore, but found it quite impossible, on account of the mangrove swamps and swampy flats, for the horses were quite unable to travel; they got up to their bellies in the swamp; killed one; lost three sheep here, and we start on Wednesday.

20*th*. Mr. McKinlay said that any of us who liked to try on foot to get to the sea could do so, but none of us did, as we all thought if it had been practicable that he would have done it himself. Hodgkinson and Poole were sent off to the salt flats for salt, so that we shall have some for our homeward trip, to relish our hard fare, for I suppose we shall have to live on horses, having only two bullocks left, and they will not last us into Port Denison. Mr. McKinlay says he thinks we are about four or five miles from the sea, and he goes by way of Port Denison home, as it is so much shorter than to return to Adelaide.

Many natives on the northern side of river to-day. McKinlay, by dint of great perseverance, got three of them over to this side, and they were regaled with sheep's head, and decorated with some old boots, and pieces of tartan on their heads. This constituted their sole attire, save a fish-hook stuck in their hair. These natives seem to be of the same caste as those we saw on the lakes, and during the early part of our journey, except that the language was different, they had not the front teeth knocked out, and were scarred on the face and bodies; they were not circumcised either, like our former friends. After getting all they could, they recrossed, and we saw them no more. The governor could not get any information out of them; they did not seem to be able to take their eyes off us and all the traps about the camp. They were too much engaged with their eyes to talk.

Hodgkinson and Poole came back in the afternoon with about fifty pounds of salt. The camels are getting quite lame from having to cross so much burnt stubble.

21*st*. Hurrah for civilization, home and beauty,

good grub, and bottled ale! We start to-day for Port Denison, where I hope we shall all arrive in safety, and *shortly*, or we shall eat all the horses. I dare say they are as good as the bullocks; we shall be able to report to our friends what we think of them. We retrace our steps thirty miles to the falls, where we shall cross over to the east. Just as we were starting this morning, the natives were in numbers on the other side of the river, up in the trees, giving us a farewell shout. This is all splendid country about here, the grass nearly up to our necks, with plenty of excellent water in the lagoons which abound here. I wish we had fifty more sheep, so that we could go back straight to Adelaide, from whence we started; but needs must when you know who drives.

CHAPTER X.

HOMEWARD BOUND—CARPENTARIA TO PORT DENISON.

Editor's Remarks—A Camp of Landsborough—June 5th, The Flinders (of McKinlay)—6th, The Binoe—13th, Gregory's Ranges; Mount Wildash; Hawker's Bluff; Morphett's Peak—16th, The Gilbert—the Old Camel served up—20th, Stuart's Creek—22nd, etc., Most difficult Country—25th, etc., Ice during Night—28th, Frank and George Creeks—July 5th, Strike the Burdekin—15th, A Platypus in the Burdekin—27th, Cross the Burdekin on a Raft—30th, Last Camel, Siva, killed for Food—August 2nd, Reach Harvey and Somers' Station, near Port Denison.

UNABLE to reach the sea, although so near to it, or even to get a glimpse of it from the low and swampy ground on which they have arrived, the party turns its back on the northern waters, and joyfully takes the homeward course. This course the leader had already decided should be by way of Port Denison, the remaining stock of provisions being inadequate for an attempt to return by the route by which they had arrived. Reascending the Leichhardt to find a crossing place, they came, on the third day's march, upon the tracks of Landsborough, in his preceding south-easterly route, which, however, they immediately lose by keeping more to the east. Here may arise some confusion. McKinlay comes upon a considerable river, which he crosses and recrosses repeatedly, and which he considers to be the Flinders, and so names accordingly. Landsborough falls in with another, and still larger river, evidently the main stream, which he too calls the Flinders. Between these two branches or supposed branches of the same river system, Walker came upon a third, which he called the Norman, while Burke describes a fourth, the Cloncurry, flowing from the south and west. The Flinders, therefore, embraces a very considerable watershed. We can hardly do better, towards avoiding a confusion of names, than by changing the Flinders of McKinlay to the name of its discoverer, and this without much apprehension from the rival claims of a lesser stream that pursues its unknown course somewhere about the centre of the country.

As the expedition advances eastward, a remarkable change is found in the features of the country. The grassy plains are succeeded by a country of the most rugged and difficult character, consisting of endless successions of hills, rising in some parts to considerable elevation, and presenting all but impassable obstacles to travelling. The Upper Burdekin is reached, rolling its fine clear waters through a country of the same character. Following this guiding channel, the travellers at length arrive amongst the settlements just after the last camel—defiant, contentious old Siva—had gone into the pot, as the last horse (save two) and the last bullock had done some time before, and when the exhausted stock of provisions had already been the subject of some anxiety.

Passing through a range of latitude varying from 17° to 20°, the climate of the country is remarkable. The intense cold, especially at night, is constantly alluded to. For instance, on 27th May, "cold keen wind, south-south-east," and on 28th, "bitterly cold," etc. Subsequently, on three different mornings, there was ice on the water in the pots, and the dew was frozen upon the blankets. Although the season was the middle of winter, this degree of cold, so frequently recurring, is unusual in other parts of the world in so low a latitude, and in positions of no great elevation above the sea level. But once more to the Journal. "*Revenons à nos moutons*," as Mr. Davis would have said most heartily, if the literal of the phrase could for once have been substituted for the figurative.

22nd. (Return Camp i.) This is a magnificent morning. Started early, but going over the same, I have not much to say. We camped about three miles north of our camp, going up a creek with plenty of water. Mr. McKinlay tried to cross the Leichhardt in one or two places, but failed, so we have to go down to the falls; the banks very precipitous. Came to camp on a lagoon.

23*rd*. Started on a bearing of 135°. We had an awful job to cross at the falls; the rocks were so rugged and slippery that several of the bullocks fell and barked their legs between the rocks; it took us a long time to get over. After crossing, a marked tree was observed, and the remains of an old camping place; the trees were cast about, and much bruised; the large tree was marked—

↑
L
EE 15
1862
C 5

the arrow pointing upwards; so up one of our fellows got to see if anything was hidden, but after a long search, nothing was found. This was one of Landsborough's camps.

We went a short stage to-day from the detention at the falls, and camped at a lagoon with plenty of duck, teal, etc. I forgot to mention that we found a broken bottle at the foot of the tree, and we imagined that there might have been documents left in it. This we afterwards found to be erroneous, when we saw Landsborough in Melbourne, as he had not buried anything there. The horses' tracks were not yet obliterated. We marked a tree close to Landsborough's, MK, with a knife.

24th. The Queen's birth-day; very sorry we cannot drink her health. Started early; went twenty-two miles, and camped on a creek. There was a heavy dew last night; lots of game, but very wild, and difficult to be got at; natives burning all round, but none to be seen. Passed over stony ridges and flats; crossed a small creek and lagoon, with plenty of water; country well grassed, with plenty of light timber scattered about, and some bushes. Then over open country, rather swampy in places, soil very good; after that stony spinifex ridges for the rest of the way to camp, passing a creek or two, and a regular town-ship of ant-hills, of all shapes and sizes, to camp 3·30.

26th. (Camp v.) Passed through some curious country to-day, pebbly but well grassed, low ranges on both sides of us, then across a large plain, and camped on a swamp about seventeen miles from old camp; natives still firing about us, but none to be seen.

27th. Was nice and cold this morning; had to make some leather boots for the camels; they were very lame indeed. We went some thirty miles to-day, for we could not find water; when we did, it was so muddy that dire necessity alone made us drink it. We started at about 8·30 A.M.; came to a fine creek, well grassed and timbered, but very boggy where we struck it, and we had to take a small spell before Mr. McKinlay could find a crossing place; crossed, and soon after came upon another large one, two hundred yards wide, full of reeds and grass, but with no water where we crossed; we had a job to find water. Mr. McKinlay tried various belts of timber, in the hope of finding some, but without success. He says, "This is the most deceptive part of the country—every five minutes you are in the expectation of coming to water, but it has been our fate to find nothing but this muddy little drop; plenty of birds about, so there must be water somewhere." I don't recollect mentioning anything about our little sheep and their travels; they have gone as much as thirty-two and often twenty-five miles per diem, and were quite jolly; I wish we had some now. Ned and the bullocks not in to-night.

28*th*. Just after sunrise the bullocks came into camp all right, and men with them. The governor went off to look for water, and found two splendid lagoons a quarter of a mile from camp. He soon came back with the intelligence, so we saddled up, and were off for the nearest lagoon in a south direction. Maitland not up. We shall stop at this new camp some time to recruit the camels, as they are very lame, and there is plenty of feed for them; we shall also kill a bullock, and jerk him here—"Boxer, your doom is sealed!"

Middleton unwell again. Maitland came into camp late this afternoon, looking rather the worse for wear, quite knocked up. The governor says had we been obliged to go on a stage without luckily hitting on this place, I think he would have gone frantic, as he appeared in a sad state of mind on his arrival.

29*th*. (Camp viii.) Spelled here at this fine lagoon; it is a pretty sheet of water, with plenty of lilies growing on it. Three or four of the lads are taken ill with shivering and a. kind of ague. Mr. McKinlay says "it is an awkward part of the world to get ill in." Getting the meat jerked to-day. These chaps being ill we are rather short-handed. Our solitary bullock does not seem to feel lonely. He came into camp, saw his old mate, and then went off to feed quite quietly. Bell went to look after Maitland during the day, and returned without seeing him at the old camp, he having orders to go no further. He found a curious fruit—nothing but stone and skin; so, unless the kernel is good, it is valueless. N.B. The stone only contained two or three small seeds; no one tasted them. Liver and cold water for tea, but the men who are ill cannot touch it.

30*th*. Repairing pack-bags and saddles. On going out this morning after the camels, I found an old acquaintance—a pretty little tree, bearing a red seed with a black eye; I knew it directly; it is called by the blacks in the West Indies "crab-eye." I took a lot of them to camp not thinking much of them myself; finding that none of the party had seen any before, I sallied forth again, and gathered a good supply.

We had some good bathing here, but very cold; it did us a power of good, though. The three men still ill. The governor says—"If these lagoons are permanent—and no doubt there are many more—this is a splendid pastoral country." Feed good enough for any stock, and timber to suit almost any purpose. There is a large bean here, the same, Mr. McKinlay says, that poor Leichhardt used instead of coffee.

Repairing to-day and shoeing some horses, and getting everything ready for an early start to-morrow. I hope the sick folk will be better. We had a first-rate breakfast this morning—potted bullock's head. You may laugh, but it was most excellent. It is true there was not much spice in it, but it went down well with a good appetite.

June 1*st*. (Camp viii.) Shall not start to-day after all. Getting the things ready repacked. Spelling the sick men and animals as long as we can. The camels being so lame, the governor ordered the hobbles to be taken off, consequently one of them is *non est* to-night. He won't be very far, as he is very lame; I daresay planted in some of the bushes.

A number of natives visited us to-day; the most curious fellows imaginable. There seemed to be only one spokesman among them, and he was an elderly gentleman, the younger ones making a kind of noise between a whistle and a hiss. Saw no lubra among them. There were many more males in the trees to the rear of our camp. Gave those who came up some old horse-shoes, and some bullocks' horns; the latter they seemed to think a great curiosity. The governor could not make much out of their motions and hissing. They soon left us, and promising to return. They are not such fine men as those on the lakes. They did not like the appearance of the camels, and looked on them with great awe, and wanted them to be driven away; they happened to be the only animals in camp when they came up.

Sick men not improved, but I fear we must start to-morrow, whether or no, as it will not do for us to remain camped too long, with only one bullock for food. Some old horse won't go badly should we be driven to that.

2nd. Found camels early this morning, so we shall not be detained, and eastward ho! again to-day. I hope we shall not stop any more till we get to a station. I am far more jolly writing this to-day than I was when jotting it down in pencil in my pocket-book. Over my shoulder are peeping rather a nice lively pair of eyes, belonging to a certain young lady of my acquaintance. Ah! what does Tom Moore say—let me see if I can recollect. Oh! here it is:

"If woman can make the worst wilderness dear,"

The other line, slightly altered,

"Think, think, what a heaven she'd make of this here."

I hope we shall soon see some merry faces and laughing eyes at Port Denison. Pretty creatures, what should we do without them!

Our path is through a good deal of scrub to-day, and we came only about twelve miles, on account of the sick men, and camped on a lagoon, in which all those who were well had a bathe, as usual, whenever there was water enough. It was very cold; a most tremendous dew last night and this morning; everything was wet through, and McKinlay's waterproof over his bedding had a gallon of water resting on it in the hollows. I never experienced such a heavy dew in my life. There was also a thick fog; could not see ten yards ahead of you. The fog lifted between 8 and 9 A.M., when we prepared to start. Palmer ill with the fever, making four on sick-list.

"Although this country is rather too thickly wooded to be called open forest, it is still an excellent pastoral country, the grasses sweet and plenty of water, the lagoons being covered with nymphans or water lily, and the soil sandy. We passed many patches of burnt ground, some burnt earlier than the rest, having green grass nine to twelve inches high.

"Saw nothing of the natives this morning before starting. Several palms seen through the forest; a few close by this camp of no great height. The feed in general is very dry, except in the neighbourhood of the creeks or lagoons."

3rd. A heavy dew last night and this morning, but not so bad as the night before. A long twenty-seven miles walk to-day—not very comfortable for the invalids. Passed through lots of spinifex and timbered ground, but not so dense as yesterday. Here we lost a fine horse, Harry: he had been ridden into camp, and began to blow a good deal, and died at 9 P.M. He was poisoned or bitten by a snake. We passed several creeks with very little water in them. Fortunately the governor ordered us to fill our canteens, and he was right; for we camped without water, and found what we had brought with us quite a godsend. We had to keep a sharp look-out after the horses and bullocks. This is nasty work, as it is nearly dark. Kept the fire in all night. None of the horses got away, and the camels being tied up, we shall get away early to-morrow morning. The female camel, Krishna, very lazy, and would not go along by fair or foul means. She is nearly done up. I expect we shall have to leave her behind. She ought to be jerked. It fairly tires me leading the old brute.

Came only about six miles to-day; have

come to a water-hole, and not finding water up or down the creeks, Mr. McKinlay thought it best to stop there. Old Krishna is to be let go her own way, and high time too. We filled our canteens and bags with water, and then let the animals drink. It being only a small hole, soon got muddy. How the poor things go into the water ! they not having had any since the morning.

4th. (Camp x.) The silk cotton, which I have seen growing in India, is here with its beautiful red blossom, and having no leaves while in flower.

5th. There is a creek on our right; then we come to a large one, with a little water in, where we camp, as there is good feed for the camels, for they have been tied up for the last two or three nights. Sick men mending, except Kirby, who is very weak. This river here, Mr. McKinlay says, is the "Flinders." It has lots of paper-barked trees on it, and some very fine ones on its banks: we camped in its bed. We got a bath to-day in a hole; water as clear as crystal. We passed several frames, six feet long by four feet wide, and three feet from the ground, on forks, making a kind of sleeping-place; the darkies are refined up here.

6th. Kirby still continues very weak; no energy left. The rest better. Passed through plenty of scrub as usual, and crossed the Flinders twice to-day. Struck another river, the Binoe.

The country open, timber, well-grassed. Camped on a small creek running into the Binoe. Few lagoons close by covered with yellow lilies. Plenty of water in the small creek, but none in the Binoe just here. Any quantity of corkscrew or spiral palm. The old camel not in yet. A native companion shot this morning. Very little game.

7th. (Camp xiii.) Started about 8 A.M., over some rough country, low ranges, with thick scrub, some very lofty barren ranges to our left, some eight miles off, very rocky, timbered to the top. We crossed the Flinders at a very wide branch, and crossed and recrossed the Binoe. Camped on the Flinders, at a long sheet of water; quantities of the bronzed stones strewed in our path to-day. We shall kill our last bullock, and then for "old horse." We must make the most of him; he is rather wild sometimes, rushing among the horses, and going through them sideways, etc.; so the sooner he is killed the better. Native fires ahead, but no darkies to be seen. Killed the bullock; not an ounce of fat on him.

8th. All hands jerking bullock. Patients better. Mr. McKinlay out on a *ramble*. Brought home a snake eight feet long. This is a fine sheet of water, 400 yards long and thirty wide. Lots of large bean vines. Very pretty it is, cut up into small islands, with the sandy courses going all round them. Some of them have fine gums growing on them. Some traces of game here—kangaroo, wallaby, emu, etc.

9th. (Camp xiv.) In camp spelling, mending bags, and finishing beef. Good roast beef for dinner; it went well without mustard, salt, or pepper even. Shoeing horses. Governor and Middleton out on a cruise to see the country.

Mr. McKinlay says:—

"I took Middleton with me to go out to reconnoitre and feel our way for next stage through the hills a-head. Found that the water-course comes from north, or a little west of north, from between the heavy-timbered ranges to north and west, and bald hills, or nearly so, to north and east, and probably winds round nearer its source more to the east. A number of thinly-wooded hills, with small creeks running from them to west and south appear to run round south for some distance, perhaps ten to fifteen miles or more. Beyond the highest, in the distance, the natives are busy burning, and this leads me to suppose they are on the other or principal branch of the Flinders River; but I shall know more about it in a few days. Abundance of water in the small creeks, as far east and south as I went to-day, and some lagoons in the flats. The natives commence their range of fires from 20° west of south to 30° east of south, and I think I shall find that it will meet me on my course. Wind in the afternoon from south by east, strong occasionally; towards evening it died away. Beef now dry. We start from here to-morrow if all is right, and we have nothing more to detain us. The horses are shod, except one, and that one, one of the best, no shoes being large enough. I hope he will be able to get along. Our food now consists of about 230 lb. of dry and salt beef, everything else in the shape of food gone, but I think we will have sufficient to carry us into the settled districts of Queensland, on the Burdekin River, where we will be able to get a fresh supply. We have a little salt, and amongst the lot about half a pound of soap."

10th. We are off to-morrow. I hope the bullock will see us to a station, but I doubt it; the meat is well jerked. Sun very hot. Bathed of course. Making all ready for an early start to-morrow morning.

11th. Started early. Country well wooded. Crossed two creeks. The bed of one of them was one mass of conglomerate, with large boulders of iron-stone, as if they had been thrown up by fire lately. Lots of quartz, sandstone, etc. The creek resembles very much the one we left, with the small islands, sandy bed, and fine trees and shrubs of all kinds. Our way lay through open forest and plains, intersected by small creeks. Passed also lagoons now and then on the plains.

Mr. McKinlay again says:—

"Over first stony ridge at 10·10, and considerable sized double creek at 10·17, dry at crossing. Top of next high range at 11·15; five and a quarter miles. Very extensive view. Spelled on top of hill waiting for the camels for forty-five minutes, till noon. Then started on bearing of 127½° for south-west end of large range in the distance, that would otherwise come right across my original course. There is an immense large black circular range from 127½° round by east to west-north-west, with reaphooky faces and scrubby tops, and a number of detached conical and coronet-topped hills. At 1 P.M. water in a rocky creek close to the right. Watered the horses. Spelled ten minutes, till 1·10. Crossed creek at

1·15. Sandy, scrubby forest. Crossed another sandy creek at 1·57. Crossed another sandy creek at 2·3. At 3·15 on top of rocky mulga hill, with granite and mass of quartz pebbles. Some difficulty in getting over and down a rocky range (granite principally). Struck a small creek, with sufficient water for our use, and good feed, and camped at 3·50 at distance of ten and three-quarters to eleven miles on last bearing. Distance travelled about sixteen miles. Course of the ranges close by, the one that we last crossed, and the one just close by before us, 40° west of south, with the drainage in same direction."

12*th*. (Camp xv.) We went only six miles to-day, and camped on a very pretty deep running stream; well wooded all about here; nearly all of the trees paper-barked; some of them were broken off at their tops twelve or twenty feet. There must have been a tornado, and high too, only just to have broken the tops off. We are now in the ranges, scrambling, climbing, ascending and descending, and getting over rocks and precipices as well as we can. Arrived at a large isolated hill; the governor ascended, and we spelled for some time, while he did the climbing. He says you have an extensive view; the whole country is black and dismal in every direction. A large range in the distance, with large gaps; drainage all to the south-west. We started again round this hill, and here we came on the tracks of horses; traced them going west. The ground must have been very wet when they passed. We soon got to a fine valley, well timbered and grassed. We were obliged to camp at this short distance, for Maitland, who had stayed behind, was nowhere to be seen. When he does come up he will catch it and no mistake; *i. e.*, if he ever does, for this is no country to track in, unless for a native; the ground very hard and stony; the camels leave no prints, only a stone turned over here and there.

13th. Came a long day's journey to-day over a most awful country as ever was seen for poor beasts to travel over; immense boulders to cross over somehow or other; the scenery magnificent and grand. We travelled from 8 A.M. to 5 P.M., and found no water; I dare say we have come twenty-five miles in distance, but only about twelve on our course; we were continually tacking, for to go straight was impossible. We camped at last on a little bit of a creek, with about a quart of water in it, in a small hole under a rock; we dug and got enough for the horses, camels, etc., and enough for ourselves. There were some little fish, an inch or so long, dead; round this and several other holes plenty of feed for the animals.

This day's work was so intricate that I must leave Mr. McKinlay to describe it:—

"*13th.* (Camp xvi.) Dewless night; wind from east by north. I take this to be the main branch of the Flinders, the hills on its right proper banks are very bold and must be over 3000 feet high. If they are not before named, I have called them Gregory's Ranges, after Augustus Gregory,

Esq., now Surveyor-General of Queensland. The point I changed my course at yesterday I have called Mount Wildash, after F. Wildash, Esq., of Queensland. Immediately east of Mount Wildash, close by, is another bluff equally high, which I have called Hawker's Bluff, after the Hon. G. C. Hawker. Started at 7·58 A.M., on bearing of 100°, for the southern end of dark range in the distance; at 8·30, south of conspicuous sandstone rocky peak, which I have called Morphett's Peak, after John Morphett, Esq., of Adelaide; dip of about 35° in the sandstone to about north-east or a little more east. Kept the above course three miles over good travelling country; spelled a few minutes, then up and down and over very rocky ranges, in many places precipitous and most intricate travelling from 9 A.M. till 11·30; three and a half miles further, then table-land till 1·50, the drainage is to the east, no doubt to go south after it has cleared the rocky ranges. Spelled, watering the camels, from 2·25 to 2·45 P.M., up to this eight and three-quarters miles further. Commenced ascending another mass of similar rocky ranges; stopped at 3·40, two and a quarter miles further, to look out a track to endeavour to get out of this awful place. Started again at 4·55 P.M., after spelling one and a quarter hours, could not get the animals over. Went back till 5·22, one mile on our track, or to sixteen and a half miles on bearing 100°, to try another place, southerly and westerly along and over very rocky ranges till 6·15, about two miles on average bearing of 215° to 220°. Came to a small sandy creek, then another, where by digging we will be able to give the animals some water; there is plenty of feed. It has been a very distressing day for the poor brutes. Distance, sixteen and a half miles on course of 100°, and two miles on 220°. Gave each of the animals from two to five buckets. Although when first seen the little water that was visible did not exceed a quart, with a few small dead fish about one and a half inches long, after digging, and clearing away the sand we got sufficient for to-night and to-morrow morning. It has been close and oppressive, which has added to the distress of the horses and camels. One of the latter, an old Indian, could hardly be persuaded to come along. Very light rain commenced about dark or a little after, but I doubt whether it will come to anything; however, it will damp the grass for the poor animals, and make it more palatable."

14*th*. Came over country as bad or worse than yesterday, till we arrived at a creek. Went down it four or five miles. Craggy and rocky hills. Our pack bags fearfully torn yesterday coming through the scrub and stringy bark. Passed through lots of fine timber to-day. We had to spell a time. One of the horses bolted with his packs; he took fright at something, and off he was like a shot; tore the bags off him, burst his girth bucking, and in the end got all his traps off but his halter. This occurred in a thick forest of small stringy bark, by the side of a creek. Palmer and Bell went after him, and he was at last caught, how or where I never asked. We were soon on the road again after he was brought in. One of our horses, "Boco" by name, completely knocked up, poor devil! He could go no more, so we took off his load and set him free. We never saw him any more. The next part after leaving the nag was rugged and steep, then over sharp rocky ridges; in fact, the roughest country that could be travelled over was the track to-day. Found lots of water in holes in a creek. The scenery very fine. The sides of creek eighty to a hundred feet high.

We had to go through some long water-holes, and in passing through, old "Nano" the camel fell, nearly done up, and would not or could not rise. We had to send to camp, which was not very far from this, and unpack the brute, and carry all the things into camp. Just before we got there we had to make them jump down five feet, a sort of a fall in the rainy season. They did it very well, and we got to camp all right, but weary and glad to rest. We lost for a time to-day Mr. McKinlay's carpet-bag and Kirby's valise. They must have been torn off by the branch of a tree. We had to go back for them, which detained us a long time. We, with the camels, passed another horse done brown, and left to take care of himself, the softest and most useless of the lot, though he cost £50. There are two more horses on the give-up system, and will have to be left behind should we have any more severe country to go through. I fear it won't change yet, for there is nothing but ranges to be seen. Everywhere we seem to be in the midst of a mountainous district with grand scenery; but we have no time to think of pictures. I said to one of our fellows, "What magnificent scenery!" "D—— the scenery, I want my dinner." Horrid broth! Went nineteen miles to-day, sixteen on our course, so did not do so badly. Having to go such long stages for water, and through such a country, plays old Harry with our beasts. No good grass for horses, all coarse. Camels eat it and seem to like it.

15*th*. Looking very much for rain this morning. I hope we shall not have much, as the travelling is bad enough now; only went short, following the large creek down the bed, up to the horses' knees in sand; several of them *hors de combat* accordingly. After we got to camp and dined, Mr. McKinlay went up to the top of a high hill to take a view round. He says :—

"After getting to camp, ascended the hills on the right, or eastern side of the river, and never beheld such a fearfully grand country in my life—nothing but towers and pinnacles of sandstone conglomerate, fit for nothing but wallaby and euro; and if it is for a thousand years from this time, it can be used by no other animals but them and the natives, as it is at present. The apparent course of this river, from the greatest height I could get to, is about 305°, going, in the first place, after passing the camp, a little more north for three or four miles. It is a terrible country. Should the river, on a closer examination to-morrow, prove to go as I imagine it does, I have nothing for it but to retrace my steps, and go up the main branch, and try and cross the range at top. Still very cloudy, and looks as if it would rain every minute. I wish I had a little more food. If I had I would give the animals a week here, but I have barely sufficient for six days. Oaks have been seen to-day in the bed of the river, since the junction of the two channels. The river runs below the junction of the two branches for some distance, but here it is dry its full width, which is about 150 to 200 yards, and is very picturesque, with beautiful drooping gums, papery bark trees, and various others, and the bold cliffs towering one above the other with awful grandeur. No one can conceive how much effect the travel of the last few days and the shortness of nourishing food has had upon our animals, which, ten days ago, were fit for anything—always excepting this description of awful country. Wind from all points of the compass."

This river is the "Gilbert," I expect, and we shall stay a few days to recruit the horses. They want a spell badly.

16*th*. (Camp xix.) I hope old "Nano," camel, will be left behind, he is quite done for, and has never stirred since we camped yesterday. His feet are quite raw, as if they had been cut with a knife, from the rough country we have been going over. He is an old worn-out brute, and has carried many a ton of forage and rations for our troops in India, I'll engage, long before he went exploring; it is time he went to grass. It rained heavily last night, and Bell and I took the precaution to build a tent, where we slept quite snugly, while the others who camped out got soaking wet before they well knew it.

The scenery up and down this creek (the Gilbert) is grand, and the feed better than we have had for some time. [We refer our readers to the illustration, copied from a sketch made by one of the party on the spot.]

The old camel is to be killed! Old and worn out, with sores all over him, he will be a nice morsel, without the slightest bit of fat to be seen. What would Mr. McGuire say to this as part of the Coronation banquet? He is dead, and we

SKETCH ON THE GILBERT

are to have his liver and kidneys for our evening's meal. Well, I have eaten many curious things, but never a bit of old camel. I was once offered some tiger, but I thought that too much of a joke. Rhinoceros I have eaten, and cats, no doubt, in pies; but to have to help to eat a portion of this old ulcerated quadruped goes against the grain. Remarks piquant and racy are made, and we all sit down round the pot, and get our portions, served out in our tin plates, of camel's flesh. All helped, but no one seemed inclined to begin. At last, the governor said, "What's the matter, boys?" and he put a piece of liver in his mouth. We all looked at him, and at it we went; a few still held back, when I made use of the word of command to make the camel lie down, "Ushe, Nano!" That was a settler; for one or two that was enough. I tried to finish mine, but the liver really was so tough that none of us could eat it. I saw McKinlay try several times, but it was no use; he had to pitch it away: the heart and kidneys were better. We shall have to cut the beast up to-morrow, and bury a lot of our traps, medicines, etc., etc. This night, for the first time for many a day, there was meat left in the pot, and the cook coolly tells us that we can "help ourselves"!

17*th*. (Camp xix.) Rained pretty smart last night; the men cutting up meat for jerking; very bad day for the purpose, for it won't dry. We had some more of him for breakfast; meat rather tasteless, but the heart, roasted for dinner, was as good as a bullock's. Mr. McKinlay says the party, after starving two or three meals, have taken quietly to him now, and rather like—like it!—yes, in preference to starvation.

18*th*. Waterloo-day. Still in camp. We played too, and drank water, keeping up the day with a vengeance. Heavy dew last night. First part of day repairing saddles. Mr. McKinlay and Middleton sorting out the most useful things to take, the rest will be buried under an old dead tree, forty yards up the bank. The camel won't be good for much; what with the dew and no sun, it can't dry.

19*th*. Missed one of the horses this morning, and on looking for him found him quite dead, perhaps bitten by a snake. He was one of our best pack-horses, and always in good condition the whole way. Mr. McKinlay was very much put out at this, but it cannot be helped. Two of our best dead, two left behind; leaving only twenty-two, and two camels.

Started up a tributary, and then struck into the main creek about ten miles; bad work for the animals, but they did it very well. We buried this morning all sorts of rubbish at the foot of an old dead tree, and medicine, too, and a tin box, in which most of the things were placed, and then it was consigned to its resting-place, till some hardy bushman finds the tree, and the mark where to dig for some treasures of the McKinlay expedition. A large arrow marked on the tree denotes the spot where the tin box is to be found. Mr. McKinlay remarks under this date :—

"I never saw animals fall off so suddenly in my life. Followed our tracks back to the junction of the two branches about two and a half miles, then took the left hand or south-east branch ; found it improve much more than I had anticipated. The rocky hills recede occasionally and leave a nice bank of grass—but most of it recently burned by the natives. On our left, the rock appeared now to be chiefly slate, while on the right it still remained sandstone and quartz ; the bed is broad and generally very open and sandy, upon which we have principally to travel ; followed it for about eight miles in about an east-south-east course. From here (camp xx.) for some distance (seen from a hill here) the river appears to receive, from the east by south generally, plenty of water at intervals, and generally at those places running ; no doubt, all the way it runs either over or under the land. Where we are now encamped the river is upwards of 150 yards broad. We found on turning out the camel meat to air that it was quite putrid, and had consequently to throw the whole of it away ; at this time it is a very great loss to us—the loss of upwards of seventy pounds of food. Even with the spell our horses have had they come along very indifferently, and I am almost afraid some more of them will have to be left behind, as I have not sufficient food to wait spelling for them till they get flesh ; there does not appear to be the same nourishment in the grass that there is almost anywhere else. Saw the smoke of natives a few miles ahead of us ; I suppose we will see something of them to-morrow. Some figs were got by some of the party this morning before starting ; I ate one of them apparently ripe, it was very insipid, the principal part of them were full of small flies. Distance travelled by bed of river, not direct, about ten and a half miles."

20*th*. (Camp xx.) Heavy dew again last night. We followed the creek up till we struck a branch. We went up till we came to an impassable barrier of rocks. Here we spelled a short time till Mr. McKinlay returned from a trip beyond the rocks. He told us the country was utterly impassable for animals, so we had to retrace our steps a short distance, and ascend the hillside. On the top we had to stop again to see our way out. Mr. McKinlay went ahead to look out for a road. Off again up the bed of the creek, and camped at a small pool. Another horse knocked up. I think he was ill, for he was a good nag; we had to leave him for he could go no further. The travelling in the sand takes it out of the nags awfully. Distance about ten miles. We saw a few kangaroo to-day.

"Started at 8·10 A.M.; at three and a quarter miles came to a barrier right across from range to range, and after considerable detention succeeded in finding a road on our left round the range that the barriers form from; at four miles came to where one branch (the largest) comes from the south, with plenty of water in its bed in the stone and rocks; the other branch is considerably to the east, so will try it, although it does not at all look a watery branch, but is much more in the direction I want to go. About same course; over much more open country, hilly, and thinly clad with small ironbark timber, and is chiefly of slate formation and well grassed, but no water in its bed as far as we went, say about five and a half miles further; where we fortunately got sufficient at the junction of a small side-creek with the main water-course to suit our immediate wants. It is perfectly surprising to see such a broad channel with such ranges close by and no water. One other of our best horses obliged to be left behind to-day; he has been ailing for some short time, and all at once refused to proceed. A few kangaroo seen to-day. I trust we will fall in with plenty of water to-morrow—our horses never do so well as when they can go to water themselves, instead of watering out of buckets. For some distance the creek bears to north of east; in fact, the next bend, about a mile long, is from north or so, when it appears to turn to south and east. We managed occasionally during to-day to get upon the slopes from the hills on either side of the creek, which was much better travelling than in the soft sandy bed of the creek, which I have called Stuart's Creek, after Mr. McDonall Stuart, the indefatigable explorer of South Australia. This part would make a good sound sheep country, if water at all times was obtainable. A number of oaks all along this branch, and more just here on our left side of the creek where the water is, and we are encamped."

21*st.* Here we go! three more horses left behind. Go it, ye cripples! So that we don't have to walk it won't signify; but if we go on as we are doing now, burning the candles at both ends, *i. e.*, eating the camels and horses and leaving them behind, and with *nothing else to depend on* for grub, we shall soon be in serious difficulty.

It won't do to be wrecked in sight of home, so, lads, cheer up and keep your peckers ditto; that's the way to pull through a difficulty; and when we are on the last horse, it will be time enough then to think of going to David Jones, Esq., and he will have a nice lot if he gets us. We had a few drops of rain this morning; kept course of creek, and camped at a water-hole, our distance some thirteen miles. One of the camels seems very C D; he had to be thrashed to get him on. A very rough day's travel, but the country is pretty. One of the horses left behind joined the others during the night, and was with them driven into camp, but was too weak to go on, so we left him with good water and feed, but there is none for the camels now; I think they are too knocked-up to eat.

22*nd*. (Camp xxii.) Weather cloudy before starting. We had to lighten the camels by leaving the *greased* tent; the other was left on the "Gilbert." There are a few oak trees just above our camp. Passed through well-grassed country, with iron bark, open forest, making for the foot of a range in the distance. We arrived at this point, and of all the places for horses to climb up, this was the worst; it was almost like the side of a house. Here we had the devil's own row; two of the horses nearly got killed. They, instead of going up the road that had been somewhat cleared for them, took it into their heads to go their own way; they made up the steep ascent, and after scrambling and trying their best to get up, came head over heels down this infernal pass. I thought they were both killed; but no, they were all well, and on their legs, but very much frightened. Bell, I thought, must have been killed; he was close under them when they fell, but he had his wits about him, and watched to see which side of a tree they were coming; he then darted just in the nick of time, and escaped being smashed, which he certainly would have been had he not done as he did.

However, we all at last got to the top of the hill, although with the greatest difficulty as regards the camels, and we repacked them. The question was how to progress, so the governor, as usual, rode ahead to see what was to be done, and we spelled. I thought we should have to go back, which was almost impossible; but our leader never goes back on the course. Had he come to a scrub, such as Stuart describes north, if he could not have gone *through* it, he would have gone *round* it.

Country splendidly timbered, and the scenery grand. I forgot to mention that all the jerked camel had to be thrown away, which was a bad loss to us in our crippled state.

23*rd*. (Camp xxiii.) A great event is to happen to-night, a horse must die, and Mr. "Buckeye" must be sacrificed to the insatiable appetites of your explorers. The nag was soon caught and killed, and the heart, liver, kidneys, etc., made into a stew without salt. We had a small spoonful of pepper which we added. It was not so bad, and a steak or two not to be despised. We shall camp here two or three days and jerk him. It is a very cold-looking country about here.

24th. Cutting up and jerking Mr. Buckeye. Worked up course and distance with Mr. McKinlay (dead reckoning remember). I found we ought to be some forty miles from the Burdekin River, the nearest point, having travelled 260 miles since we crossed the Leichhardt Falls. Camp is not a nice one, the grass up to our necks nearly. The country well wooded with iron-bark trees. Middleton and Kirby still continue very unwell, they being continually sick. We are obliged to cook in turns, for our cook is ill also. Some of the horses got lamed.

25th. The dew very heavy last night, and ice in our pannikins about the thickness of half-a-crown. The meat is drying well, as the DAYS are hot. It is always rather dull in camp during this process. Mending what we have, which is little enough, and very little to mend with.

26th. In camp all day looking after the meat, except early in the morning, then after 10 A.M., then 4 P.M., when I visited the camels. Heavy fog indeed, and got fearfully wet going through the high grass, but had no change of raiment, so were obliged to dry our clothes on us. Men still very sick. We shall start in the morning, as the meat is jerked, and weighed sixty-nine pounds, with six pounds of beef, seventy-five pounds; about six days' grub, so that if we don't hit a station in that time another nag must die.

27th. Up early. Breakfast, and immediately got the animals and passed through some beautiful country, well watered and admirably adapted for pastoral purposes. One of our camels rather lazy, "Coppin;" he won't last long I fear. He is a magnificent beast, and pluck to the backbone, like his former owner, G. Coppin, Esq. I shall be sorry if we are obliged to kill him.

28th. (Camp xxiv.) Started early on our course, and went about ten miles over magnificent country, well watered and wooded, and very pretty. Crossed several running brooks, evidently fed by some large swamp here. We also crossed a large fast-running stream, which Mr. McKinlay has called Frank, after Mr. F. Marchant, of Arkaba; he could not have called such a fine stream after a better fellow. I had the pleasure of seeing him on our trip up; he is the *beau ideal* of the Australian bushman. A few miles further on we come to another fine creek called George, after his brother George, of Wilpena, whom we had also the good fortune to foregather with on our northern trip, and have since our return had the pleasure of meeting him in Adelaide. We soon after got to the top of a rocky range. Extensive view of level country. Camped after passing over a large boggy swamp, striking another large creek, sandy bed with some water in it. Two more horses nearly knocked up. There is plenty of excellent food for the animals.

29th. (Camp xxv.) Up and away in good time, over fine country the whole way, well wooded and grassed. Old Jack, a horse that has carried the governor many and many a mile, and travelling has carried me, is to die to-day, a fine plodding old brute, but, alas! he can hold out no longer, it was a labour to get him along, so I expect we shall be soon having another horse ragout.

30th. A little dew last night, and wind light. Crossed a creek shortly after starting, thickly timbered, but not so good as lately. Afterwards ridges of sandstone and granite, then crossed an oak dry creek, east-south-east, and a little further on another—plenty of kangaroo—then to a swamp with a water-hole, with water in it sufficient for our purposes, and camped. Maitland so ill he could hardly stick to the pigskin. Kirby about the same, he is come to a shadow, and Palmer and Hodgkinson both complaining. Distance about nine miles. Bad travelling on account of the slopes being so steep, and we are going down in the water-courses, pretty well grassed though and good sort. Killed old Jack. Although a mere skeleton he will make some soup for a few days, with a little liver (*but no bacon*), and give the sick men a spell, and time to recruit at all events, and they want it badly.

July 1st. (Camp xxvii.) No dew last night. Bell better, but complaining, and so am I a little;

Middleton quite well. Stiff wind from north; men busy jerking the remains of poor old Jack. Saw some large kangaroo, but very shy. Fine timber about here. Sorry to say the maggots got into the horse-flesh, which did not improve it in appearance, but it is of no use being particular now. Oh! for a rump steak, plenty of mustard, pepper, and salt, mashed potatoes, and TWO bottles of stout. *Never mind!*

2nd. This is called "Jack's Swamp," after the old horse. It is a splendid fine day, and the jerking going on well. Maitland is better, but Kirby and Palmer only about the same. The horses seem to be doing pretty well.

3rd. Still in camp. Little dew last night; the hills round here have the appearance of decayed sandstone, very precipitous, and in some places even overhanging. Shall finish jerking to-day. Kirby is improving a little; Maitland much better, but Palmer is not quite so well. I hope they will all feel equal for to-morrow's trip.

4th. Started early this morning. The weather looks fine. Great quantities of quartz to be seen. Passed a rugged range ten to eleven miles. Struck more creeks, with an island of dark coloured abrupt rocks. Some way down it receives a deep tributary from the west, so we had to go into the main creek to pass it. Here we camped. Lots of feed and water. Here we found a fine creeper running over trees and bushes, bearing a beautiful scarlet fruit. We thought we had found a prize, but of all the vile tasting things I ever met with this was the worst. It is very handsome, and would look nicely over a verandah. We took plenty of seeds.

Mr. McKinlay and self went up a high range after dinner and had a most extensive view—hill and dale, forest and plains. Saw plenty of native smokes to the north, and here we had for the first time the sight of what must be the Burdekin River, the stately gum trees of enormous height well defining its course. Very hot travelling to-day.

5th. Followed the creek down, when all of a sudden we heard the governor sing out that there were two horse-tracks in the bed of the creek. Was there not a shout of joy, inasmuch as we expected soon to see a homestead, or a hut at any rate; but, alas! "as the sparks fly upwards," we were doomed to disappointment; and we had to camp as usual with only old horse and water for supper. We ascended the side of the creek, and found a tree marked with a K roughly cut in the bark, also the remains of a hut.

After having seen these the *first* signs of civilization for so many months, we travelled over some open country with spinifex and grass up to the horses' bellies. The country undulating, the creek out of sight, and at last we struck the long-wished-for Burdekin. We went a few miles down it and camped. The sand in the creek was very heavy, and fatigued the nags much. Mr. McKinlay says from here the river appears to flow 15° north of east. The bed of the river at this part is about ninety to a hundred yards wide, and a very strong current running. A few small fish to be seen. Magnificent gums on its banks, and plenty of excellent timber in every direction. This will be a most difficult part of the country for drays to travel, on account of the very steep-sided creeks, and at anything like a flood quite impracticable. The K we supposed to be the initial of some party exploring, and we were not wrong in our judgment, for we met Mr. Kennedy and had a long talk with him, in fact he asked us if we had seen his "K."

6th. Came over a nasty country to-day. Poor little "Coppin" was so weak that, from touching his pack against a stump as he was going down the steep bank of a creek, he fell into a deep hole, and there he was quite helpless. We had to unload him the best way we could to get him up. This was done, and all went on well again. Soon after this accident another horse fell into a deep hole, and we had to dig him out. The country was well grassed, but cut up with deep water-courses. One of our horses, "Spider," the one Bell was riding, can go no further, so we shall kill him, and spell a day or so to jerk him; there will not be much of him, as he is only a bag of bones.

We camped on the side of the "Burdekin." It was a pretty spot, quite like fairy land. The gums on the river magnificent, and plenty of good grass, but no green fodder for the genus *homo*.

Old Spider is now dead, and we shall have, as usual, a stew of his liver, kidneys, etc. I think we are beginning to like "dead horse," some prefer it to bullock. I forgot this morning we had an addition to our soup in the shape of one salted bullock's hide, cut up in slices, and it improved the flavour of our otherwise insipid and scanty breakfast. The country, although difficult travelling, was well wooded. Crossed a creek which flows into the Burdekin.

8th. Started down the river. "Coppin," the camel, very bad, can hardly go at all; he is regularly baked, and no mistake. Travelling very rough, up sides of steep creeks, and down rocky ravines, and crossing a deep creek from the south-east, camped on the Burdekin again.

9th. We came upon a lot of native spears on our arrival last night, which I forgot to mention, and also an oven full of baked roots, something like the sweet potatoe, which were very soon devoured by us. The natives must have been alarmed at the noise the camel made coming into camp, or they would not have made off in that way, leaving

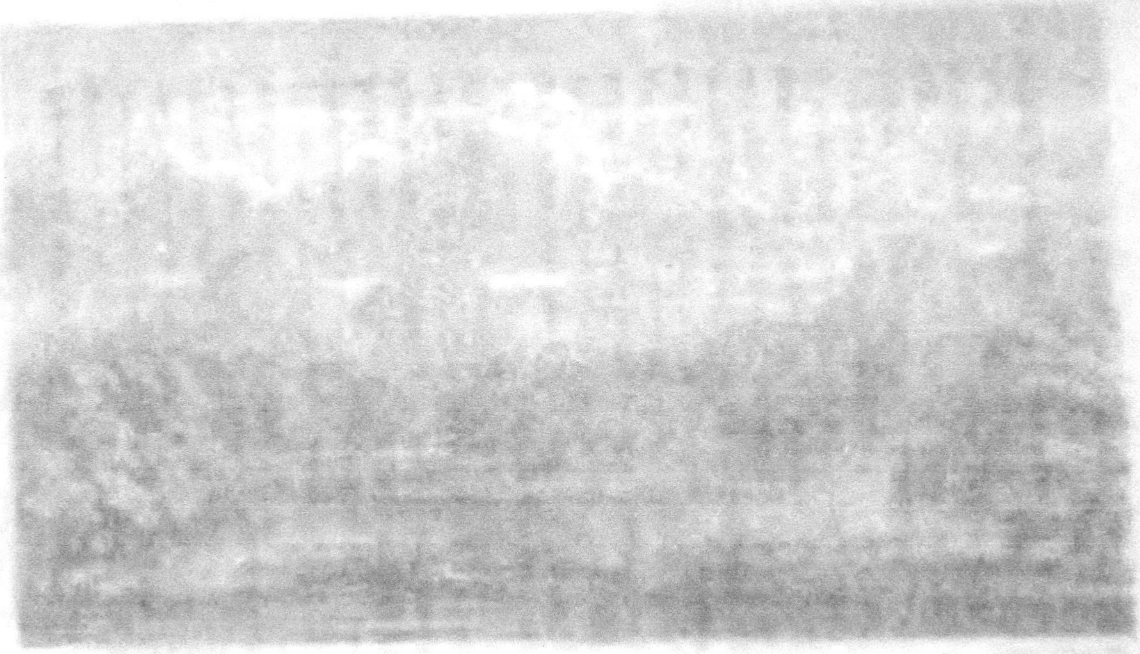

W Wyatt del.   Vincent Brooks lith.

A CAMP ON THE BURDEKIN.

their weapons and grub. We saw nothing of them, and kept no watch.

We shall leave old "Coppin" to take care of himself, there is plenty of good grass and water; he is a plucky beast, and I hope he will do well. All the old clothes, a heavy cavalry sword, and many other things too numerous to mention, will be buried here, with the camel saddle hanging on a tree to mark the spot; so that if any one passes this way they will find one good camp oven, sword, and a pair of buckskin breeches. Distance eight miles.

10*th*. Oh, was it not cold this morning! ice in our quart pots, and over the tarpaulings. Farewell, old "Coppin," you are a noble little beast; many a long mile you and I have travelled together. Breakfast this morning—crows, bullock hide, and jerked horse; not bad, only there was not enough of it, that was the only fault. Country not so bad for travelling, a few pinches here and there. Only one camel left—"Siva."

11*th*. A heavy dew last night. Started at 8·15 A.M., through a good and well-grassed country, the river wide and picturesque, majestic gum-trees, and creepers of every description. "Goliah," one of our horses, is *done;* so we shall kill him to-night. It won't do to leave him, as we are now reduced to four pack-horses. We tie him up for an hour, and then he is laid low with a revolver bullet, and then as usual the old feast of liver and kidneys.

Camped in the bed of the Burdekin, and shall stop here to jerk the horse; his head will make a great stew, for it is about the largest one I ever saw. This camp was a very pretty one, and we had some nice bathing, which suited us all well, and refreshed us.

12*th*. In camp to-day, drying seeds of the large red fruit. Caught some fine bream to-day. Heavy dew last night, but as we camped under a large "tope" of trees we did not get much of it; lots of excellent fish caught. We start to-morrow morning, meat being nicely jerked, the weather having been fine for the purpose.

13*th*. This is about the nicest camp we have had on the Burdekin. I hope we shall go a good long stage to-morrow, if the ground is anything at all like decent.

14*th*. (Camp xxxiii.) Started early, after a good breakfast composed of—what do you think, reader?—you will never guess, so I may as well tell you: five crows, one shag, one pigeon, some bullock hide, and jerked horse; not a bad mixture, you will say. The country was good, undulating, and well grassed, some table land, and then scrub. Crossed two creeks, with corkscrew palms on the banks; then we follow close under the ranges, well grassed, then over a nice flat beautiful grass, but thinly timbered, and some of it rather swampy. We struck the river again, and camped at a place where it is from 700 to 800 yards broad.

15th. Some fine bream were caught to-day by the men and the governor. Most of us, with the exception of the cook and two left in charge of camp, were out with rod and line fishing for our supper. A little rain with some thunder; plenty of hawks and cormorants. The governor saw a platypus in the river this afternoon, the first during our long journey. Distance fifteen miles.

16th. (Camp xxxv.) Started early this morning; very cold and misty, and after travelling some six miles came on some dray tracks. Did not our spirits rise! Three to one and five to one was offered and taken that we had damper and coffee or tea this evening; but no such luck, for we camped on a small river that flows into the Burdekin. Lots of horse and sheep tracks; in fact, we are camped close to where there has been a large flock. I fancy they must have gone on the other side of the Burdekin, and so have escaped us.

17th. (Camp xxxvi.) Came over some very fine country, adapted both for agricultural and pastoral, the soil very rich, and I believe would grow any thing. Camped on a fine river flowing into the Burdekin, after having crossed two creeks. I dare say we have passed stations, but it will not do for us to go out of our way (course) to look for them in our present plight; the only plan is to go on, and chance coming on one *en route.* Distance to-day about twenty-two miles. Saw more dray tracks to-day, probably made by the same dray as the others were made by.

The old proverb sayeth that "hope deferred maketh the heart sick;" but I say that bad grub, and little of it, maketh you yearn after something better. We made a sweepstakes of £1 each, seven of us, each taking a day of the week determined by lots, and the holder of the ticket of the day on which we first make the habitation of a white man takes the £7.

18*th.* Fine cold morning, ice in all the pots. We found a very pretty fruit, a plum of a beautiful colour, and very good eating; the tree was covered, and we stopped under it for twenty minutes, one up in the tree throwing the fruit down, and we below stowing it away in bags, etc.; none of it quite ripe, but still when we got to camp we found it very good when boiled. After dinner we tried some roasted, and they were better. Wylde and I had a tent some fifty yards from the rest, and we were roasting them nearly all night. In the morning what was our surprise to find our teeth, which were quite black over night, as white as snow, and every one was the same—some peculiar acid I suppose.

Here we killed Hodgkinson's pony, and shall

remain a day or two to boil him down, as we have buried our jerking ropes some time ago. We must carry it in that way, otherwise it would not keep, for though the nights are very cold, the days are hot. All the country down the Burdekin is much the same, well-grassed, with rocky creeks and water-ways.

19*th*. Here we shall spell to boil the horse down. Nights still cold, and days warm. All of us cutting up the animal. Then some went away fishing, some roasting plums or mending the remains of their clothes. The quantity of fruit we have eaten I should have thought would have made us ill, but it is quite the reverse. Poole caught some fine fish. Only about twenty-two miles from the "Fanning," says the governor; so perhaps we may have some substantial food to-morrow.

20*th*. (Camp xxxviii.) Started at 8 A.M. over a rocky creek through fine undulating country, with creeks, spiral palms, and oaks, which at eleven miles struck the river high range on the other side. Crossed creeks, two, and camped by some oaks. The timber here is not so fine as above. The river nearly 800 yards wide, with strong current on right side. Cold boiled horse, and a quart of superior Burdekin water for dinner. Fifteen fine bream caught—not a bad supper.

21*st*. We had frost last night; our blankets were quite white with it. Crossed many sandy creeks with paper-bark trees, gums, and palms;

a beautiful and well-grassed valley on our left, highly timbered, plenty of limestone here, and at sixteen miles camped on a little water in a small creek.

22nd. (Camp xl.) Started about 7·30. Crossed the west creek to the one we camped on, and in eight or nine miles struck the Burdekin again. Country pretty, open in places, rough in others. No traces whatever of horses or stock of any kind on this side of the river. Another horse must be killed to-day, and we shall stop here to boil him down. On these days of slaughter, and when in camp, we fare sumptuously every day, as we have as much as we can eat from the head, bones, etc. In fact, all goes into the pot except the hoofs. After we leave the camp we are then on our old rations, twelve pounds per diem for ten men.

23rd. (Camp xli.) Governor and Middleton rode out on the other side of the river, and report lots more fresh cattle tracks. Where are all the settlers, I wonder? We are only stationed ninety miles from Port Denison, so we shall not starve, but may have to ride and walk by turns if we eat any more horses.

24th. Travelled eighteen miles, and camped in the bed of the Burdekin. No "damper" yet, nothing but boiled horse. The country rugged, thickly-wooded with iron-bark. The Burdekin narrows just below our camp, two high round-topped hills on the right. Here we are, poor forlorn explorers, left with only two pack-horses and one camel! Yes, reduced to this extremity from twenty-six horses, twelve bullocks, one hundred sheep, and four camels.

27th. Spelled here to boil down old horse. Mr. McKinlay, Middleton, and Wylde went up river to see if they could find a crossing, for we cannot go any further down this side, as it is completely blocked up with boulders and rocks, to say nothing of hills too steep for the beasts to climb up. Instead of finding what they wanted, what do you suppose they saw? Three or four full-grown alligators! Pleasant that, as we shall have to swim the river, and raft the things across it; rather took away our appetites when we heard of it. One of these brutes eighteen or twenty feet long. The governor says he gave them a shot or two.

We have a raft to make to-morrow, and little or no wood to do it with; there is one pretty good tree and some dry stuff. We put the water-bags and "billies" (tin saucepans) inverted underneath to make it as buoyant as possible.

28th. Now comes the tug of war; to be or not to be, that is the question. The raft is loaded with a few things, as much as it can bear, with grass at the bottom to keep the goods from the water, and macintosh cover over all. Palmer, Hodgkinson, Wylde, and self, naked in the water loading; it is a very gingerbread affair. Now all is ready, Hodgkinson and self start with the first load, he towing the said machine, and I behind helping him along, both doing our best to get to the other side as fast as possible. I never expected to get across; I thought that one of us must certainly go, as the alligators were close to us. We did not get across very fast, but at last landed on a spit of sand, and felt more at our ease. This was to be my place, for to the raft was attached a long string, composed of every available rope, fishing-line, bridles, etc., so as to make it long enough to reach the nearest point, I remaining to pull the raft across, and another fellow paddling back again to the other side. I took what we had brought up a kind of inlet, and landed it on *terra firma;* so I had to be dressing and undressing, in and out of the water all day.

Well, we got all across safely, and camel, but the nags would not come, and night closing on us we had to defer bringing them till to-morrow. Mr. McKinlay, Bell, and Poole are over there. How cold it was. I had to strip and pilot the governor through the intricate passage, and land him safely with the other goods. Old Kirby had got a good fire, and we made ourselves comfortable, but alas! I had to take the three men's dinners to the spit, where Wylde was waiting to row the concern over with the grub to the fellows

[illegible] all [illegible] carried, [illegible] closing [illegible] them till [illegible] are over [illegible] passages, and [illegible] Old Kirby [illegible] we made ourselves com-[illegible], but alas! I had to take the three men's [illegible] to the [illegible] was waiting to [illegible] the concern over with the [illegible] to the fellows

Vincent Brooks lith.

The Alligators were close to us'

on the other side. This was a fearful day's work. How we escaped, God knows. After giving the grub over to Wylde I returned over the rocks to the bivouac fire, and had a good feed of "Joe Buggins." We had to kill him yesterday. The camel too is almost done. He can't go much further, as it seems there are only ranges ahead of us. Middleton and Hodgkinson had a good deal of swimming to-day, and I think they are about the best two that could have been selected, being strong swimmers. The governor says the horses would not cross, so left them and hoped for better success. It is a difficult, intricate, and dangerous place, and if they cross in safety it is more than I expect.

29*th*. (Camp. xlv.) It was a work of difficulty, and no mistake. First we had to get the horses to the spit; that was not so bad, but to get them to the place where we were camped, that was the rub. We had to get three lines fastened to each horse; one in front to guide him to the landing-place, and one on either side to keep him straight, and keep him from swaying. It is a vile place, and I hope I may never see it or its like again if I have to get horses through it. Went about thirteen miles.

30*th*. (Camp xlvi.) Camped on a small stream running into the Burdekin, 100 yards off. Wylde and Hodgkinson are to dig a hole, for here everything is to be left behind and buried, and only the clothes we stand in and our blankets, those carried on our horses, to be kept. We take old "Siva" on to our next camp, and there he is to die, poor old fellow! he is to be lightened of everything; for on the first onset we have to climb a high and very steep hill, and were he loaded he could not by any means get up it; so this is the reason why we are leaving all our household goods to be buried. I wonder if we shall find a station near enough to send for them—seeds, stones, curiosities of all kinds, some brought hundreds of miles.

Started about 10 A.M., and had to skirt the hill, for the horses could not carry us straight over; the old camel got on well. Up a steep ascent, down into a valley, then over another, and so on till we camped. A very heavy day for all of us, as we had to walk the greater part of the time.

We camped at a running stream of beautiful water; there we shall kill our faithful ally "Siva." I shall be sorry to see him drop—he has been such a noble animal. We have a fine shady camp here; fine trees, with leaves twelve to fifteen inches long by ten inches broad; these leaves smoke well, as I learned by one of our party (Ned) coming to me and asking for my pipe. I lent it to him, and soon discovered him blowing a cloud; and happy he looked, with a knowing smile on his face, as much as to say "have a whiff." I was not long in trying it, and it turned out first-rate. Quickly did all the rest gather some leaves; and that night we had a good smoke of this ***very fine*** substitute for the nicotian weed.

There has been an old native encampment here. The remains of ancient whirlies are to be seen, etc., etc. Had some "Siva" for supper; his tripe very good, so we shall have all the rest prepared to-morrow, which, with his feet, will make one good meal, and his head, etc., another. Our spell here will do the horses good too. We shall boil down the meat, and each man carry so much on his saddle. The governor, in fact, will handicap us.

31*st.* Spelled here in this comfortable cool camp. Very convenient finding these leaves to smoke. Natives not far off, firing the grass in different directions.

August 1*st.* Boiling down camel all day. Poole sick with a touch of fever and ague, and cannot eat anything. There is not much choice, that's quite certain. Mr. McKinlay and Bell off for a ramble over the hills to see what they can see. On their return, they report the country ahead pretty level. Preparing for a start to-morrow. Four days' meat left, so that if we don't hit a station in that time *look out* those that have not good boots, as we must kill another horse. So we shall all have to walk in our turn. My boots, happily, are good.

2nd. Started early this morning; last man taking with him on his saddle in front a certain quantity of boiled camel, as we are now reduced to one riding-horse and one pack ditto. He carries the few necessaries of Mr. McKinlay—books, papers, etc.

After travelling for some ten miles we suddenly came on some cattle tracks, and shortly after were gratified by seeing the animals themselves, with two of our own countrymen "tailing" them. Were we not jolly! The station is situated on the "Bowen," a stream running north into the Burdekin, and belongs to Messrs. Harvey and Somers. Mr. Somers was from home when we arrived; but he soon made his appearance, and hospitality in the most extended sense of the term was the law. We had already astonished some cold roast-beef, etc., etc. The murphys were fine, and you may be sure we did justice to the novel fare.

Singular enough, here we met Mr. Brahe, a gentleman who was out in that fatal expedition with Burke, and, as many of my readers may remember, was stationed at Cooper's Creek, where he waited *till he could wait no longer*, but he was blamed for leaving. I don't see that the *slightest* blame can be attached to him; that is my opinion, and also of many others whom I have conversed with on the subject.

The flour we eat in the shape of bread, puddings, etc., has had a most curious effect on us all. We have been in the greatest pain; it would not digest somehow or other, and, strange to say, all are suffering from swelled legs and feet.

And now, dear reader, having brought you into the settled districts again, with just one concluding chapter I shall take my leave.

CHAPTER XI.

THE RETURN HOME—PORT DENISON TO SOUTH AUSTRALIA.

James Morrill, Narrative of Seventeen Years' Residence with Natives; Shipwrecked; Sole Survivor; Aboriginal Manners and Customs—Account of Port Denison, and Town of Bowen—Strathmore Station—Squatting Hospitalities —Embark in the "Ben Bolt," of 20 tons, for Rockhampton —Many Islands—Broad Sound—Rockhampton, Sydney, Melbourne, Adelaide.

WHILE the expeditionary party are enjoying their short respite at the station of Messrs. Harvey and Somers, and doing ample justice to the roast-beef they had so often consumed in imagination, when in reality only a tough old camel was between their hungry teeth, we shall make a digression to relate an interesting occurrence connected with the time and the place. About six months after the party's arrival, and a little to the north of their present quarters, a man suddenly presented himself to two shepherds at the outpost of a sheep-station. Quite naked, and of a reddish yellow hue, he was seen to be no aboriginal native. On the shepherds seizing their fire-arms, under a sense of possible danger, he called out in English, although speaking with difficulty, that he was their countryman. He then informed them that he had lived for seventeen years with the Aborigines in the neighbourhood, being the sole survivor of the crew and passengers of a ship that had been wrecked, so far back as the year 1846, upon a reef off the adjacent coast. He had been wandering over the country about Mount Elliott, a lofty hill, above 4000 feet in height, near the mouth of the Burdekin, and he must have been but a short way to the east of McKinlay's party, as they passed down the river. His name was James Morrill, and he was born near Maldon, in Essex, England, and had been a seaman of the wrecked vessel the "Peruvian." He was supplied with clothes by his new friends, and after a short interval taken to Port Denison, where a subscription was made on his behalf, and where both himself and his narrative were the subject of very general interest.

The captain of the "Peruvian" had warned the watch against "broken water," that dangerous symptom of this coral reef coast. The vessel was wrecked during the night, after the watch had indeed detected the fatal symptom ahead, but too late to be of any avail. There was a considerable gale blowing; the two boats were lost, and with them the first and second officers. The construction of a raft was the next resource. It was promptly made, launched, and loaded with its living freight, but it broke away from the wreck before any adequate supplies of either provisions or water had been secured. There had been fourteen of a crew and seven passengers, and for forty-two days these miserable creatures were drifted to and fro, until at length the raft, with a small remnant of survivors, was cast ashore on the north side of Cape Cleveland. They had prolonged their lives mainly by catching three sharks, part of a legion that followed the raft for the sake of the dead bodies that were at intervals committed to the waters.*

Ashore at last, they were for a time undisturbed, and subsisted on shellfish; but after a fortnight they were discovered by the Aborigines. They were by this time reduced to four—the captain and his wife, Morrill, and a boy. The natives, after gratifying an intense curiosity by examining all of them, from head to foot, behaved kindly after their rough fashion, and took them to the great tribal camp in the neighbourhood, where they again underwent a thorough inspection, their white skins causing a general astonishment, and

* The editor may here state that he perfectly recollects the circumstance of the "Peruvian" being missed in 1846, while he was residing in Melbourne. The passengers were all from the Port Phillip district (now Victoria), and were supposed to have all perished by shipwreck in Torres Straits.

inspiring some with such terror that they at first ran away. For some time the neighbouring blacks were arriving in streams to gratify the common curiosity, but there was no violence used, nor was insult ever offered to the female. Meanwhile the poor outcasts were at first supplied with food, and afterwards were shown how and where they could find roots and other edibles for themselves.

Exposure and privation caused much suffering, especially when their clothing, gradually falling to pieces, had disappeared, and left them entirely naked. The poor wife, the only female of the party, contrived to retain to the last a few scraps of covering. Severe rheumatism attacked them all, and in a little more than two years Morrill found himself sole survivor. The captain had died before his wife, and she, thus desolate and forsaken, survived him but four days. Morrill had a strong frame and a good constitution, and survived the trying ordeal of his new mode of life.

His narrative of his life among the natives is interesting in its account of native manners and habits. He forms a very low estimate of their qualities, as they are cruel and treacherous, even to each other of the same tribe. "There is," he says, "a sort of partizanship of private friends and private foes in each tribe. Some individuals are occasionally the victims of these enmities, but many more are preserved by the watchfulness of friends. He himself had both friends and enemies, and would have fallen on many an occasion by the hands of the latter, but for the vigilance of the former, who threatened the direst vengeance in case any injury happened to him. As already mentioned in our Introduction, he confirms the now perfectly authenticated cannibalism of the Australian natives. He brightens the dark picture a little by stating that they will not kill their fellow men merely for the sake of eating them. In eating their friends or chiefs, after death, there seems some vague notion of appropriating yet something of the virtues of the deceased; all at least that the grasping appropriator death has left them.

It is remarkable that he scarcely ever heard reports of his countrymen, many of whom must have traversed the country at no very great distance from the scene of his protracted wanderings, not a few having from time to time been murdered, or killed in hostile attacks. This circumstance is to be accounted for, perhaps, partly from the desire of the natives to withhold information of his countrymen from him, as they seem really to have valued his presence amongst them; and partly from the mutual hostility, or at least the alien feeling generally prevalent between the various tribes, which greatly restricted any intercourse, and prevented the spread of news, however wonderful. At length, however, reports meet his ear, which he cannot misunderstand. The new settlement of Bowen, about two years before his deliverance, had attracted the natives' attention, and Morrill was certain his countrymen must be somewhere near him, and that the continually advancing wave of colonization had at last rolled up to his neighbourhood. There was a twofold difficulty in reaching the settlers, however; for not only were the tribes he lived with unwilling that he should leave, but he could hardly venture any distance away without falling among natives unfriendly to the tribe he was identified with, and thus endangering his life. After some time he transferred his residence to a friendly tribe, living between Cape Bowling-green and the Burdekin. He seems to have been on the outlook nearly a year with this tribe, when he hears of cattle being seen feeding and drinking at the Burdekin, and a white man with a whip attending them. Soon afterwards two females describe some sheep as among the long grass, a short distance to the south. One of them he induces to accompany him; but at sight of the sheep, she will go no further, fearing to be murdered by the whites; and earnestly advising Morrill too, by all means, to avoid the wicked intruders. She returns therefore, and Morrill goes on, presenting himself to the shepherds, as already related.

Morrill describes the natives as in great dread of the whites, from an incurable notion of their cruelty and murderous intentions towards them. He greatly regrets this feeling, and alludes to a recent massacre of a number of blacks by the colonists, in order to show that it has too good a foundation. He returned to the tribe after the interview with the shepherds, and advised the natives to keep out of harm's way, stating, for the sake of peace, that the power of the whites was something far beyond what the natives could resist. The poor creatures seem to have had some sorrows at leave-taking, looking on Morrill as a kind of protector, and begging him to arrange for them with his powerful countrymen that the poor natives should be left in possession of the swamps and salt water creeks at least, if they gave up the rest of the country. Morrill's views for the future seemed to be to spend the remainder of his life in the country so long familiar to him, acting under sanction of the Colonial Government as a protector and interpreter for the Aborigines.

From these adventures of Morrill's let us return to those of our travellers, who now, with freshened energies, direct their steps to Port Denison, to enjoy the hospitalities of Bowen, the young capital of this tropical part of Australia. Port Denison is an inner harbour on the west side of Edgecumbe Bay, and is well protected seawards by islands, with excellent anchorage for the largest fleet of ordinarily sized shipping, and a depth of twenty-seven feet of water. The port was discovered only in 1860, during a coasting search for the mouth of the River Burdekin. This fine stream was found debouching near Cape Cleveland, but with a branch, previously known as the Wickham, entering the sea near Cape Upstart. As these outlets proved to be subject to the mischance common to so many Australian rivers, of having bars that impede navigation, the discovery of Port Denison a little to the southward was all the more important to the settlers, who have already begun a rush with their flocks into the vacant neighbourhood. Bowen was commenced about a year before our travellers arrived, and has already a presentable array of buildings, including of course public houses, blacksmiths' forges, and general stores. Whether that very early necessary of a colonial town, a daily local newspaper, had yet appeared we are not told, but "our own correspondent" for somewhere else was already on the ground some months before the expedition's arrival, and in writing, on 27th May, 1862, to a Rockhampton paper, this universal and *aimable inconnu* describes the little township as having been first settled about ten months previously, and as possessing already a population of 120, of all ages, whose numbers are steadily increasing by arrivals from Rockhampton and Sydney.

Let us now follow Mr. Davis for the last time. He is still as far as ever from Adelaide, his starting point, having more than 2,000 miles of sea to traverse; and although his patience is occasionally tried by the slow coach system of the "Ben Bolt" and other impedimental tubs that "express" the traveller in these out of the way latitudes, yet the last of the journey is perhaps quite as pleasant as the first, with a substitute of hospitable colonists for natives, and the varieties of a good dinner table for old Siva and his jerked brethren.

We remained at this station for one day quite enjoying ourselves. Mr. Somers has our warmest thanks for the kindness shown to us, and may the station flourish! No one could have been more kind than he. He gave us everything we wanted—more power to him. We then changed our camp some five miles to another station owned by Germans, called "Strathmore," Mr. Selleim being the chief of the firm, and a Mr. Trussaint the other partner. Here we remained for a week eating and drinking, etc., only the beef was as tough as old leather. The other things were good, and we are beginning to pick up, and are looking quite different men already. The same fine country between the two runs past through by us.

At this station, "Strathmore," there is a station of "native police," under the command of a European sergeant. Here we got some police horses and men, and a native trooper went for the things we buried two stages back.

During the week past here we were eagerly ready for the news from papers lent us by Mr. Selleim, for all the latest English news, Yankee war, etc. It was here we first heard of the death of Prince Albert. Mr. McKinlay, after remaining here for two days, started with Poole and one pack-horse and a spare nag for Mr. McKinlay, to push into Port Denison. This place is some eighty miles from the port, the most northern settlement of Australia; it will be a pretty little town by and by.

The climate, they tell me is magnificent, for all the summer months. Whilst it is piercing hot in the interior here, this little spot is blessed with the most magnificent sea-breezes. Port Denison is situated on Edgcumbe Bay; the bay is very shallow, having to wade out a long way to get to a boat to take me off to a vessel.

The squatters soon came in to welcome Mr. McKinlay, many of them knowing him personally, and many more by report. They gave us a dinner to welcome us back to the land of the living. Lots of speeches, songs, etc., and we passed a jolly and happy evening; and we did not break up till 4 A.M. Some thirty gentlemen sat down to table to do honour to our worthy commander. The squatters here looked quite fierce with their long knives stuck in their belts, and revolvers at their sides. We passed two pleasant days here at the Port Denison Hotel.

The "Ben Bolt," a small coasting "ketch," of some twenty tons, was the only vessel in the harbour. She trades regularly between this place and Rockhampton, a town lower down the coast, and sprung up since the great Port Curtis rush to the Canoona goldfield. She also carries the mails. This is the vessel that is to bear Cæsar and his fortunes. We embark to-morrow, 17th August, for Rockhampton. Nineteen of us in all to be in this small boat. How we shall stow I don't know. How Mr. McKinlay will stow is a puzzler. He is 6ft. 4in., and the berth about 5 by 6, and very narrow. He will have to take to the deck, or else put a knot in his legs. We had a Mr. Bierly, a gentleman who had been up taking out runs (tracts for pasture) in the district, and now returning to Rockhampton on business, Mr. Ham, a young squatter up here, and Mr. Finlay, who was going down for cattle to stock a run. The anchor up, and with three cheers for Port Denison and its inhabitants, we sail from the harbour with a flowing sheet.

Our little vessel sailed well for the first two days, but there came head-winds and baffling gales, and the little craft could not do anything against them. We sighted many islands, too numerous to mention, even had I known the names. It was interesting now and then to hear a sailor spin a yarn that on that island poor Jack so-and-so got killed by the d——d blacks. It gave a kind of interest to the island. Mr. Bierly had a friend murdered on one of them not very long since. We passed close to one island, and were pointed out by the captain, Tom McEwin by name, the remains of a steamer and a quantity of coals lying high and dry on the beach. What steamer it was no one up to the present time has ever been able to discover. She was of iron, at least all that remains of her ribs are of iron. We were knocking about this part of the world for some ten days.

Our provisions getting short, our water nearly done, so the skipper put into an island called L Island. There we went on shore, for at low tide the gallant barkie was quite dry, as the tide recedes a very long way here. Put in a supply of water, which one or two of us found out, for be it known we went and explored the island. It was pretty well grassed and seemingly tolerably watered, for there was plenty of water in a creek, and in several large holes in the rocks. We had to take the puncheon up some three hundred feet to fill it, for the water was high up the mountain. We soon filled it, and we had a job to get it down again; however, it was got down safely and put on board, where we embarked some dampers for use on board.

The captain had laid in enough provisions for some twelve days, consequently we were now beginning to look short in the locker. The beer and porter, however, were holding out well, and other liquors. It was now determined to make for a place called "Broad Sound," where there was a bush public store of all kind of "omnium gatherum," where was sold everything, from a bottle of "Lea and Perrin's" sauce to paper collars. To this spot the skipper determined to make, and lay in a fresh supply of the good things of this life.

I forgot to mention that McEwen had put on board a sheep, but had forgotten to put any grub for it; and thereby one poor fellow, who was sleeping in the hold on the ballast, lost his blanket, and could not make out where it was till it was discovered the sheep had nearly eaten it, so we had him killed and eaten.

Very shortly after this sad catastrophe of the blanket, we landed at another island—Middleton, Harding, Finlay, and myself, with two sailors,—to get some more water if we could find any, but alas we only found a little in a hole, about half a gallon, which was no use to us. On this pretty spot, for it was a pretty island, well grassed but not well timbered, we discovered a large beam of white pine timber squared off. It was about eighty feet long, and fifteen inches square. Evidently some ship had been lost coming through Torres Straits. Covered with timber there was also on the same island a piece of a large built ship's mast, which must have belonged to a large ship, perhaps to the very one that got wrecked loaded with timber. Who can tell?

Started for Broad Sound, where we arrived two days after. Broad Sound is the lower part of a river. Here we found a Sydney brig lying, the "Fortuna," having taken up stores to Port Denison, Broad Sound, and Rockhampton. There was also the wreck of a topsail schooner, the "Comet," lying up the river. We all went on shore, of course, and played quoits for bottles of rum, for that was the only drink they had. We start at the making of the tide to-night. The "Fortuna" also starts to-night for Sydney. We drop down the river.

We are all right at last. We are now going up the Fitzroy River, on which is the town of Rockhampton. This is at present rather a straggling town, but will soon be a fine prosperous place. There are already some one or two brick houses in it, and others being built.

None knew anything of our advent at Port Denison, for we were the first to bring the news;

and to the astonishment of the population (for we landed some way below the town), who wondered who the devil such a ragged lot could be. We entered the town and put up at the Royal Fitzroy Hotel, and glad were we to get a good breakfast and some beer. The hotel is kept by Mr. and Mrs. Gardner, and a nicer house or more civil people you could not well meet. They were very kind and attentive to us all, and did the best to make us comfortable.

We stopped in this town some week or so, waiting for a steamer to take us to Sydney. Up to this time no one knew where we were, never dreaming in Adelaide that we should come out at Port Denison. They will indeed be surprised to hear of our advent at this part of Australia. Two steamers came in, the old "Balcutha" and the "Bomerang." We go in the "Balcutha," at least some of us, as McKinlay stops for a dinner to be given to him, and the steamer can't wait. I take on the telegram to send to Adelaide, leaving him with one or two more, for some of the men remain behind here, and, as I forgot to mention, two had remained at Port Denison. We are reduced now to six, McKinlay, Middleton, Kirby, Wylde, Poole, and myself, the others being left, as I said before, at Port Denison. Messrs. Bell and Hodgkinson remain here.

We start from the wharf at 4 A.M., after having

a bout of champaign and songs till that hour in the hotel, when we wish good night to all. We start down the river on board the "Balcutha," but we strike on the bar; so, early, say 8 A.M., a boat containing Captain Trouton, as jolly a tar as ever walked a deck, starts for town again, as to-day is the Rockhampton races; and we go with Middleton and others off for the races. The dinner to McKinlay takes place to-night, and of course Trouton and I stop.

We arrived in Sydney harbour early in the morning, and the sight of it is well worth a voyage from the old country. It has been so often described that it would be superfluous to try even to do it, but of all the harbours I have ever seen, this is the most beautiful. Glad were we on arrival at the wharf to hear that the "Calcutta" was going on the next day to Melbourne. So we shall start for Melbourne to-morrow afternoon with Trouton.

We arrived in a couple of days at Melbourne, Captain Trouton making us as happy as possible, more power to him! We found the "Hannibal" steamer just leaving for Adelaide, but we are just too late to go by her, and have consequently to stop here for a fortnight. Oh! won't our time fly? Melbourne's the place to make it go well. Went up to the Criterion Hotel, and I should advise any one going to Melbourne to go there. Everything first-rate there, no two ways about it. We stopped here a fortnight, and enjoyed ourselves much.

Here we are now on board the "Havilah" steamer, bound for Adelaide. Four days of it, the sea as smooth as glass, lots of passengers. We arrived all safe and sound at Port Adelaide very early in the morning. No one to be seen hardly, but we have to wait till eight for the train to take us to town. We go and have a nobb or two with friends, who are glad to see us all. Here we are back again.

My chapter concluded, good reader, farewell.

THE END.

INDEX.

www.ingramcontent.com/pod-product-compliance
Lightning Source LLC
Chambersburg PA
CBHW031958300426
44117CB00008B/814
* 9 7 8 3 7 4 3 3 1 9 7 8 3 *